WITHDRAWN

D1214574

The Book of
SMOCKING

3 3501 00015 5836

The Book of
SMOCKING

Diana Keay

NORTHWEST BOOKMOBILE CENTER
SOUTHEASTERN OHIO REGIONAL LIBRARY
40780 SR 821
CALDWELL, OH 43724

ARCO PUBLISHING, INC.
New York

Published 1985 by Arco Publishing, Inc.
215 Park Avenue South, New York, NY 10003

© Diana Keay 1985

All rights reserved. No part of this book may be
reproduced, by any means, without permission in
writing from the publisher, except by a reviewer
who wishes to quote brief excerpts in connection
with a review in a magazine or newspaper.

Library of Congress Cataloguing in Publication Data
Keay, Diana, 1922-
   The Book of Smocking
   Bibliography: p.159   Includes index.
   1. Smocking.   I. Title.
   TT840.K43 1985   746.44   84-18629
   ISBN 0-668-06264-9

Reader: Fiona Holman
Design: Yvonne Dedman
Line artwork: Sue Baker

Filmset by SX Composing Ltd, Rayleigh, England
Printed and bound by Printer Industria Gráfica SA,
Barcelona, Spain

D.L.B. 712-1985

Frontispiece Smock, dated 1830-50

Title page Detail of the back of the smock
illustrated on frontispiece

Illustration Sources and Acknowledgements

The author and publishers would like to thank the following:
Bankfield Museum: 32 *(below right)*; Bethnal Green Museum: 12;
Margaret Bowman USA: 138, 139 *(2)*; The Burrell Collection, Glasgow:
6; City Museum and Art Gallery, Birmingham: 19 *(below right)*;
Martin Dohrn Photograph: 11 *(above)*, opposite 48, opposite 49,
opposite 64, opposite 65, opposite 89, opposite 96, opposite 97, 97 *(2)*,
98 *(2)*, 99 *(2)*, 100, opposite 112, opposite 113, 118, 119 *(2)*, opposite 128,
opposite 129, 139, 140 *(2)*, opposite 144, opposite 145, 152 *(2)*, 153 *(3)*,
154 *(2)*; The Embroiderer's Guild Collection, Hampton Court Palace:
11 *(above left)*, 16 *(above left)*, 16 *(above right)*, 28 *(centre)*, 28 *(below)*, 30
(2), 32 *(centre right)*; Gallery of English Costume, Platt Hall,
Manchester: 20; Edith Garland: Project 6: Floral Dress and Project 13:
Gingham Dress, between pages 88 and 89; Guildford Museum: 16
(below left); Maggie Hall: Project 4: Smock, opposite 65; Maxine
Henry: Project 5: Christening Robe and Bonnet, opposite 88; Project
20: Ribbon Waistcoat, opposite 145; Hereford and Worcester County
Museum, Hartlebury: Frontispiece, Title page; Diana Keay: 30 *(2
photographs)*, 32 *(photograph, centre right)*, Project 1: Sampler,
opposite 48; Project 7: Formal Dress, opposite 89; Project 10: Cocktail
Dress, opposite 97; 97 *(2)*, 98 *(2)*, 100, 118, 119 *(2)*, 148 *(photograph)*;
Liverpool Museum: 21; Joan Lomas: Project 11: Green Bag and Project
12: Black Bag, opposite 112; Project 15: Black Belt, Project 16: Suede
Belt, Project 17: Blue Belt, opposite 128; Louvre, Paris: 8; Luton
Museum: 15; Geoffrey Magnay Ltd, Chipping Norton, Oxfordshire:
38 *(below right)*; Julie Milne Collection: 32 *(above left)*; Museum of
Costume, Bath: 10 *(below)*; Museum of London: 9; Vanda Palmer:
Project 3: Lampshade, opposite 64; Priory Gallery, Bishop Cleeve,
Glos: 34; Private collection: 26; Maggie Shaw: Project 19: Mexican
Blouse, opposite 144; Janet Simms: Project 2: Honeycomb Cushion
and Project 8: Round Cushion, opposite 49, 152 *(2)*, 154 *(above)*;
Smocking Arts Guild of America: 31; Madge Taylor: Project 14: Blue
Dress, opposite 113; Joppa Valk, the Netherlands: Project 18:
Volendam Blouse, opposite 129, 153 *(3)*, 154 *(below)*; The Victoria and
Albert Museum, London: 11 *(below right)*, 27, 28 *(above)*, 29;
Warwickshire Museum Costume Collection: 10 *(above)*; Anne
Watson: Project 9: Blouse, opposite 96; William Morris Gallery,
Walthamstow: 17; Jennie Woodcock: opposite 88, between 88 and 89.

Contents

1

The History of Smocking

Clothing in the beginning of time was simply cut. Later, garments became more sophisticated and it was this sophistication which brought about extra fullness. Fabric had to be draped or moulded to a figure, so in order to accommodate this extra fabric a system evolved. This took the form of pleating or gathering to hold the excess cloth in place, and to enhance this further, various forms of decoration were used; either sewn on to the surface of the material or through a prepared foundation. These decorations could be either elastic or firm. Any form of decoration on or through the fabric which makes the fullness a decorative feature, whether elastic or non-elastic, may be termed decorative smocking and is found not only in Europe but throughout the world.

The form of decoration most popular today is called English smocking which has been done in Britain for three hundred years (See baby cap and bib, on p.10) but how far back it goes we do not know for certain. To piece together the history of smocking, one has to go back to the origin of the name, to the garment called a 'smock'.

The Oxford English Dictionary states that the word 'smock' is probably related to the Old English 'smugan' meaning to creep and the Old Norse word 'smjuga' to creep into, or to put on, a garment – a woman's undergarment, a shift or chemise.

Smocks were worn as an undergarment by the wealthy and as an outergarment by the peasant. The word 'smocking' does not appear until the nineteenth century and in order to trace the history of smocking, a study of the costume of the wealthy and the peasant has to be made. As textiles are among the most perishable of materials, we have to depend on representations in art and references in literature, for our knowledge of smocking in earlier times.

The Fourteenth Century

One of the earliest references to a smock in art is shown in the *Luttrell Psalter* (circa 1340) in which a man ploughing is depicted wearing a loose garment of a smock type. While in literature, Chaucer describes a woman wearing a smock in the *Miller's Tale* in 1386:

> Fair was this yonge wyf, and therwithal
> As any wezele hir body gent and smal.
> A ceynt she werede, ybarred al of silk;
> A barmcloth as whit as morne milk
> Upon hir lendes, ful of many a goore.
> Whit was hir smok, and broyden al bifoore
> And eek bihynde on hir coler aboute
> Of colblak silk, withinne and eek withoute.
> The tapes of hir white voluper
> Were of the same suyte of hir coler;
> Hir filet brood of silk and set ful hye.

This passage describes the smock as being white and embroidered both on the front and the back and on the collar in coal-black silk. The 'barmcloth' referred to was an apron worn by countrywomen in the thirteenth and fourteenth centuries. It was long and narrow, reaching to within a few inches of the hem and was usually white, being made of coarse linen or hempen with 'seckcloth', 'dowlas' or 'lockram'. This rural apron had a peculiarity of its own: it was 'honey-combed' – that is gathered at the waist and over-stitched with the basic stitch of 'smocking' to a depth of several inches as depicted in the *Luttrell*.[1]

The Fifteenth Century

Paintings of the second half of the fifteenth century give an insight into the types of garments worn at the

Opposite Detail from 'The Rest on the Flight into Egypt', *circa* 1465, by Hans Memling, showing smocking on the Virgin's dress

1. Alma Oakes and Margot Hamilton Hill: *Rural Costume – Its Origin and Development in Western Europe and the British Isles*. (Batsford, London and Van Nostrand Reinhold Company, New York, 1970). Pages 160, 175.

time together with further details about the dress of the period. Elizabeth Birbari in her scholarly book *Dress in Italian Painting 1460-1500* gives informative details about the dress of this period. She explains that during this period in Renaissance Italy, paintings of fashionable women show them wearing an under-garment called a *camicia* or chemise. This was a simply cut and full garment reaching sometimes to the ankle. It could be worn to sleep in, or at home in the privacy of a house in suitable weather, or under a dress. There were several styles.

One form of this chemise can be seen in the painting 'The Story of Patient Griselda' (in the National Gallery, London) by the Master of the Story of Griselda where the simply cut garment of transparent fabric shows an inverted pleat falling from under the arm. Elizabeth Birbari shows how this garment would have been constructed by folding a length of material double (the fold being at the shoulder), cutting a square out for the armhole and using the square for the sleeve. As this would have made the bottom of the armhole too wide, a pleat was formed, thus allowing the released fullness to accommodate the hips. After the neckline had been shaped, the simple pieces were sewn together and the neckline gathered.

A chemise could also be worn under a dress. In this form it was finely gathered and for the wealthy it would be made of fine linen. Towards the end of the fifteenth century the chemise was very full, elaborately trimmed and embroidered to display its beauty. The over-dress was cut lower to expose as much of it as possible. The sleeves being very full, those of the over-dress were slit to show the richness below.

The simple chemise style, whether plain or elaborated, can be seen in many Italian and other European paintings of the second half of the fifteenth century and the early sixteenth century. One of the most informative paintings of this period showing costume detail is 'The Rest on the Flight into Egypt' (in the Burrell Collection, Glasgow) by Hans Memling (circa 1430-1494), who painted devotional pictures showing calm and piety, in the Netherlands style typical of the late Middle Ages or Renaissance period. The Virgin is depicted wearing a long, simply cut gown with a slightly gathered neckline and plain sleeves. But at the waistline at a point under the sleeves, extra fullness has been inserted in the form of a godet (a triangular piece of fabric) on which honeycomb smocking is clearly visible. For a garment of this cut, the insertion would be in keeping, as it would provide the extra fullness required across the hips. The dress is similar to that shown in 'The Story of Patient Griselda' where pleats are used rather than a godet. But both treatments served the purpose of giving extra fullness over the hips.

'The Rest on the Flight into Egypt' is the earliest painting I have seen that shows smocking so unmistakably and clearly – the execution of the painting shows distinctly the drapes of the gathers falling away from the honeycomb stitches. One marvels at its appearance at this date, but the craftsmen and women of the Renaissance period were very talented. It is no surprise that garments requiring fullness, as was the fashion, should display rather than conceal, an outward and visible embellishment as a form of controlling such fullness.

But this painting provokes questions such as: What name was given to the stitch or technique? Who embroidered and smocked the garment? Was it made in the home or in a workshop? Was it worked by a man or a woman? What kind of thread was used to embroider it?

Other paintings of great interest were painted by Dürer (1471-1528) who lived and spent most of his life in Nuremberg in Germany. He was a meticulous painter and observed great details of decoration on costumes of the time. In 1493 he painted a self-portrait (now in the Louvre, Paris). This is reputed to be his betrothal portrait because in the painting he is holding a flower in his hand. He is wearing a jacket and, underneath, a shirt with tight gathers across the rounded neckline. These gathers are edged with

Self-portrait aged 22, 1493, by Dürer

ribbon or braid, and on those closest to the braid a zig-zag stitch can clearly be seen. Could this have been diamond stitch still used in smocking today? Whatever it is, it would appear to be a decorative stitch over the gathers.

In 1498 he painted another self-portrait (in the Prado, Madrid) which shows his shirt finely gathered to a depth of several inches. It appears to be edged with a ribbon or braid, but this time there is no decoration discernible over the gathers. In 1499 he painted his friend Oswold Krel (in the Pinakothek, Munich), who wore a similar type of shirt, though the gathering appears to be less deep. However, one can just discern a tiny decoration at the top of the gathers.

These clear examples of decoration of gathers depicted in paintings of the fifteenth century are a very early record of smocking.

The Sixteenth Century

Fashions, however, do not change abruptly on the decade or on the turn of the century. At the beginning of the sixteenth century 'The Mona Lisa' (in the Louvre, Paris), painted by Leonardo da Vinci between 1503 and 1506, still depicts a rounded neckline which is gathered and edged with braid, ribbon or a band, while on the gathers a form of decoration can be seen. Other paintings of this period show very full chemises worn under dresses, and shirts worn by men with decoration controlling fullness at the neckline. This can be seen in Lucas Van Leyden's 'The Card Players' (in the National Gallery of Art, Washington) painted circa 1520. But this decoration might have been a separate piece of embroidery applied as a band to the fullness.

Such gathers may be seen in the paintings of Holbein the Younger (1497-1543), particularly in 'Edward VI as a child' (in the National Gallery of Art, Washington). However, in two of his portraits of Jane Seymour, Henry VIII's third wife (in the Kunsthistorische Museum, Vienna, and the Mauritshuis in The Hague), the paintings depict a dress with a square neckline and a narrow flat edging extending beyond the neckline. This may have been her smock, worn to protect her fine dress. Furthermore, the sleeves of the dress in both portraits show large areas of an undersleeve which could have been part of the undergarment, or even a separate piece.

While the chemise or *camicia* was used in Italy in the second half of the fifteenth century as a loose garment, 'smock' was the name used in sixteenth-century England for a woman's loose garment, though of course the term had been used long before. However, at this time its function becomes obvious as there are explicit references to the 'smock' in writings and

Fragments found amongst Tudor material in London

inventories of the period. We have seen, too, that it is shown in paintings, depicted with rich embroidery and lace. Although this garment did not show smocking as we understand it today, it was a smock garment in the sense that it was loose fitting.

Later in the sixteenth century smocks were cut higher, some having a high neckband with attached frill which later gave way to a separate ruff. In portraits of the period these changes in the style of the smock are evident, as Janet Arnold points out in her article on *Elizabethan and Jacobean Smocks and Shirts*.[2]

She explains that at the same time, men were wearing shirts similar in cut and decoration to women's smocks, the only difference being the width over the hips. In a man's shirt the sides would be straight, whereas in a woman's smock the sides might slope outwards or extra fullness allowed for (as Janet Arnold has shown in her diagrams). The embroidery, in some instances, was placed in the same position in both garments, and Janet Arnold suggests that they were made by women who used the same designs for each.

During Henry VIII's reign inventories mention 'shirtes' and in Elizabeth I's reign, New Year gifts given to the Queen included 'smokes' and the embroidery on them is described as being 'wrought with' all kinds of silk and metal thread.

A boy's shirt of the middle of the sixteenth century exhibited in the Victoria and Albert Museum in London shows fullness at the neck beneath an embroidered band edged with a frill. An early man's shirt dated between 1585 and 1600 is in the Museum of Costume in Bath. This shirt is made in white linen, embroidered with black silk thread. The embroidery

2. I am indebted to Janet Arnold in her article 'Elizabethan and Jacobean Smocks and Shirts' in the journal *Waffen und Kostumkunde* Vol. 19 1977 (pages 89-110) for much information in this section.

designs show the Elizabethans' delight in coiling stems, roses, oak leaves, insects and birds.

Three fragments of smocked twilled wool, now in the Museum of London, were found amongst Tudor material in London in the early twentieth century. These pieces are most interesting as they are not English smocking as we know it. These fragile pieces are very tightly gathered and decorated with surface stitchery, in a zig-zag pattern, rather like smocked pattern darning, but unfortunately, they are too delicate to examine properly. There are small metal decorations on one fragment. However, nothing further is known about these pieces.

The Seventeenth Century

Around 1600 Shakespeare wrote *Much Ado About Nothing* in which Leonato describing Beatrice says, 'For she'll be up twenty times a night, and there will she sit in her smock 'til she have writ a sheet of paper,' and in 1604 in *Othello* the moor says to Desdemona, 'O ill starr'd wench! Pale as thy smock!'

It is evident, therefore, that at the beginning of the seventeenth century the smock was an established garment. Several smocks of this period have survived and are exhibited in museums. In the Museum of London is a smock of 1603-15, made of white linen and trimmed with needle lace. A smock made of white linen embroidered in red silk and dated 1615-25 is in the Warwickshire Museum Costume Collection, Warwick.

However, it is in the seventeenth century that we now begin to see the first evidence of English smocking as we understand it today. In the Museum of Costume in Bath, there is an enchanting baby layette consisting of eleven pieces, two of which are smocked, one being a baby cap and the other a long bib. The crown of the cap is smocked in seven bands, each band consisting of one row of stem stitch, one row of cable stitch and one row of stem stitch. The bib has the same pattern repeated in a small area in the front. Both the cap and the bib, as well as the other pieces are edged in an embroidered couched trailing design in fine cord. Also, of this period there is a child's set at the Victoria and Albert Museum, London, amongst which are two baby caps, one long and one short, each with smocked crowns.

The Eighteenth Century

An early piece of smocking as we know it today can be seen on another child's cap of circa 1700 at Platt Hall, Manchester. The crown is smocked in stem and wave stitch. From this and the few other pieces of smocking

Above Smock of white linen dated 1615-25 in Warwickshire Museum Costume Collection

Below Cap and bib from the Museum of Costume, Bath

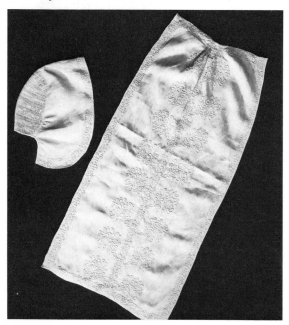

Detail of a baby's bonnet showing smocking with buttonhole loops, 18th century

to have survived from this period it is possible to see how it was worked and what use was made of it.

Examples of baby clothes at this time show the use of a restrained form of smocking on the inside of baby gowns where it was used to hold the fullness neatly. Upon examination of these garments the gathering of the fine fabrics is so beautifully executed, that one does not expect to see the smocking hidden away. Stem stitch is commonly used to control this fullness on the wrong side to hold the gathers in place. This is also seen on the inside of gowns.

Baby bonnets of this century, again executed in very fine fabric, show smocking very simply arranged around the exquisitely embroidered crowns, some of which were worked in hollie point, a very fine needle lace. Stem stitch is used again on the gathers and sometimes it is further enhanced with a buttonhole loop over the gathers, as seen in the baby bonnet in the Embroiderers' Guild Collection.

An interesting polonaise of circa 1785 in the Bankfield Museum, Halifax, shows honeycomb smocking worked on a striped silk fabric as a decoration on the deep trimming on the cuffs.

Words used to describe a loose garment are confusing; smock until the eighteenth century referred to a woman's undergarment, after which time it was called a shift and later a chemise. Men, however, still wore shirts while frock, the name given to a full-skirted coat worn by men until the end of this century, was replaced by a new form of garment with decoration, known as a smock-frock or smock.

Towards the end of the century George Morland (1763-1804) painted *genre* scenes showing figures wearing loose garments but he shows no clear definition of decoration on them although some by this time were ornamented. One such smock is from Mayfield in East Sussex. It is dated 1779 and appears to be the earliest smock showing true smocking. Though

many generations of the family have worn it, it is still in good condition for it is a wedding smock and as such has been treasured and, therefore, preserved.

The Nineteenth Century

The popularity of the decorated smock became widespread in the first half of the nineteenth century. Smocks were made of tough material and many have survived and are now preserved in museums throughout Britain. They were written about, painted, drawn, and later photographed, and therefore from the nineteenth century there is much evidence about smocks.

Many writers of the period referred to smock-frocks. In *The Two Drovers* (1827) Sir Walter Scott wrote: 'Robin Oig returned to Heskett's Inn [in Cumbria]. The place was filled at once by various sorts of men ... among whom was Henry Wakefield, who, amidst the grinning group of smock-frocks, hob-nailed boots and jolly English physiognomies ...' Charles Dickens wrote in *The Old Curiosity Shop* (1840): 'men who lounged about all night in smock-frocks and leather leggings'.

In *Burne-Jones Talking – His Conversations 1885-1898*, preserved by his studio assistant Thomas Rooke, we read: 'On a Sunday afternoon once, when I was at Oxford (about 1850) I came to a church in a meadow

The Mayfield smock, 1779

. . . I waited until the end for the congregation to come out . . . and when it was all over there came out about six old men (and perhaps a woman or two) dressed in smock-frocks and nice fluffy hats, with pretty embroidery on the smock-frocks.'

Thomas Hardy, too, in *Under the Greenwood Tree* (1872) writing about an earlier period described stalwart ruddy men and boys assembling for choir practice as: 'mainly in snow-white smock frocks embroidered upon the shoulders and breasts in ornamental forms of hearts, diamonds and zig-zags.' And in *Far From the Madding Crowd* he wrote that in Weatherbury: 'the long smock frocks have nearly disappeared.' Another reference appears in his poem 'An Unkindly May' which begins: 'A shepherd stands by a gate in a white smock-frock:/ He holds the gate ajar, intently courting his flock'.

In *Lark Rise to Candleford*, Flora Thompson describing the 1880s wrote: 'The carter, shepherd and a few of the older labourers still wore the traditional smock-frock, topped by a round black felt hat, like those formerly worn by clergymen. But this old country style of dress was already out of date; most of the men wore suits of stiff, dark brown corduroy, or in summer corduroy trousers and an unbleached drill jacket known as a "sloppy".'

Painters of the nineteenth century depicted a full loose garment in many a *genre* scene, but it is difficult to see any precise stitching on them which might indicate decoration on the gathers. Good examples of various forms of the smock garment can be seen in the following paintings: In 'Woburn Sheep Shearing,

'Snowballing', by John Morgan, showing several little boys in smocks

1811', George Garrard depicted shepherds and others in smocks with decoration; John Crome (1768-1821) painted 'View on Mousehold Heath near Norwich' in which the fullness of the garment suggests a smock; James Ward (1769-1859), brother-in-law of George Morland, painted 'Sheep Shearing' in 1828, showing shepherds in loose-gathered garments with a little decoration discernible; 'Village Choir, Bow Brickhill Church, Buckinghamshire' by Thomas Webster (1800-1886), exhibited in 1847, shows one man in a smock; Samuel Palmer (1805-1881) suggests a smock-like garment in 'The Sleeping Shepherd – Morning' in 1857.

Small boys in smocks are delightfully portrayed in many paintings right up to the end of the nineteenth century. The pictures tell us so much about the occasions on which boys wore smocks, which appear to be smaller versions of an adult's. In his painting 'Snowballing' John Morgan (1823-1886) painted four figures wearing gathered smocks enjoying their sport despite the cold while other figures are clad in a different style wearing trousers, short woolly jackets and scarves.

In 'A Dame's School' by Thomas Webster (1800-1886) several little boys are shown in gathered smocks while other boys are also in a different attire. A painting by W. Hopkins and E. Havell, 'Weston Sands, 1864' shows two youths in what would appear to be smocks. Alfred Downing Fripp (1822-1895) in 'The Piping Shepherd' shows a romantic youth in a bluish-green smock with contrasting smocking, complete with a patch across the side seam and open flap-pocket. In John Reid's 'A Country Cricket Match' of 1878, there is a marquee with spectators near the village green. One adult is wearing a smock, and two

small boys are in full smocks. Another artist, Charles Edward Wilson (1854-1941) painted young boys in smocks in several of his works including 'A Rustic Angler', 'Rustic Anglers' and 'No Luck Today' which show would-be anglers trying their luck in a brook. 'The Fight' by John Morgan shows a scene near a cricket field with adults separating the so-called offenders, three of whom are wearing smocked garments. Helen Allingham (1848-1926) was another artist who portrayed children in smocks.

As well as paintings, there are many drawings and engravings of the period in which artists drew people wearing smocks. An illustration in the *Illustrated London News* of 1851 shows 'Agriculturists at the Exhibition' (the Great Exhibition at the Crystal Palace) showing countrymen and boys in smocks.

Towards the end of the century *Cassells Family Magazine* in 1893 showed a picture of 'A new sheep-shearer' wearing a smock. In the same magazine, a vignette shows two smock-clad figures driving sheep along a country road. This magazine was not simply aimed at country dwellers but at townspeople too. The nostalgic feeling for a folk costume fast disappearing was haunting artists intent on preserving an image of rural 'Merrie England'.

There are many photographs, too, of venerable old men in smocks and these are preserved in various museums. Many show ageing veterans in an agricultural era when the countryman worked long hours to make a living. One such photograph in the Buckinghamshire County Museum, Aylesbury shows Robert Hinton, born circa 1774, in a smock in 1856. Other photographs show bent old men still working at their labours, as well as boys in tattered clothes. However, towards the end of the century photographers became aware of the attractiveness of the vanishing folk costume of the countryman and instead, captured workers in their smock garments in romantic cottage settings – taking tea beside the fire, outside thatched cottages, drinking ale – or shepherds with their sheep dogs.

The predominantly rural and somewhat idyllic setting for the smock or smock-frock can, therefore, be visualized and seen in references in literature and art in the nineteenth century. For the countryman 'was surrounded by pastoral beauty' – his manner of living was, in essence, simple, and what communications there were did not greatly impinge on his life. So, living in rural England or Wales he kept to his conservative ways and though changes were afoot in industrial areas, he was content to carry on the customs and tradition of his area. The smock garment, in which the style tended to become localized, continued to be worn. Sometimes, however, farm workers might move on to another area when job

Detail from 'Agriculturalists at the Exhibition' – as illustrated in the *Illustrated London News* of July 1851

opportunities arose, taking with them a particular type of local smock.[3]

It would seem that few smocks were recorded as being worn in the north of England, although Sir Walter Scott noted in 1827 in Cumberland (now Cumbria), 'a group of smock-frocks'. Lady Stanley of Alderley,[4] writing in 1851 of her return home to the south of England, having lived all her married life in Cheshire, says '. . . had the pleasure of seeing the smock-frock in numbers which my eyes had not seen since I left Sheffield.' She was referring to Sheffield Park in Sussex. Elizabeth Gaskell, a few years later, in *North and South*[5] writes about Margaret Hale from Hampshire describing her new home in Lancashire as 'There were no smock-frocks even among the country folk.'

Sadly, because the smock was worn mainly by agricultural labourers who did not give much thought to their preservation, there is little exact documentation about the garment. The information that does survive is verbal and details rely only on recollections from memory. Ownership may be known, but details of stitchery are almost negligible.

The Workwoman's Guide written in 1838 (see Bibliography), however, gives details of a 'waggoner's smock' with the following description: 'made of strong linen, similar to that used for sheeting, and the biassing upon it is worked with the strongest glazed thread or cotton that can be procured. This work must be firmly and regularly done, as the price of these frocks depends on the quantity and quality of the

3. Anne Buck: 'Clothes in Fact and Fiction'. *Costume* 1983. Page 95.
4. Anne Buck: Ibid. Page 95.
5. Anne Buck: 'The Countryman's Smock'. *Folk Life* Vol. 1 1963. Pages 19, 20, 21.

work in them. The shoulders and wrists as well as the back are biassed with strong, glazed thread in various patterns. . . . The plain part between the biassing and the armhole is worked in chain stitch, as also the collar in various patterns. These frocks are to be met with at clothing warehouses, and cost from 9 shillings to 18 shillings each, the price depending on the quantity and quality of the work put in.'

The detailed drawings accompanying the article clearly show the cut, the smocking and the embroidery on the 'box' – the area at the side of the smocked panel, collar and cuff. This, with the description, give a clear picture of what an early Victorian smock looked like. However, while the illustrations show smocking as we understand it, the explanation given for 'biassing' in another section of the book, describes it as being worked on gathers in an entirely different way.

A man might possess two smocks – one for Sunday best and one for working. The best one, usually made of white linen, would be for Sundays and special occasions such as weddings, funerals and national celebrations. In the Warwickshire Museum Costume Collection, Warwick, there is a smock of circa 1850 made in white linen for a wedding anniversary and for Sunday wear. Another, also made in white linen, was for Sunday best and for playing the fiddle for Morris dancers on the green. Another smock in the same collection belonged to a Warwickshire farmer and has as accessories, a blue and white check scarf marked with his name, a pair of cream knitted socks embroidered with his initials and a pair of white linen spats.

The everyday smock, made in twilled cotton cloth or drabbet, could be in varying colours from white to brown including a greenish-brown colour, blue and also black. Mary Mitford in *Our Village* (1824-32) describes how a carter 'sometimes in cold weather throws over all a smock frock . . . one of that light blue Waterloo such as butchers wear.'[6]

George Ewart Evans writing about 'Dress and the Rural Historian'[7] writes of Mrs Reynolds, born in 1891 at Westerham in Kent: 'She told me, for instance, about the smock that the farm workers wore in her part of Kent: the smock was made of twill. But I'll tell you what they did – if they were – well, very poor people they used to do marvellous smocks in thick, unbleached calico – and do you know, they were most attractive because the unbleached calico had flecks of white in it, and I can't tell you how effective that was in these smocks. But I as a child have seen, on a

winter's day, some of the cottage wives with bandages on their fingers: they had been doing smocking with that stuff. With the cold weather, their hands – they'd got their hands in a really bad state through forcing the needle through the smocking. They were beautiful to see. They were very warm, perhaps too warm in summer.'

Anne Farwell in an article 'A Gathering of Smocks' describes an 88-year-old Berkshire labourer reflecting on his childhood: 'I did use to have to walk from Wheatley to the factory at Oxford with a bundle of those heavy smocks, as I'd waxed the thread for and ruled the lines on in chalk. Mam only fetched in ninepence a smock.'

There is another report from this area from a man whose mother made two smocks per week, for which she received 2s 2d for each. As a boy he used to help his mother by waxing her needles so that they pierced the heavy fabric more easily.[8]

A story related by Elizabeth Bishop in 'A Family Heirloom' refers to her great-great grandmother who lived in the early nineteenth century. She made smocks for members of her family and for many of the labourers who lived in the Sussex area for 1s 6d a time.

A Warwickshire smock made for Mr William Hanson Sale by his wife was used by him when he was wool grading. This is an example of a smock being made in the home for the family, and as was customary with many a treasured smock it would be handed on to the next generation.

There were specialist smock-makers such as Mary Bufton who worked in Hereford before 1835, who is said to have taken orders for smocks from a sample smock. There is also a smock in the Warwickshire County Museum Costume Collection made by a young woman as part of a Diploma Course taken at an Agricultural College late in the century.

There were towns where the smock-making industry centred around factories making cloth. At Newark-on-Trent in Nottinghamshire, records show that there were ten smock-makers listed between 1819 and 1872 – the earliest mention of a smock-maker in the town being 1807. Linen for the smocks was woven in Newark, the dyeing took place locally, and the smocks were made and sold in the town to farmers and agricultural workers. The designs for the embroidery on the smocks were stamped on with sheet metal pattern printers which still exist. A dark-blue smock showing one of these designs is in existence in the Newark Museum. There was another smock-making industry in the market town of Haverhill in Suffolk.[9]

6. Anne Buck: 'The Countryman's Smock'. *Folk Life* Vol. 1 1963. Page 24.

7. George Ewart Evans: 'Dress and the Rural Historian'. *Costume* 1974. Page 39.

8. Christine Bloxham: 'Oxfordshire Smocks' Oxfordshire Museums Information Sheet No. 16. 1980.

An unmade smock showing part of the construction

A smock industry also existed in Abingdon, Oxfordshire, where the Census returns in 1851 state that the wives and daughters of labourers and craftsmen of the town and surrounding villages were employed as outworkers making smocks and garments.[10]

Museum records list many occupations for those who wore smocks – mostly concerned with outdoor pursuits. Many were farmers, judges of livestock, shepherds, stockmen, agricultural labourers, ploughmen, cowmen, gardeners, woodmen, waggoners and carters. Fishmongers and butchers were tradespeople known to have worn them too.

Smocks were put to a variety of uses and were much sought after and highly prized. They were worn by a bridegroom at his wedding; worn by pall bearers and others attending funerals – several villages are known to have had sets of smocks for pall bearers. They were given as prizes in ploughing matches and smocks are also recorded as having been worn when performing at local concerts.

The smock at this time was a garment for protection from the weather – perhaps the forerunner of the raincoat, for some were already oiled. Gertrude Jekyll in *Old West Surrey* (1904) wrote about the nineteenth century: 'The old carter's smock-frock or round frock, still lingering, but on its way to becoming extinct . . .

no better thing has ever been devised for any kind of outdoor wear that admits of the use of an outer garment. It turns an astonishing amount of wet.'

In order to protect the wearer, the smock was cut very full and to control this fullness the fabric was gathered up and decorated, thus giving elasticity to the garment. Various expressions were used to describe the technique of decoration on gathers. In 1838, the word 'biassing' was used, and in 1851 'gauging', and the first recorded use of 'smocking' is in circa 1880. The older name for smocking appears to be 'plaiting'.

In *Proverbs in the English Tongue* (1546), John Heywood quotes 'I shall cut my cote after my cloth.' Throughout the centuries and into the nineteenth century, cloth was laboriously woven by hand on a loom, the width of the loom dictating the width of the cloth. The proverb above means that every piece of precious cloth was used. And so it was with the countryman's smock: according to the width of the loom, so every piece was cut as economically as possible into oblongs and squares, the selvedges being no exception as they added strength to the seam and saved extra sewing.

Three styles of smocks, with variations, have emerged and are to be found in different areas of Britain. Though these areas are not defined by precise boundaries, there are certain recognizable variations in the garment, possibly influenced by weather and tradition.[11]

One type of smock was the 'round smock'. Basic oblongs and squares used to make the pattern for this smock consisted of the following pieces: front (1); back (1); shoulder straps cut double (2); sleeves (2); cuffs cut double (2); gussets (2). The smocking would be placed in the centre, front and back. Embroidery, elaborate or otherwise, would generally enhance the 'boxes' at either side of the smocking on both front and back, and sometimes on the collar and shoulder straps as well. Smocking would draw the sleeve-top in as well as at the cuff.

This type of smock was sometimes called a 're-versible' smock. As it was the same both back and front, it could be turned back to front so that it wore evenly, and if the front became dirty, also – both very practical reasons in those days. There were many variations in the details of the length of the neck opening and how it was finished, the collar, type of pocket, buttons and of course length. One unusual version of this style is in the Warwickshire Museum Costume Collection, Warwick and is a white linen smock, reversible with a stand-up collar.

9. Anne Buck: 'The Countryman's Smock'. *Folk Life*. Vol. 1 1963. Pages 22, 23.
10. Christine Bloxham: 'Oxfordshire Smocks'. Oxfordshire Museums Information Sheet No. 16. 1980.

11. I am indebted to Anne Buck in her article 'The Countryman's Smock' (*Folk Life* Vol. 1 1963) for much of the information on types of smocks in this section.

Above 'Round' type smock – Buckinghamshire, 1810
Below 'Surrey' type smock

Above 'Coat-smock' type of heavy natural linen, 19th century

Another type was the 'coat-smock' which was cut in much the same basic way as the 'round smock' except that, being a coat style, it opened down the front. Made in strong linen, it was a heavy garment and meant for practical use, rather than for best. It was worn in the western counties of England and Wales where protection from a wetter climate was essential. There were variations in the style; these showed larger collars with embroidered tucked ends. Others developed cape-like collars, and still others replaced these by large collars with enormous epaulettes. All these garments were richly embroidered to the extent of decoration between the buttonholes – a spectacular sight on the hill farms of Wales and nearby.

A variation of the 'coat-smock' was one made with parallel tucks instead of the smocked area. This would give the protection required from the weather.

Another style is called the 'Surrey' type, as it was commonly worn in Surrey. This was a much simpler garment – it was more like a man's shirt. The cut was also simpler, the fabric being cut in one length the width of the cloth and folded at the shoulder, thus obviating the need for a seam. An opening for the neck was cut as well as short openings down the front and the back. Over the shoulder fold a strap was superimposed. The sleeves with cuffs were cut out like the other styles, with a gusset underneath.

The 'Surrey' type is very restrained, both in smocking and embroidery, compared with the two types of smocks already described. In the 'Surrey' type, the smocking which is placed either side of the neck-opening ranges from only 1½in to 4in (4-10cm) in depth with only approximately 2in (5cm) in width. The embroidery, used to decorate the strap, collar and cuffs simply, is very delicate and of a linear form. This style was in use across the Surrey border into Hampshire, and one from that county, and said to have been in the family before 1800, is of this style and is still owned by the family.

These three versions with many variations show the style of the garment as it appeared in the nineteenth century in England and Wales. In constructing the garment most were seamed by hand. Sadly, the fineness of the hand-sewn seams and finishes on the garment showed a skill which was to slowly disappear and towards the end of the century machine stitching was introduced. This can be seen on a coat-smock in the Warwickshire Museum Costume Collection, Warwick dated circa 1880.

On these garments, the smocking, together with the embroidery, was the outstanding feature and it was finely executed. It developed and reached a peak between 1830 and 1870 but disappeared towards the end of the century – perhaps the invention of the sewing machine contributed to the decline.

The smocking, whether in large or small areas of the garment, worked closely together or sparsely, gives a unique richness to the smock. The stitches used for the smocking were the basic smocking stitches that we still know today – stem, outline, cable and wave. All these stitches and permutations of them make rich textures with the play of light of self-colour against self-colour, such as white smocking on white linen, and natural-coloured smocking on natural linen.

To prepare for the smocking decoration, the fabric would be gathered up accurately either by counting the threads or by eye. The thread used to smock with was generally linen, with the same thread being used for the embroidery.

The embroidery on 'boxes', collars, cuffs and yokes was an outstanding feature on these smocks. The designs showed the usual, simple folk art decorations such as geometrical designs of circles, diamonds, lozenges, squares, zig-zags, spirals, whorls and stars. Hearts were popular as well as leaves, floral motifs and pine cones. The stitches used were simple basic stitches such as feather, chain, stem, herringbone, and French knots.

Several smocks have survived embroidered with 'VR' and a crown. These garments were evidently intended for very special occasions, such as the celebration of Queen Victoria's Accession in 1837 or her Jubilees in 1887 and 1897. For the Great Exhibition in 1851 two of the very finest were produced by Hannah and Esther Stimpson for Harris and Tomkins of Abingdon, near Oxford. Designed by Thomas Watson, they show numerous mottoes and devices together with oak boughs, acorns, a wheatsheaf, a hive of bees, a rose, a thistle, and a shamrock. All are most exquisitely and elaborately worked.

Some boy's smocks are preserved in museums. One, dated 1870 in Gloucester Museum, shows deep, smocked panels, front and back and with a front opening to below the panel. The skirt has two tucks decorated with feather-stitching near the hemline – this would have been useful for letting the hem down. The yoke straps are heavily embroidered and the sleeves are long and smocked at the top and at the wrist. The scarcity of these tough and practical boy's smocks suggests that in large families this garment would be handed down until it had outworn its use. In *Old West Surrey* (1904) Gertrude Jekyll referring to country boys of the nineteenth century said: 'Boys had short round frocks like small smock-frocks over suits of corduroy; these short frocks were sometimes called by the old name "gabardine".'

The smock as a garment is associated with artists in various ways. William Morris (1834-1896) was known

William Morris in a smock of the 1870s

to wear one in the 1870s; the wife of the artist G. F. Watts (1817-1904) who herself was a painter, is shown wearing a smock and palette in hand, in a photograph circa 1887; and Dante Gabriel Rossetti (1828-1882) depicted a smock in his painting 'Found' (in the Bancroft Collection, Wilmington Society of Fine Arts, Delaware, U.S.A.).

At the end of the nineteenth century the decorated smock had declined in popularity as a practical garment for countrymen, but its influence could be seen in other strata of society. In considering these one has to look back to the beginning of Queen Victoria's reign and study the dress of the fashionable woman then. It was not so much what the outward appearance showed, though this was restricting enough, with sleeves set below the shoulder line and thus restraining the raising of her arms, but her underpinning.[12] This, of course, was the laced corset worn to produce a 'wasp' waist and so restricting and uncomfortable that it was no wonder the poor creatures had the 'vapours' or fainted on couches and had to be revived by smelling salts.

Though other parts of a woman's attire changed, the corset remained throughout the nineteenth century in one form or another. Doctors were concerned about the ill effects they produced and dress-reformers tried their best through magazine articles and societies to change fashion. Eventually women sympathetic to dress reform led the way by dispensing with the fashionable corset and crinoline and, with natural waistlines restored, took to wearing comfortable, full dresses of a flowing kind. Sleeves were set in at the natural sleeve line thus giving ease of movement. There was an emphasis on 'hygienic' dress and the Aesthetic Movement of the 1870s and 1880s encouraged women to dress more comfortably but without sacrificing beauty.

Liberty's, founded in 1875, opened a dress department in the store in 1884 to cater for the needs of those who wished to buy their beautiful imported silks. These silks were ideal for the gowns of those who did not wish to adhere rigidly to the demands of fashion, and the firm also offered a dressmaking service. In 1894 their first fashion catalogue was issued showing on each page a drawing of the garment with price and details, as well as a perforated side for tearing out and using as an order form. Their styles were undatable and smocking was very much in evidence.[13]

The following, from *A Writer's Recollections* (1918) by M. A. Ward (Mrs Humphrey Ward), sums up the setting: 'For nine years, till the spring of 1881, we lived in Oxford ... We gave dinner parties and furnished our houses with Morris papers, old chests and cabinets, and blue pots ... Most of us were very anxious to be up-to-date and in the fashion, whether in aesthetics, in housekeeping or education. But our fashion was not that of Belgravia, or Mayfair, which indeed we scorned! It was the fashion of the movement which sprang from Morris and Burne-Jones. Liberty stuffs, very plain in line, but elaborately "smocked" were greatly in vogue, and evening dresses "cut square", or with "Watteau" pleats were generally worn, and often in conscious protest against the London "low" dresses which Oxford – young married Oxford – thought "ugly" and "fast". And when we had donned our Liberty gowns we went out to dinner, the husband walking, the wife in a bath chair drawn by an ancient member of an ancient and close fraternity – the "chairman" of old Oxford!'

Liberty's had led the way with a dressmaking and catalogue service showing smocked garments. At that time amateur dressmaking was in its infancy, so other services were required, and in 1887 Weldons published the first of four books on *Practical Smocking*, stating: 'When the rage for artistic dressing set in a few years ago, smocking was revived and brought into requisition for the ornamentation of ladies and children's summer costumes, for lawn-tennis dresses and holland blouses; and so greatly has it increased in favour that it is now a recognised style of fashionable dress.'

This same book contained drawings and directions for all manner of articles, such as smocked bodices, children's dresses, a muff, drawers and even a bathing suit. For the latter, 10 yards of 27-inch serge or flannel in navy blue 'smocked with red wool, silk or ingrain cotton stands the sea-water better than any other colours', is part of the description which goes on to define the smocked areas of this two-piece as being at the knees for the knickers, and at the neck for the blouse.

The second series showed a 'Home' or 'Tea Gown', flannelette knickers as well as children's wear of a smocked pinafore, a smock for a boy, a boy's smocked dress (aged 2-6), a boy's American blouse and a smocked evening cloak.

The third series depicted dresses, bodices and a 'diamond pattern' for smocking on a plastron (a bodice front), as well as children's clothes of Dorothy Mantle, a ploughboy's blouse and a smocked granny bonnet for a child of 2-3 years.

In the fourth series elaborate aprons and a lady's dressing jacket were illustrated using various stitches to illustrate the technique – stitches which are still used today.

---

12. I am indebted to Stella Mary Newton in her book *Health, Art and Reason* (John Murray, London 1974) for much of the information in this section.
13. *Liberty's 1875-1975 – An Exhibition to mark the firm's centenary*. Victoria and Albert Museum, London 1975.

From *Weldon's Practical Smocking*, 1887

Smocking obviously was the rage, and Weldons, in their first series of 1887, gave clear instructions on how to set about the technique: 'One method of proceeding is to take a piece of perforated cardboard', and goes on to mention, 'Quite lately, for convenience in smocking, Mr Briggs has issued sheets of transfer papers imprinted with small dots at regular intervals.' This appears to be the beginning of the use of transfer dots in smocking and they are still used nearly 100 years later. It is interesting to note that Deighton's, another transfer firm, has also been in existence a long time; it has been manufacturing smocking dots for around 100 years as well as being involved in the manufacture of general needlework transfers since 1870.

Weldons' smocking instructions went on to mention that, 'If a lady can succeed in satisfactorily working her own smocking, she can pass it over to her dressmaker to be made up, and the result will probably afford gratification.' Furthermore it adds that, 'Smocking may be worked upon almost any material, the Liberty silks, pongee silks, and Umritza cashmere being especially suitable.'

It is not surprising that Weldons' magazines, of which *Practical Smocking* was one, found their way into odd corners of the globe, as is implied in their page entitled 'What others say of Weldons Paper Patterns and Publications', with snippets from as far afield as Java, 'in the bush', the 'Antipodes' and Italy.

Smocking had arrived and was soon to establish itself; ever since it has been a form of decoration much-loved by the needlewomen in Britain and elsewhere – a technique handed on from mother to daughter and synonymous with Liberty's.

Liberty gowns with smocking exist from the post-1880s. An early example of 1881 in the Victoria and Albert Museum, London shows a 'Liberty Indian washing silk with a white stripe, square neck with smocking on the bodice and puffed sleeves, a looped up overskirt.' A tea gown of 1891 in the Metropolitan Museum of Art in New York is of 'pale pink silk barathea and white china silk semi-fitted over a smocked and embroidered under-dress.' The label reads 'Liberty and Co. Artistic and Historic Costume Studio'.

Gowns from other sources, especially wedding gowns of the period, show the rich decorative use of the technique. One wedding dress shows the whole sleeve richly worked in honeycomb stitch with tiny pearls for the spots. The stitch alone was used for rich panels and insertions to enhance the rest of this already elaborate garment. Another wedding dress, of ivory crêpe de Chine, shows the simplicity of honey-

A richly-smocked Victorian wedding dress, *circa* 1880

Green aesthetic dress of between 1893 and 1898

day, *Queen* (1880) had this to say: 'Smocking so popular one or two years ago for lawn-tennis costume has now found its way into children's dress', and *Ladies Treasury* of the same date commented: 'The fancy of the moment is for children to wear the new provincial smock made exactly like the carters' or waggoners' dowlas frocks . . . they are decidedly not becoming to little folks.'[14]

In the Museum of Costume in Bath is an interesting little girl's dress made of woollen cloth with smocking and embroidery; this early dress, dated around 1830, makes use of the smocking as a trimming.

Two years after Liberty's opened their dress department in 1884, their catalogue shows a Mab Smock with smocking at the yoke and on the wrist. In 1887, largely inspired by Kate Greenaway's books, they issued a catalogue called *Artistic Dress for Children* and showed a 'Kate Greenaway' dress with smocked yoke and sleeves.[15]

In the traditional style of a smock, *Weldons Practical Smocking* (third series) of 1887 illustrated and gave instructions for a Ploughboy's Blouse for sizes 2-10 years, describing it as, 'This little smocked pinafore or blouse is made exactly after the style of the smocks worn by countrypeople, and it is exceptionally pretty for boys in petticoats as well as for those wearing suits, as it forms a thorough protection and at the same time is very dressy.' They recommended 2¼, 2¾, 3 and 3¼ yards of 36-inch linen and advised preparing the material for smocking by drawing lines on the wrong side from right to left, then crossing these by perpendicular lines ½-inch apart for gauging the size of the pleats.

Several smocks for boys are seen in the Warwickshire Museum Costume Collection, Warwick. These belong to the late part of the nineteenth century and show how the style was being perpetuated. A boy's smock in natural-coloured linen and smocked and embroidered in natural-coloured thread with hand-sewn seams is in the traditional round-frock style. Dorset wheel buttons fasten the short opening at the back. This garment won a prize at 'the local institute'. Another smock from the same museum is made of white linen and decorated with embroidery and smocking in white thread. It is also in the style of a round frock with a short back opening. Interestingly, the boxes are of double-thickness fabric.

Generally, the fabrics used for making smocks for both adults and for boys were of plain material, so it is interesting to find a child's smock of the 1890s in patterned fabric. This smock, now in the Museum of

comb stitch. This was worked at intervals, in peaks, around a full flounce with a train at the bottom of the skirt, as well as on the sleeves at the elbow. Another wedding dress exists with inset panels worked in honeycomb.

A green aesthetic dress of between 1893 and 1898, with rich smocking on a rounded neckline and deep waist, shows the fullness and elasticity that this technique can give.

Several tea gowns in the Castle Museum, Nottingham show how smocking was used on these leisure gowns. One dated 1890-4 is a gown in pink silk with dark green velvet, the smocked decorations being at the waist and neck in honeycomb stitch worked in a pink thread on the green velvet. Another tea gown of between 1892 and 1900 is of pink silk richly embroidered with an ivory silk-panelled front. This is deeply smocked in ivory honeycomb stitch at the neck of the panel.

A blouse in the Liverpool Museum of between 1890 and 1910 is of fine ivory silk deeply smocked in various stitches in ivory across the top and at the wrists.

Not only was smocking seen on adult garments but on children's too, the technique being ideal for comfort and growth. It is not surprising that it was adaptable to clothes for the young. In magazines of the

14. Phyllis Cunningham and Anne Buck: *Children's Costume in England 1300-1900.* A & C Black, London 1965.
15. Alison Adburgham: *Liberty's – A Biography of a Shop.* Allen & Unwin, London 1975. Page 53.

Child's dress, *circa* 1890

the same subject painted some years earlier. It shows Red Riding Hood in a long, golden-yellow dress with smocking at the waist.

At the close of the nineteenth century smocking had become firmly established as a technique. It had surfaced on the countryman's smock in the early years of the century, and come to a peak in popularity about 1850. The smock was becoming obsolete as a male garment towards the end of the century, so causing the art of decoration on these clothes to deteriorate. Sadly, the industrial age had arrived with machines for use on the farm and for sewing. There was little need for these full, flowing picturesque garments – they were not safe to wear for the new mechanical tasks. Slowly they were discarded and although still worn into the twentieth century, for country people change their habits slowly, they became the exception rather than the rule.

From the fashion point of view, the dress reformers found smocking an ideal and artistic way to decorate their flowing garments as well as a practical decoration for their children's clothes and for the clothes for their dolls. Thus, when the smock ceased to be a working garment and was discarded, it found a new role in the world of fashion and this was to be extended into the twentieth century.

The Twentieth Century

At the beginning of the twentieth century the use of smocking continued in the fashionable field of clothing for children and adults. One child's dress in the Warwickshire Museum Costume Collection, Warwick existing from this period is made of ivory silk worked in cream silk and the style, with a yoke and puffed sleeves, could well be found in the present day.

The Butterick Publishing Company Limited (Paris, London and New York) mentioned smocking in a booklet published in 1902, saying, 'the recent revival of smocking or honeycombing has resulted in a number of pretty arrangements', and goes on to mention 'the two methods of making the smocking or honeycombing – the American and the English – the former is rather the simpler, but the result is exactly the same.' The difference appears to be slight and is only in the way the gathered fabric is held, that is with the gathers either in a horizontal or in a vertical position.

A scheme for the revival of the traditional smock was initiated by Mrs Sarah Bere, the wife of the vicar of Bere Regis in Dorset, in circa 1906. She set out to teach local people how to make replicas of the old smocks which they then sold or sometimes exhibited. In 1916 she gave up The Bere Regis Arts and Crafts Association, as it was known, to devote herself to war

Costume in Bath, is made of indigo-printed linen, said to be designed by William Morris, has a turned-down collar and long sleeves. It is smocked in two shades of blue thread at centre front and back, shoulders, and the wrists of the long sleeves.

Smocking for children's clothes was very popular in the 1890s – as can be verified from examples in the museums. The *Queen* magazine of 1890 wrote: 'Nothing could be daintier for a damsel of one or two years' old than a little smock of white washing silk . . . pretty blouse-waisted frocks for boys and girls or made either pink, blue or white smocked at the throat.'

A frock, made in circa 1890 of white flannel for a four-year-old, now in the Bethnel Green Museum, London, shows smocking below the yoke, at the waist and on the long sleeves, together with embroidery worked in white and brown silk. It was designed for Marshall and Snelgrove, a large London store. Also of a similar date, there is in the Liverpool Museum a child's dress in fine red-and-blue check wool, smocked in a strong red thread in surface honeycomb, making an interesting effect on the deep rounded neckline and sleeves. During the same period in 1890, G. F. Watts painted 'Little Red Riding Hood' (in the City Museums and Art Gallery, Birmingham) which appears to have been a larger version of a painting of work, but some of the villagers carried on with the craft of smocking.[16]

In *Embroidery*, edited by Mrs Archibald H. Christie, and published by James Pearsall & Company in 1909, an article on 'Smocking – a revival of an old English Craft – Part 1' comments, 'in these days, when revivals of old arts and industries are so numerous, lovers of good needlework may be glad to have their attention called to a branch of an old English handicraft which perhaps more than any other has suffered from neglect and misuse, and is in consequence, in danger of being altogether forgotten, or so misrepresented by modern adaptions as to lose all its historical and much of its decorative value.' The article goes on to describe the history of the smock which cannot be separated from the technique. In Part II the article recounts the story of an old lady who in 1905, at the age of 90, made her last smock just as she had always done for 'father and grandfather', and it also gives directions for smocking and embroidery stitches.

On colour, one was advised to avoid 'aesthetic shades' – it is preferable to work in blue on white or white on blue, or dull green or dark brown on light drab, or deep blue on deep blue linen, and, 'she will appreciate the severer charm of a pure white linen, richly embroidered in fine white thread'. Alice B. Evans, the writer of the article, goes on to warn, 'those who wish to see a genuine revival of smocking must realize that it is in danger of becoming a lost art, and must not be led astray by modern "practical" handbooks, which tell us that smocking has now reached such perfection that it can be adapted to tea cosies and numerous other things.'

Her comment on this last suggestion was that, 'the fine old English art that has come down to us unspoiled through so many centuries deserves a better fate than that.'

One of the most charming items of this period owned by Mrs Sheila Lovett-Turner is a delicate shell-pink silk umbrella, which in its combination of elegance and frivolity is the epitome of the Edwardian age. The trellis smocking in a matching colour is worked around the bottom edge of the umbrella, and the enchanting effect belongs to an age of style and leisure which was to disappear a few years afterwards. One wonders what Alice B. Evans would have thought of this departure in smocking.

Artists still drew on the sentimentality of the traditional smock for *genre* pictures depicting little boys in embroidered smocks.

The smock style for children was made during the first quarter of the century. One example for a girl is smocked in yellow thread on cream silk and wool

16. Maggie Hall: *Smocks.* Shire Publications Ltd, 1979. Page 30.

THE CHILDREN'S FROCK PARTY

U Ursula—says she has come up to town
For mother to buy her a Liberty-gown.

V Is Vera—the sweetest of tiny wee tots,
Is longing for fun, and wants lots and lots.

The Children's Frock Party, from Liberty's catalogue 1906

fabric; another of white twill cotton is more in the traditional style, smocked in white; others for children are of linen, smocked and trimmed in a colour. In Liberty's catalogue *The Children's Frock Party* published in 1906, the caption under U reads, 'Ursula says she has come up to town, For mother to buy her a Liberty-gown.' The gown shown is smocked.

Liberty's, always the leader of fashion, showed the changing mood of the times in their catalogues. In 1913 just before World War I, an elegant rest gown called 'Lousette' and a tea gown called 'Old English' are depicted. This was to be the end of an era and in 1915, a simpler, smocked gown is shown. By 1916 their catalogues displayed, among other items, several smocked work coats. The war had created a demand which Liberty's answered. Some land-girls were depicted, too, wearing lightly smocked overalls.

Clearly the war had taken the glamour out of smocking and it was preserved for working garments and for children's clothes. A revival smock for a young boy in 1918, a smocked woollen dress, and a smocked silk dress for young girls show that smocking was still being used.

During this time articles in journals and booklets appeared on the use of the sewing machine as a means of preparing the foundation for smocking. These advised using eight stitches to the inch for a fine fabric, which would give a fullness three times the width, or for coarser work on coarser fabric six stitches to the inch which would give four times the fullness. The idea was to thread the machine, set the tensions and machine each line, making sure each line was started at the same position. Then, when it was all machined, a sewing needle was threaded and the machined shirring undone ahead of the needle which now used the holes as a guide. This was reputedly an accurate and easy method.

Embroidery books of this period show smocking 'useful for children's pinafores and dresses'. Certainly, dresses survive made in cream silk and cashmere. As for the countryman's smock this had almost completely vanished, a few areas only having reported the use of the garment.

In the Buckinghamshire County Museum, Aylesbury there is a coat-type smock made of white cotton, with smocking either side of the front opening above the chest and on the long sleeves, and also embroidered. It is dated prior to 1919 and was worn by a lady when milking the cows on her husband's farms, perhaps helping with the war effort.

An article in the *Embroidress* published by James Pearsall & Co. Ltd and the Old Bleach Linen Co. Ltd in 1924 was entitled 'Smocks past and present'. In it Mrs J. D. Rolleston, the editor, commented that smocking was applied 'almost exclusively to garments worn by artists and children, the agricultural labourer and the shepherd having abandoned their beautiful smocks altogether, but they have left us a legacy of which we should be proud and which should form the basis and inspiration of all our modern smocking.' She advised studying the old smocks. Regarding colour she said, 'it is a mistake to use more than two colours on the same garment or the interest of the stitches themselves will be lost. Red and blue always look well together or alone, or red and black, two shades of blue or bright brown and black, but I should say if your smock is of linen or some strong cotton material, never use tender shades as leaf green, terracotta or mauve . . . for silks and lighter fabric, they are not primitive enough for heavier materials.' Two smocks for a child were illustrated, one of white linen embroidered in red and blue and the other of holland (a linen fabric) embroidered in blue.

Three ladies' smocks surviving from this period are of interest as they reflect what Mrs Rolleston was advising for the 'artistic' smock. One in brown holland linen was embroidered in orange; another in fine blue linen was embroidered in white. An interesting example of another smock (in the Embroiderers' Guild Collection, Hampton Court Palace), made in natural linen, is embroidered with cotton thread in orange, rust and blue. The design is based on the traditional smock with smocked panels but without collars, the neckline being boat-shaped and finished with two rows of chain stitch. The embroidery design consists of S shapes and squares.

A booklet written by Alice Armes called *English Smocks with Directions for Making Them* and published by Dryad Press in 1926, was a contribution to the revival of the smock. The booklet was sold complete with transfers of copies of the old smock designs, though the linking of specific designs to trades and callings is now disputed.

At this time Liberty's were again to the fore in their catalogues: in the early 1920s blouses with smocking were illustrated, and in 1928-9 'an afternoon dress' as well as smocked children's clothes were depicted. Many magazines of this period show smocked garments for both children and adults. The present Queen was photographed when she was a child in a dress with smocking.

In 1934 the Needlework Development Scheme was started in Scotland. This was formed to encourage greater interest in embroidery and to raise the standard of design. A collection of embroideries, both British and foreign, was formed to which Art Schools, Domestic Science Colleges, Training Colleges, Women's Institutes and schools had access. By 1939 about 900 embroideries had been collected. The scheme closed during World War II, though plans were afoot in 1944 to revive it. However, after a very successful period during which the collection had increased to 3,500 pieces, the Scheme was disbanded in 1961. The pieces collected were distributed to various museums interested in embroidery, the largest share (475 pieces) being given to the Embroiderers' Guild. Smocking was one of the many traditional techniques collected by the Scheme worldwide. The Scheme influenced teachers of embroidery and as a result smocking came to the fore again.

An interesting outfit of the 1930s for a boy in the Bethnal Green Museum, London consisted of a green linen smock top with coloured smocking together with matching linen short trousers. Also of the same period is a girl's dress made of green velvet which is decorated.

In 1936 a section devoted to 'Smocking as Decoration for Children's Smocks' in *Quilting and Smocking* (published by James Pearsall and Company) starts by stating that, 'smocking is never more popular than it is today', and goes on to say that, 'collars and cuffs resort to smocking. And many smart little capes and scarf draperies are elaborately smocked, whilst in the newest evening modes the skirts have fullness in front confined by smocking ... The fashion of using smocking on grown-up garments is one that comes and goes, but it does seem as if there is nothing quite so charming and suitable as the smocked frock for young children.' The writer continues, 'the most popular materials for little folk are linen, good quality crêpe de Chine and shantung silk.'

In *Bestway Smocking Book* the author, describing a model dress, wrote, 'Another idea would be to make the frock in black crêpe de Chine with the smocking in rich Hungarian colourings,' a reference to peasant embroidery from Europe which was very popular in the 1930s. Blouses with a full neckline in a 'peasant' style were richly smocked and embroidered in bright colours. Dresses of crêpe de Chine were brightly smocked at the neck and wrists, as well as at the waist. There was also rich embroidery. The pattern books of the period illustrate these styles and others.

Liberty's was, of course, leading the field with fabrics and it was the ambition of every mother to dress her daughter in a tana lawn dress with rich, deep smocking. But when World War II broke out in 1939, imports were restricted. Clothing and fabrics were obtainable only on a strict, clothing-coupon allowance. However, even with rationing, some mothers were not deterred from sacrificing their precious coupons for fabric to make children's garments to be decorated with smocking.

After the war maternity smocks with smocking became popular and the time-honoured tradition of smocking on baby and children's clothes continued. At this time, new fabrics, such as nylon seersucker, were appearing; they were labour-saving as they could be easily washed by machine, and drip-dried. On the other hand these fabrics were not really suitable for clothes worn on a summer's day or in a warm climate as they could not absorb body moisture. Nevertheless, these synthetic fabrics gradually superseded the silks, crêpe de Chines and cashmere.

In the 1950s factories making children's clothes sent the smocking to be done by hand to out-workers. There was no prepared foundation of dots for the workers to follow but after the first row or so had been gathered by eye, the fabric was stretched between two stands and the smocking worked freely by hand. The results were extremely good and were seen on the most expensive party dresses of the day.[17]

For the home embroiderer Reads' Smock Gathering Machine was available in 1956 from a large London store at the price of £7 10s. This machine had sixteen needles which could gather as many lines in one operation. 'Hours of work in a few minutes', its instruction leaflet read. This machine is still available today.

The National Federation of Women's Institutes, in its book *30 Crafts*, published in 1950, advised, 'it is not sufficient to know how to smock' – a knowledge of 'how to make up' was stressed. The Women's Institutes in Britain have always given prominence to smocking in their handicraft programmes and still promote the craft in classes, competitions and exhibitions. In 1955 the organization produced a small leaflet, *Smocking Traditional and Modern* which set out the basics of smocking.

In the embroidery books of the 1950s, smocking was always mentioned as a technique. Winsome Douglass in *Discovering Embroidery* (1955) says, 'Today, of course, we use smocking, mainly on children's clothes, blouses and aprons, and also use gay colours which add very often to the decorative quality of smocking' and continued that most smooth cloth is suitable for smocking.

Throughout the 1950s other books, such as *The Chella Thornton Smocking Book* published by Van Nostrand Co. Ltd (Toronto, New York and London), showed interesting designs for smocking, advising for boys' dresses, 'These can be cut on a girl's pattern by reversing the yokes to make the dress open down the front.' There were simple, semi-advanced and advanced smocking designs. During this period, too, pamphlets on smocking by 'Penelope' were generally available, as were smocking dots.

In 1963 the magazine *Embroidery*, produced by the Embroiderers' Guild, reviewed a revised edition of *The Chella Thornton Smocking Book* published by McClelland & Stewart (Toronto) as follows: 'This book is attractively presented with a jacket design printed in colour, and opens to reveal a full-scale pattern for a dress for a one-two year old. Though the author has based her directions on English traditional work, some of her methods, such as that of gathering, and the use of stranded, rather than twisted thread, are different from those generally used. A most useful part of the book is the large number of clear photographs of border patterns showing an interesting variety of designs for dresses of all ages.'

In *The Craft of Embroidery* published by Mills and Boon in 1961, Alison Liley in her introduction wrote, 'The aim of this book is to provide an outline of the craft which will serve as a starting point for all serious students, and provide a basic grounding sufficient to meet most demands and standards up to and including those of the City and Guilds Hand Embroidery Examination.' There is a clear section on traditional

17. Kindly told to me by Mrs Archibald of Glasgow.

smocking setting out the preparation and stitches together with sketch ideas for nightdresses, children's wear and aprons.

The City and Guilds of London Embroidery Examination has always included smocking as one of the techniques in its syllabus. In this way, the nationally recognized examination held since 1907 has helped preserve and uphold standards, and kept to the fore the craft of embroidery, including smocking.

In *English Smocking* by Grace Knott, published in 1962 by Muller (London), the author says, 'There are no limits to the number of designs that can be created in smocking by continuing these basic stitches in various ways. Similarly, all our countless musical selections are composed by the coordination of the various keys on the piano.' Her book is full of clever combinations of smocking stitches and colours which have delighted many an embroiderer.

In 1965 Mills and Boon also published *English Folk Embroidery* by Aenone Cave which gave an interesting history of the smock garment through the ages, together with designs inspired by the embroidery on the 'boxes' of the nineteenth-century countryman's smock. There were present-day ideas using traditional smocking for children's dresses, a romper suit and a skirt as well as other household items.

But changes were rapidly taking place. The 'Swinging Sixties' had arrived. Anything and everything was worn by the young, and sometimes the not-so young. It was fashionable to wear long dresses throughout the day, no matter what the weather. The caftan became popular and commercial patterns were available showing this style of dress with smocking incorporated. Dress was casual and so was the smocking. But despite this casual approach, fashion magazines showed garments incorporating honeycomb smocking.

Up to this time, smocking as a technique had not progressed in any way; it had continued to be worked in a manner, which, though attractive and functional, was formal, traditional and rather conservative. The same classic little girls' dresses were made as they had been throughout the century; clothing for boys was more or less the same; from time to time there would be a 'revival' smock. In the 1930s, with the peasant influence displayed in embroidery, it had become livelier, but apart from that there was no attempt to break away from the same traditional patterns of smocking. Nothing new had emerged.

However, in 1969, Lynete de Denne in *Embroidery* demonstrated how a child's smocked dress could be made, using both machine and hand embroidery. A decorated line by machine was worked, first of all vertically between the dots used for preparation (these lines falling in the centre of the cell) and then honeycomb stitch worked by hand. This was quite a new approach.

The next decade was to experience a break-away from the traditional way of using smocking. Embroidery was taking on a very experimental and textural look and artists looking for new ideas turned to smocking for these exciting effects. Margaret Thom in *Smocking in Embroidery* wrote: 'Smocking is seldom incorporated in today's embroidered hangings and panels, although most other traditional methods have been developed and adapted to meet contemporary needs. For too long the usefulness of smocking in dress has hidden is latent possibilities as an exciting addition to free embroidery. Its textural qualities and adaptability make smocking potentially a valuable asset to the embroiderer.' This then was a lead, and artists and students resurrected the technique and the flow of ideas was endless.

Members of the 62 Group, the exhibiting group of the Embroiderers' Guild, had been experimenting with smocking. Audrey Tucker's work, 'Dead Blue Tit', showed a very creative use of smocking to simulate the feathers of the bird. Another artist, Ingrid Rowling, made a gown called 'Foxglove' in palest foxglove colours, the shoulders gently smocked with added crochet foxgloves, enhancing the charming shaded effect.

In 1973 'The Craftsman's Art' was exhibited at the Victoria and Albert Museum in London. This exhibition consisted of new work by British craftsmen. One of the exhibits was 'Three Dimensional Landscape Picture' (110 × 110 × 12cm) by Carol Blackman, designer/maker. This was a fascinating huge piece of honeycomb smocking which had been dyed, and in places padded, together with added embellishment to the surface.

Hannah Frew in her book, *Three-dimensional Embroidery*, gave a great boost to creative smocking by saying, 'a certain embroidery technique may be the starting point for an idea ... a technique such as smocking, which makes use of the effect of drawing up material into folds, and using the folds as a foundation on which to work, could be the starting point for a design idea. The application of this technique has become linked almost exclusively to children's clothes, blouses etc. and has not been investigated sufficiently as a free means of expressing movement in materials. The rhythms of folds catching the light and creating ripple effects could become the basis for an imaginative composition, combining the technical skill of the embroiderer with the essential qualities of pliability and surface texture contained in materials.' She went on to explain about added stitchery, other than traditional, and no obvious stitchery at all. This was a great lead from an artist of international repute.

Smocking lends itself to dramatic textural effects and so it is natural that theatrical costume designers should turn to this technique. At the Royal Shakespeare Theatre in Stratford-on-Avon, it is used on costumes which are handsomely smocked in honeycomb and theatrically painted to highlight the texture of the folds so that when the lights come into play, one colour against another is shown in an exciting way.

On the creative side, smocking in the 1970s had made great strides – artists, teachers and students were experimenting on panels, on 3-D articles, and on clothing with interesting results.

At the same time, however, the traditional ways were not being abandoned, but it was now being realized that smocking could be developed and extended in ways other than those that had been practised for centuries.

An article in *Embroidery* in 1971, entitled 'Clive Couture Collection 1971' expounded, 'Softness was the keynote, the softness of suede, cashmere and hand-smocking ... Smocking was used not only in the traditional way but also to create a fabric in itself, for a peplum of a jacket, for example.' A photograph was reproduced in the magazine of a hand-smocked white cashmere lawn dress, worn with a terracotta sunflower and white printed wool coat.

Several fashion designers used smocking during this decade, but sparingly, together with embroidery to complement it on blouses, skirts, dresses, loose jackets as well as on up-to-date smocks. The smocking was understated in the fashion world. There was also a renewed interest in the countryman's smock for both adults and children.

In 1976, when my grandson was born, I gave my daughter beautifully smocked linen and silk baby dresses lovingly made by her grandmother and aunts which she and her brother had worn in 1948 and 1950. But, I was told a 'Babygro', which was an elasticated garment covering the entire body like a space-suit, was the order of the day! Nevertheless, an easy-to-launder, little, white, polyester cotton dress which I smocked is much appreciated.

It is noticeable in the mass-produced market of the 1970s that there were children's dresses of polyester/viscose or polyester/cotton with smocking which was done by machine. A thread was applied across gathers and held down by machine stitching.

The home dressmaker was created for in the form of kits. The fabric used in the kit was pure cotton, machine-washable, with the dots for smocking already printed on the cloth. There was a smock style with a printed fabric inspired by the embroidery designs of the countryman's smock. The fabric was ready for smocking and making-up, and proved very popular with the young.

The 1970s was therefore an exciting decade for smocking. On the creative side artists were using the technique in a way that had not been seen before and on the fashion front designers were using it in a restrained way together with embroidery. There was a revival of the smock in its traditional form by smockmakers specializing in the art, and there were kits incorporating smocking, as well as commercial patterns, available for the home dressmaker.

These changes were also carried forward into the 1980s. In 1980 Beverley Marshall's book *Smocks and Smocking* included an interesting history of the subject and smock patterns which could be easily followed. Her advice is still followed today. In the same year, *Embroidery* published an article about 'Free Smocking' by Jean Littlejohn. She wrote, 'The visual impact of smocking depends greatly on lines and distortions of lines, the basis of traditional smocking being the accurate drawing up of the fabric into regular tubes and gathers. That these gathers were originally called reeds suggests many possibilities for developing the technique.' Her piece 'Summer Grasses' shows reverse smocking, where the smocking is worked on the wrong side and the texture so formed on the right side is manipulated and held in place by further stitchery which produces a very free and interesting effect. Other work produced by her students shows fresh and innovative ways, sometimes on three-dimensional pieces.

In 1982, an exhibition 'Textile Aspects', organized by the 62 Group of the Embroiderers' Guild, showed a panel by Polly Binns which was a piece of honeycomb smocking. Explaining her work she said, 'Each piece of work is an intuitive exploration into the depth and

Panel by Polly Binns, exhibited 1984

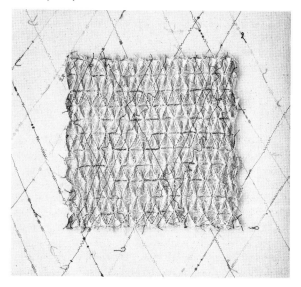

play of light on surface fabric, often enhanced by the addition of stitches, ceramic discs, Japanese papers, dyed and printed marks.'

The following year several magazines and newspapers carried articles about smocks with photographs of models in countryside settings of hay, pitchforks and rabbits with captions such as 'Back comes the smock' and 'Fresh from the Farm', showing up-dated versions of the garment, by designers such as Ally Capellino. At the same time, Prince William was pictured wearing smocked rompers and this revived a fashion that had almost died out.

The dramatic effect of texture can again be detected in Sadler's Wells Royal Ballet production of 'The Swan of Tuonela' performed in 1983, where the fantastic wings of the swan showed the boldness of a smocked effect.

Sometimes today, Morris dancers appear on village greens wearing smocks, but these are copies of the traditional type.

So, reflecting upon the first few years of the 1980s one finds that smocking is very much to the fore. On the creative side artists, teachers and students are finding new ways of using the technique; dress designers continue to use it – and some designers are giving the countryman's smock a new look. For baby boys, smocked rompers are back in fashion and for little girls an article in *The Times* in March, 1984 shows that the little girl's dress is as fashionable as it was in 1900. Liberty fabrics are still used; they have never gone out of fashion.

There are too, still smock-makers carrying on in the same pure tradition. Maggie Hall is such a person and has designed and made the smock illustrated opposite page 65. The smock will delight all those who make it, for generations to come. The garment will always be fashionable and through classes, courses, lectures and the collecting of historical data, 'The Smocking Group of The Embroiderers' Guild' aims to preserve the art of English smocking and its heritage.

Smocking Throughout the World

So far the type of smocking discussed has been the English type. However, worldwide many other types exist with variations within each type. There are three main types: the first is worked on a very tightly-gathered foundation where the gathering threads are left in, and a pattern is darned over and under the pleats so made; this is called 'smocked pattern darning'; the second type is prepared in the same way, but embroidery stitches such as satin and cross stitch decorate the pleats; the third type is called 'pattern shirring'. In this the fabric is gathered up, usually in the same colour as the background, in such a way as to form a pattern of lozenges, zig-zags and diamonds. These three types are firm and not elastic, whereas the English type of smocking is.

WESTERN EUROPE

Some of the oldest forms of decoration on gathers are to be found in Italy on linen shirts which could be of the seventeenth century. One very interesting shirt (in the Victoria and Albert Museum, London) has the top of the sleeve very closely gathered, with gathering threads approximately 2.5mm (⅛in) apart. This foundation of gathering threads is left in. In this particular garment a design of flowers, using white thread, is worked in satin stitch right through the prepared ground. It is an unusual decoration and very effective. The shirt is seamed with insertions of drawn thread work. Where the collar joins the gathered shirt front, the gathers are interestingly worked over a zig-zag which is then buttonholed.

Another shirt of approximately this date shows a decorated shirring at the wrists. It is worked in double thread and gathered in a specific way so that when the threads are pulled tight a pattern is formed. This form of shirring is sometimes called 'Italian shirring'. The rest of the shirt is of richly worked cut and drawn work, with needlepoint lace fillings and pillow lace

An Italian 17th-century linen shirt in the Victoria and Albert Museum

Above Detail of an Andalusian shirt, 18th century

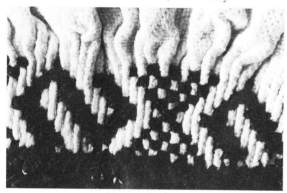

Above Detail of a Salamancan cuff
Below Detail of an apron from the Balearic Islands

edgings at the neck and wrists. It is interesting to note that in 1914 an article on 'Pattern Shirring – an Italian alternative to Smocking' appeared in *Needle and Thread* magazine. The article mentioned that in the area around Mount Arunci, between Naples and Rome, this form of decoration was still being carried out at the neck and sleeves of blouses worked by the older women in the area. However, it was dying out as the younger generation preferred to buy trimmings for their blouses. The more recent of these shirred designs were made up of lozenges and zig-zags.

In an article on 'Peasant Art in Italy' in 1913 a lace decoration was shown with an inset of what would appear to be pattern shirring.

Another form of decoration in Italy was to work embroidery designs over pleated cotton for a dress or blouse. This kept the fullness in place, with the added bonus of keeping the effect flat.

In 1975, smocking of the English type was shown on various garments in Fashion Collection in Italy. Today, smocking of the English type is very popular in Italy, especially for children's clothes, and exquisitely embroidered little girls' dresses are available in the shops. For the home dressmaker there are magazines with interesting designs to follow, one of which is called *Punto Smock*.

Spain has always had a tradition of smocking. Eighteenth- and nineteenth-century pieces show an elaborate form of an unusual smocking technique which was worked on shirts at the top of a sleeve, or at the wrist, or both. In this form of smocking the foundation is tightly gathered up into pleats and the gathering threads approximately 2.5mm (⅛in) apart are left in place. On this tight foundation a fret design is worked in stitches very close together to give an almost cord-like effect. Eighteenth-century examples from Andalusia show the shirt to be made of linen and the embroidery and smocking in silk thread.

Another part of Spain which has shown a smocking tradition is the Salamanca area, where the linen sleeves were richly embroidered in black wool. The wrists were tightly gathered and decorated with a darning pattern. Mildred Stanley in *Popular Weaving and Embroidery in Spain* (Batsford, London 1924) wrote: 'The cuffs of the Salamanca sleeves, like the shoulder pieces of the Lagartera shirts, are cunning examples of smocking; thick though the linen is, it is gathered into an incredibly small space and held by a fret, a dog-tooth, or by rows of little animal figures. Cuffs are often finished off by knitted woollen lace, black and fastened by little handwrought silver buttons. While sleeve designs vary, they are always large and bold.' Describing Lagartera in the province of Toledo, south of Madrid, she goes on to comment: 'It is a compensation to meet occasionally in the streets of the capital the quaint-looking little Lagarteranas in their short, smocked, red flannel skirts, gaily embroidered worsted stockings, black and white *pecheros* and flowered kerchiefs.'

Today smocking is extensively worked in Spain, in a technique akin to the English kind. The Spanish patterns for design are densely worked with elaborate bullion knots (bouillion stitches) for added variety. There are magazines published showing a wide variety of designs.

From Majorca in the Balearic Islands comes an apron which is made of a ribbed fabric rather like a coarse needlecord. The top part of the apron is worked in satin stitch down the vertical stripes in alternating colours of pink and gold. Superimposed upon this worked surface are motifs of a form of needleweaving, giving a most unusual effect.

In Portugal, we find an apron, part of a peasant costume from the Biano do Castelo area in the north, which is red in colour with white embroidery incorporating the word 'Amor' over the tight gathers. Herringbone stitch in blue and white is also used on the band of the apron. A child's fiesta dress shows a similar style with crude embroidery in chain stitch over the gathered tubes of the apron part of the costume. A form of pattern shirring is also found on blouses in this area.

In France a fifteenth-century *Book of Hours*, depicting occupations for the months of the year, includes a simple garment worn by a man in a harvesting scene, while in photographs and examples of the nineteenth century a fuller smock garment is noted. In 1832 the Duchesse de Berry gave a smock to her son. It was of blue linen gathered around the neck, along the shoulders and down the front, and embroidered mainly in white and red.

One French magazine in recent years carried an article showing how to make an English-type smock.

There are many regional folk costumes in Holland, one of the best known being worn in Volendam. On weekdays, the working days, the costume consists of a black skirt over which is worn a striped, cotton apron called a *bondje* which has a form of smocking at the top. This technique is explained in detail in Project 18, the Volendam Blouse *(see page 141)*. The apron, which measures approximately 1 metre (39 in) in depth and 1.20 metres (47 in) wide, is made of a cotton striped fabric in the traditional colours of black, brown, blue, green and red on a white background. The apron, which is starched, is worn wrapped around the waist with white ribbon ties brought to the front and tied in a bow.

A jacket is worn with this costume. It is made of a black cotton fabric with a design of stripes printed in white and brown. This fabric is drawn up in an interesting way, by running stitches only, making use of the stripes to surface in certain parts, and to disappear in others. It is not drawn up over the bust and sleeves are gathered in a different way. The name given to this particular form of decoration is *vlagrimpelen*. The costume is usually made in the home.

The English type of smocking is also practised in The Netherlands, and during World War II it was taught as part of the handwork curriculum in some of the schools. Childhood pictures of Queen Beatrix show her in smocked dresses. In post-war years, mothers who knew how to smock, would incorporate smocking in baby layettes as well as on girls' dresses. Today, magazines are reviving the interest.

In the Metropolitan Museum in New York, there is a rare military skirt or *waffenrock*, probably originating from Dresden, Germany, in the early sixteenth century. It is a quilted skirt with, in one area, twenty pleats held in place by two lines of heavy braid giving the effect of smocking.

Another example from Germany (in the Victoria and Albert Museum, London) is an eighteenth-century hunting pouch. It consists of two outer pockets of green silk embroidered at the corners in gold thread. Divisions are embroidered in coloured silks with animals of the chase. This interesting piece of work shows smocking on the outside as well as on the inside. The outside silk appears to have a padding or lining of leather, possibly chamois, and these two layers and a silk lining are worked together in what

German 18th-century hunting pouch

appears to be vandyke stitch, the padding giving a soft, rounded texture. The inside silk lining seems to have been worked in honeycomb stitch.

A glazed cotton apron which is part of a bridal and festival costume of the mid-nineteenth century comes from near Hamburg. It has fine pleating with darning worked through the pleats. Smocking on a blouse of 1910 shows that the English type of smocking was also worked in Germany and is also seen in Bavaria.

In Sweden during the nineteenth century, shirts were commonly made by a bride for her groom. She would incorporate their initials and the date of the marriage in the shirt. To hold the gathers in place, either under the collar, or at the cuffs, a simple form of English smocking was worked in some examples.

At the end of the nineteenth century the Swedish painter, Carl Larsson painted little girls in costume showing a form of smocking.

EASTERN EUROPE

In the vast republics of Soviet Russia there are regions where smocking has also been evident. Examples of eighteenth-century costume from the Carpathian mountain region show a form of pattern shirring; on nineteenth-century costume from Byelorussia various types of smocking were worked on the sleeves of women's garments either at the shoulder or at the wrist. This also shows a form of pattern shirring as well as pattern darning on tight gathers and a simplified form of English smocking. In the Ukraine, examples show interesting variations such as cross stitch worked over tight gathers, satin stitch worked down tight gathers, as well as the usual darning. In Lithuania a form of pattern shirring was also worked.

When visiting Russia in 1981 I did not see much evidence of smocking on clothes. The tourist shops sold blouses, but they were embroidered in cross stitch, possibly by machine.

In Czechoslovakia old caps or bonnets show a panel at the back which is closely smocked in English-type smocking in rich colours on white, almost resembling a woven piece of fabric. In the past it was also used on jackets, skirts and aprons. Another form of decoration was worked on a pleated cotton skirt. In this method elaborately worked designs in chain stitch were used.

Hungary has a tradition of colourful embroidery and this is much in evidence in their blouses which were fashionable in the 1930s and 1950s in Britain and more recently have come back into fashion. The labels on them today read 'Hand embroidery – made in Hungary'. The style of the blouse is known as the peasant style with gathered neck and short gathered sleeves. They are smocked in English-type smocking around the neck, sleeves and waist, usually in very

A richly-smocked Czechoslovakian cap

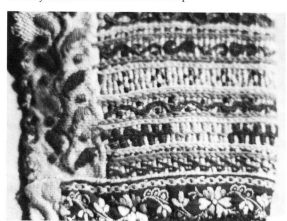

Detail of an Hungarian shirt

bright colours with matching colours for the elaborate embroidered motifs on the front of the blouse and sleeve. The fabric of the earlier blouses was sometimes cotton georgette or cotton voile, whereas the more recent ones are usually a mixture of 67 per cent polyester and 33 per cent viscose.

On older costumes, possibly nineteenth-century, a form of decoration is shown at the wrists of shirts and blouses preserved in museums in Romania. Again, this decoration consists of a tightly-gathered foundation, not very deep, with a darning pattern worked. On the more up-to-date blouses an English type of smocking is seen as well as a form of decorative gathering, not unlike pattern shirring, but the effect is looser. In this form of gathering, a coloured thread is most generally used, so that the gathering and the decoration in colour are worked in one operation.

Pauline Johnstone wrote about Bulgaria in *Embroidery* in 1962 saying that, 'In the Danube basin the ground material was drawn up into gathers, and the embroidery worked over them, but the gathers are not afterwards released as in English smocking.'

Museum pieces of Yugoslavia show fascinating decorations on gathers on blouses, shirts and aprons. On a foundation of tight gathers various stitches are used, such as cross stitch, which forms a colourful geometrical pattern on the back of a man's shirt. Satin stitches worked in spot blocks on the sleeve of a man's shirt forms a rich decoration, while other examples use stem stitch.

THE AMERICAS

There has always been a smocking tradition in the United States; it is interesting to note that there is a white linen smock at Old Sturbridge Village, Sturbridge in Massachusetts.[18] A particularly elaborate garment was worked in 1852 by Mrs Betsy Reynolds Voorhees, an outstanding embroiderer. It was made for her husband, Dr Voorhees, to wear in a ploughing match; the garment was made of homespun linen and embroidered with hearts on the collar. It had a deep panel of smocking down the front and is similar to the countryman's smock of England and Wales.[19]

Examples of children's clothes from the nineteenth century showing the use of English smocking are preserved in numerous American museums. It is interesting to note that Mary Cassatt (1844-1926), a prominent artist, depicted what would appear to be smocking in 'The Letter'.

In the *Manual of Modern Embroidery* published by the Singer Manufacturing Company in 1896, instructions are given for using the Singer sewing machine for smocking. It advises folding 'the goods to be smocked as the leaves of a closed fan are folded, making the spaces between the folds a quarter of an inch wide and perfectly straight.' This is followed by step-by-step instructions for sewing the pleats to form a honeycomb.

18. Catherine Fennelly: *Textiles in New England, 1790-1840.* A booklet from Old Sturbridge Village, Sturbridge, Massachusetts.
19. Mary A. de Julio: *A Record of a Woman's Work – The Betsey Reynolds Voorhees Collection,* Montgomery County Historical Society, USA. From Vol. 3 of the research papers of the American Quilt Study Group in *Uncoverings,* 1982.

A child's dress made in Memphis, Tennessee in 1982 and presented to the Smocking Arts Guild of America

A few years later in 1902 the Butterick Publishing Company in *Fancy Stitches* includes smocking, showing both English and American methods, though the difference appears to be slight. This method was done by hand. While in *Simplified Smocking* (1916), Helena Burcher advocated the 'one process method' of smocking. In this method only the dots required were transferred to the fabric, and the smocking was worked directly on to these dots, there being no preparation. This method is used on commercial patterns today. Her book contains many designs for blouses and smocked dresses.

Several American magazines of the time recommended a method for preparing smocking by machining lines, taking them out, and then using the holes left by the machining for gathering by hand recommended by other magazines.

Many towns in the south, such as Memphis on the Mississippi, have a long tradition of English smocking where it has been popular since the late 1920s. Commercial pattern companies, since before World War II, have incorporated smocking in their patterns from time to time and have thus continued to keep the tradition alive. *The Chella Thornton Smocking Book*

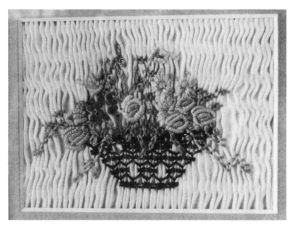

'Spring Flower Basket', by Julie Milne

Further south, the embroidery of Mexico has been influenced by Spain. Smocking is worked on a tightly-gathered foundation into which a darning pattern is incorporated over and under and across the pleats. The designs are traditionally of birds, animals and flowers, and usually worked in one colour on a cotton fabric.

In the early part of the twentieth century, another form of decoration on Mexican blouses was the use of beads on a tightly-gathered foundation, the pattern being formed by adding beads between the pleats. A typical Mexican smocked design of today, decorating a dress, shows a row of little figures holding hands. The smocking is worked in several colours on a tightly gathered foundation and the depth of the design is narrow.

(1951) did much to revive the craft in the USA as did Grace Knott's book on *English Smocking* (1962).

Nowadays there are specialist shops in numerous cities and towns throughout the USA, selling all the requirements needed for smocking, as well as organizing classes. Many books, patterns, leaflets and smocking designs, all in copyright, are privately printed and sold. The commercial aspect of smocking is far more highly developed there than in Britain.

A magazine is published by the Smocking Arts Guild of America (SAGA), an organization for those interested in smocking. It has a wide membership and over eighty branches (chapters) where classes are held – all maintaining a high level of expertise. A newspaper is published by the author of several smocking books, Dianne Durand, for Little Miss Muffet Inc., and this gives a wide selection of interesting articles. Authors and teachers such as Allyne Holland are also keeping alive the tradition of English smocking.

Today, all forms of clothing, both for children and adults, are elaborately smocked as well as articles such as Easter eggs and Christmas tree adornments; on the creative side several artists such as Joan Craft, Nellie Durand, Sarah Douglas, Lois Guran and Julie Milne are using smocking in an exploratory and contemporary way. Picture smocking is also very popular.

The tradition of English smocking was taken to Canada by British settlers. Here, as in the States, *The Chella Thornton Smocking Book* and Grace Knott's book have done much to create a new interest in smocking. The interest is still very much alive today with specialist shops supplying the wants of those interested in smocking, especially for those who live in isolated areas. As well as keeping alive the art of traditional smocking, there are Canadian artists using the technique in a creative way and there is a good deal of cross-fertilization of ideas between the United States and Canada.

Above A Mexican blouse

Below Detail of a Mexican blouse showing beadwork used on smocking

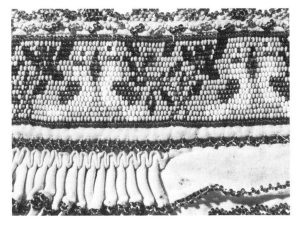

As well as the traditional form of smocking on tight gathers, the English form of smocking is now being introduced into Mexico. Another form of smocking is on flat pleats and this is explained in Project 19, *(see page 149)*.

In Guatemala smocking of the English style is taught; the older style worked on a tightly gathered foundation as in Mexico, is also preserved. While in the San Blas Islands a chain stitch or stem stitch is used to hold gathers in place.

INDIA AND SRI LANKA

Smocking of the English type was worked in convents in India. A silk nightdress with smocking which had been made in a convent was bought by my husband in Delhi in 1945. In recent years smocked garments made in India have been available in the shops in Britain. These are usually blouses, skirts and dresses worked in the English type of smocking, some with very little gathering on cheap, thin cotton fabric.

Anne Morrell, author and lecturer in embroidery, recently visited an embroidery workshop in Madras where embroidered saris and children's clothes were being made. The women, who embroidered, sat on the floor on one side of the workshop. The men, who did the machining on treadle machines, worked on the other side of the room. As there were power cuts for up to four hours a day, small industries such as this used hand-operated machines. The advertisement for this workshop reads, 'Specialists in tailoring – hand embroidery and smocking'. A child's dress of the usual classical style, bought there, was made of white cotton muslin smocked across the front in white and pale gold with embroidered trimming on the collar. The dress is seamed by machine and the smocking is worked directly on to the fabric without preparation.

In Sri Lanka smocking was taught in the convents by the nuns. Today, smocked blouses are available in the tourist hotels. One bought in 1981 was made of white cotton fabric, and smocked in the English way with added bullion knots (bouillion stitches).

THE FAR EAST

China has an ancient history of embroidery; women's silk skirts of the nineteenth century show an interesting way of holding fullness by pleating and decoration. A form of tacking (basting) was worked on the wrong side of the pleats, in such a way that when the garment was worn the pleats would expand with movement and a honeycomb effect was seen.

A silk blouse from China shows English-type smocking on the rounded neckline and sleeves. It is finely worked in one strand of silk and is embroidered with 'Peiking–China' across the front. An elaborately smocked blouse made of cotton and synthetic fibres, made in China and bought in Hong Kong in 1981, is worked in the English type of smocking.

In Japan, a publication dealing with smocking by the Ondori Publishing Co. Ltd of Tokyo, has been available since 1975, and observers have commented on smocking being seen on garments worn by the Japanese.

Smocked dresses for little girls made in the Philippines are available in both Britain and the United States. The dresses are superbly worked, using a gathering technique which produces a fine lattice pattern, as well as the English type of smocking.

In Thailand, a Meo Hill tribe skirt in blue made in 1966, collected by Herta Puls, shows an unusual form of holding the small pleats approximately 2.5cm (1in) below the waist band. The method is described on page 148.

SOUTH AFRICA

In South Africa there has been a tradition of smocking helped by the Read Smock Gathering machine which was invented there and is manufactured there. This is a machine which prepares the foundation fabric for smocking and therefore takes much of the drudgery out of the preparation. The patent for this machine was applied for in 1947. The standard of present-day smocking in South Africa is superb – no doubt the machine enabled the embroiderer to spend more time on her craft.

AUSTRALIA AND NEW ZEALAND

The pioneering women of the nineteenth century, proud of their heritage of embroidery and their embroidery skills continued the craft of smocking in Australia and New Zealand. Smocking offered a practical use which was very necessary in those days. Magazines, taking six months by sailing ship, would be sent by relatives from the 'old country', and so the art of smocking together with other skills infiltrated these far-flung corners of the British Empire.

In Australia the same traditions as those of the Mother country existed. Liberty fabrics were available and smocking on little girls' dresses was the same as that in Britain, the tana lawns being especially favoured. In the twentieth century commercial patterns from the major firms are available, enabling the home dressmaker, especially if far from the cities, to carry on with her craft of smocking allied to her dressmaking. The Embroiderer's Guild of Victoria carries on the tradition of smocking and has several interesting children's dresses in its collection.

2

Basic English Smocking

FABRICS

There are many fabrics on the market which are suitable for smocking; they may be made of natural or synthetic fibres, as well as blends of these; they may be plain or printed, thick or thin, in fact any fabric is suitable for smocking as long as it drapes well.

Cotton comes in various weights and finishes. Cotton lawn and poplin are suitable fabrics, as well as thicker fabrics such as denim, gaberdine and cotton drill, depending upon the project. The mixtures of cotton and synthetic fabric, such as polycotton, also drape well *(see Smock in cotton drill facing page 65 and Round Cushion in polycotton facing page 49).*

Linen, whether fine or thick can be used for certain garments. It is suitable for smocks, and in fact the old traditional smocks were made of heavy white linen.

Silk comes in various weights, and, depending upon the project, can be used attractively. Some have a stiff finish and are useful for evening bags and cushions, while the silks which have softer draping qualities such as crêpe de Chine, satin and Jap (or China) silk are attractive when smocked.

Wool is another suitable fabric. Wool crêpe drapes very well. Mixtures of wool and cotton are ideal for smocking, and are still widely used on children's clothes as they launder well *(see Floral Dress between pages 88 and 89).*

Synthetics come in many types of fabric. Some of the softer fabrics, such as crêpe de Chine smock beautifully. This was used in the Formal Dress *(see illustration facing page 89).* While synthetics smock well, they may not be easy to make up.

Other fabrics are those which are transparent. These can give a very delicate effect. The lining should be considered at the same time *(see Lampshade facing page 64).* Depending upon the use, a transparent

Opposite 'Captured Unawares', by Caroline Paterson (working 1878-92)

fabric of one colour can be placed over a thin fabric of another colour, and treated as one fabric.

Thick pile fabrics, such as velvet, can be used for projects requiring a bold effect.

Certain fabrics which have a pattern suitable for preparing the smocking can also be used. These may be a gingham, stripe or spot (dot) or one that has a repeating design or weave at suitable intervals. Experiment to see how the fabric alters when pulled up for smocking *(see Gingham Dress between pages 88 and 89).*

Shiny and dull fabrics give interesting textures.

THREADS

For gathering: When picking up the dots, use appropriate thread; it must be strong so that it will not break and it must be suitable for the fabric. Generally, a cotton mercerised thread will suit most fabrics. Synthetic threads can be troublesome when tying, as the knots slip. Use a contrasting colour to the background fabric for gathering.

For smocking: Stranded cotton is the most versatile thread for use in smocking. It comprises six strands of thread which can be split to any thickness suitable for the project. It has been used extensively in the projects in this book as it is suitable for most fabrics.

Perle is another useful thread. This has a twist and an attractive shiny finish. It comes in various thicknesses, No. 3 being the thickest *(see Honeycomb Cushion facing page 49).* No. 5 Perle is medium thickness and No. 8 is a fine thread.

Coton à broder (sold as Brilliant Embroidery and cutwork thread by DMC) is a fine cotton thread which also is useful. It is available as No. 16 which is fine and No. 12 which is slightly thicker. It can be used on fine fabrics, particularly fine cottons. The Volendam Blouse was smocked using No. 16 Coton à broder *(see illustration facing page 129).*

Silk threads, although expensive, are becoming available and can be very luxurious when used on silk fabrics, or in creative work.

For creative work, any thread can be used. Interesting effects can be obtained by using any metal thread which can be threaded in a needle, but beware of metal threads which are not suitable for this purpose. Very fine ribbon, either silk or synthetic, can be used in very exciting ways. Crochet and knitting yarns are sometimes suitable as well as machine embroidery threads. Watch out for unusual threads elsewhere.

Two colours, or types of thread, can be threaded in one needle. This gives an interesting effect (*see Sampler, bottom left for 'long and short diamond' in illustration facing page 48*).

NEEDLES

Crewel embroidery needles are the most useful. They have long eyes and a sharp point. They vary in sizes from 1-10, sizes 8, 9 or 10 being the most useful for ordinary smocking.

Chenille needles are short with long eyes and sharp points and are most suitable for work on coarse materials using thick threads. Sizes 18-24 are the most useful. This type of needle (size No. 22) was used with Perle No. 3 on the Honeycomb Cushion (*see illustration facing page 49*).

Beading needles are used for adding beads. They are long and fine, No. 10 being the thickest and most useful. Do not thread using a needle-threader as it can split the eye of the needle.

PREPARATION

Preparing for gathering
Smocking is decorative stitching on a gathered base. Once the fabric has been chosen, the next important step is to decide how to prepare the fabric for gathering.

The fabric must be straight at the top edge, otherwise the smocking will not be straight. If it is uneven, if possible, pull out a thread to straighten. Always press the fabric now so that there are no creases, as there will not be another opportunity to do so. If the fabric frays, protect edges by whipping by hand (*see page 48*), or zig-zag on a machine.

All markings and preparation are made on the wrong side of the fabric.

Prepare gathering so that the folds lie along the grainline. When preparing gathering, it is useful to allow two extra rows of gathering – one at the top edge which can be used for joining on to a yoke etc., and the second one at the bottom of the work to aid the smocking when the row above it is being worked.

Do not start to prepare too near an edge. If preparation is being done on a garment, keep a fraction outside the seam allowance.

Estimating width of fabric for gathering
It is difficult to estimate the width of the fabric required for gathering, because various factors have to be taken into account.

- The thickness of the fabric is very important. Fine fabrics such as silk, cotton lawn and voile may take 4-5 times the finished width of the smocking; medium-weight fabrics such as cotton or polycotton may take three times the finished width for the smocking.
- The distance between the dots has to be taken into consideration.
- The type of stitch used also needs to be considered as some stitches, such as cable stitch, are tight and others, such as honeycomb stitch, are loose.
- The tension which an embroiderer works to is another important factor. Like knitting, some embroiderers work to a tight tension and others to a loose tension. The only safe way is to work a small sample piece before attempting the smocking.

Choosing a system for gathering
There are many ways to gather fabric. It will depend upon the fabric chosen which system is the most useful. It will also depend upon individual preference as well as availability of supplies.

Listed below are various systems which may be considered. All produce dots which are used for preparing the gathering. Only the smock-gathering machine eliminates this process.

- *Transfer dots.* These came in transfer form on paper strips approximately 92 × 20.5cm (36 × 8in). The dots have a silver wax finish. When heat is applied to the wrong side of the paper, these dots are transferred to the fabric. The spacings between the dots and between the rows vary (*see diagram 1*).

When using dots, remove all other details surrounding them. Use these extra details for testing on a sampler beforehand. Always make a trial testing for the correct iron temperature. Be very careful with synthetic fabrics.

Place dots wax side down on to wrong side of fabric. Hold in place with a few pins and align with the straight edge. Press by repeatedly lifting the iron. Do not iron back and forth as for clothes, as the dots may become blurred. Unpin and quickly lift off the paper.

Dots can be difficult to remove from the fabric afterwards. A wash in diluted biological washing powder (biodegradable detergent), with many rinses in clean water, will usually remove them. Do not leave to soak. (*For more detailed instructions, see page 40*).

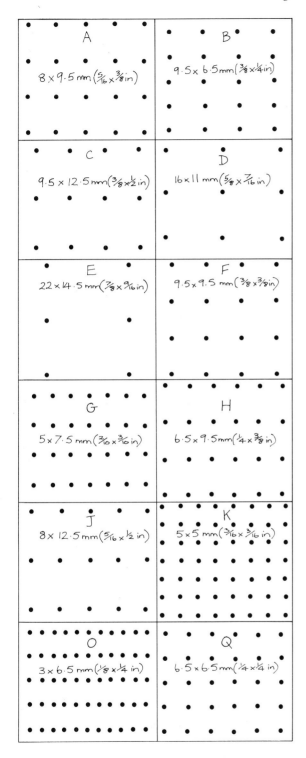

Diagram 1 Deighton's Smocking Dot Transfers are made on paper 20.5cm (8in) wide and in lengths of 92cm (36in). The illustrations above show the spacings of the dots for each of the sizes. The code initial indicates the size, and should be specified when ordering, or buying.

● *Ruler and pencil method.* This method is very useful for small areas, or for a large area when the dots and rows are far apart. For a wide area, a metre ruler or yardstick is useful. A ruler can be made from a stiff piece of card or stiff paper marked off like a ruler and used for marking. Align the measure with the thread of the fabric. Use a soft pencil and work lightly on the wrong side. A water-erasable pen can be used, being careful not to expose the marking to heat. This method was used for the Honeycomb Cushion (*see illustration facing page 55*).

● *Graph paper method.* This is easy to use and it is accurate. Place carbon paper, shiny side down on to the wrong side of the fabric. Place graph paper over it. Pin in position. Transfer by marking dots at certain points on the grid of the graph paper using a hard pencil or blunt needle. Test to see if the marks are transferred.

● *Making a grid on paper.* Take plain paper and mark lines with a ruler and pencil. This can then be used in the same way as the graph paper method.

● *Template method.* Take a piece of thin card and draw a grid with pencil and ruler. Where required, pierce holes with a stiletto which is a tool with a sharp point, or with a thick needle. Place on to the wrong side of the fabric and using a pencil or water-erasable pen, mark the dots through the holes.

● *Prick and pounce method.* Using a pencil and ruler, draw a grid on to thick tracing paper or thick drawing paper. Mark holes with a stiletto or with a thick needle. Working on the wrong side, pin the paper to the fabric. Take powdered chalk for dark colours or powdered charcoal for light colours. These can be used in little bags which are then dabbed over the holes. Talcum powder can also be used. To preserve the marks, go over with a fine artist's brush, using poster paint or water colour.

● *Gauge method.* Follow diagram 2 (*overleaf*) for making a gauge. It is a precise way. Make an accurate gauge with card and use by placing points to dots, using a pencil or water-erasable pen, and making the next row of dots in each V. Work on the wrong side.

● *Paper method.* On some fabrics, such as those which are multi-coloured florals, dots may not show up easily. In this method, the smocking dots, or prepared tissue paper, can be tacked to the wrong side of the fabric. The dots are picked up working through both paper and fabric. When all the dots have been picked up, the paper is torn away. To do this take a sharp

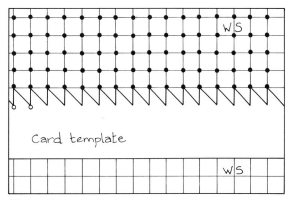

Card template

Diagram 2

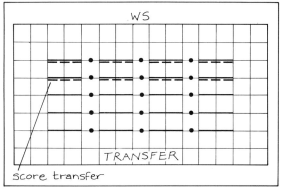

WS

TRANSFER

Score transfer

Diagram 3

needle and score on the gathering line between the dots. The paper should then lift off *(see diagram 3)*.

● *Counting the threads.* If the warp and weft threads can be counted on the fabric, this is an accurate method to use. Sometimes coarse fabric can be prepared in this way.

● *By eye.* This is more accurate than one supposes. As long as the top line is accurate, following on by eye can be used most successfully. Keep the rows straight, by marking where each row starts and ends as you work.

● *Tracing method (1).* This is used for transparent fabrics. Place the transfer under the sheer fabric and pin securely in place. Working on the wrong side, pick up the dots only on to the sheer fabric, as they can be clearly seen. Do not pick up the transfer.

● *Tracing method (2).* This is used for semi-transparent fabrics. Some fabrics which appear to be transparent can have dots marked on to the wrong side by placing the wrong side of fabric over a dot system. These are pinned and tacked together and then placed against a window pane which shows light through from the outside or on a light box. The dots will be seen more

clearly and can then be lightly pencilled in, or a water-erasable pen can be used. Sticky tape (or masking tape) can be used to help keep the fabric in place on the glass.

● *Patterned fabrics.* Fabrics such as gingham checks, stripes and spots (dots) do not need preparation by marking with dots as the print of the fabric can be used as a guide. When using gingham checks, the checks can be picked up at various equidistant places *(see the Gingham Dress page 122)*. Stripes can be picked up by working across the stripe and when the fabric is pulled up an interesting effect is achieved. Similarly spots can be picked up, usually on every alternate row. By the use of these methods a lot of time can be saved in preparation.

Look out for interesting repeating patterns. Usually the pattern has a small repeat motif which can be picked up at certain points. It is interesting to experiment with all patterned fabrics to see the exciting effects.

● *Preparation using a smock-gathering machine.* The smock-gathering machine has been in existence for over thirty years. This sturdy machine has been a tremendous help to those who smock. It is simple to use, if used properly, but certain points must be adhered to. The machine can be used on most fine fabrics but will not go through tough or thick fabrics.

To use a standard smock-gathering machine, the fabric is wound on to a dowel stick and the end of the fabric inserted between two rollers. Turning a little key or handle at the side of the machine, the fabric is fed through and gathered by up to sixteen threaded needles at one time *(see illustration below)*.

Any length of fabric can be fed through the machine. The depth of the standard machine is 14.5cm (5¾in), and the gathering can be made deeper by feeding the fabric through the machine a second time.

Smock-gathering machine

Newer machines which gather to a depth of 24 rows (23cm/9in) and 32 rows (31cm/12in) are now available.

To gather, a strong thread suitable for the fabric must be used. Mercerised sewing cotton thread is very useful. Quilting cotton thread, if suitable for the fabric, can also be used. Synthetic thread slips, and is troublesome when tying the gathering threads.

Although the machine comes with comprehensive instructions remember the following points. The machine will not go through thicknesses such as seams and selvedges. Therefore, remove selvedges beforehand. The fabric must be pressed before using. If the fabric is not fed in evenly, there will be problems. So, straighten the end of the fabric and roll it tightly on to the dowel stick. If the fabric slips, when beginning to roll it on to the dowel, keep it in place with a tiny piece of sticky or masking tape. Feed the fabric very slowly through the machine, stopping to remove gathers which collect on the needles. This is very important. If the needles become congested, they may break. If the machine is having difficulty feeding the fabric through, stop. Do not force the machine. Consult the instruction booklet.

To help keep the fabric straight when feeding it through the machine, keep it straight at the righthand side (this will become the top edge of the gathering) by ruling a line with tailor's chalk. When feeding the fabric through a second time, for a deep piece of smocking, do not thread the first needle, but leave it as a guide for distance.

Follow the manufacturer's instructions for maintaining the machine. Keep spare needles in case they are required, though if the machine is properly used the spares should rarely be required.

Preparation for a curve or circle

Smocking can be used to decorate gathers making a curve, as on a blouse or baby dress neckline, or a circle or parts of a circle which can be used for making bags and cushions (*see the bag in illustration facing page 112 and the cushion in facing page 49*).

Preparation for a curve

Depending upon the type of fabric, choose a dot transfer method which has dots wide apart so that when the extra dots are added, the distance between the dots at the top row will be the normal requirement for working the smocking.

Seam the blouse or dress at sleeve joins, and press. Measure the length of the neckline, and the depth to which smocking is required. Measure dot transfer, allowing an extra row of dots for the seam line at the neck edge.

Pin transfer to wrong side of garment, placing first row of dots on seamline. Slash the transfer from

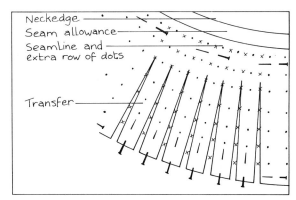

Diagram 4

bottom to top between second and third row of dots. Spread out the transfer to fit the curved neckline and pin in place. Iron dots on to garment (*see diagram 4*).

Mark in extra dots as shown by crosses. The distance between the dots will be gradually wider towards the last row.

Gather up the threads in the usual way by picking up each dot. When pulling up the threads, pull up into the desired curve by spreading out the folds. Starting on the second row, smock in the usual way, but lessen the tension of the stitching as the work progresses towards the edge of the pattern.

Preparation for a circle

Interesting effects can be obtained by gathering straight pieces of fabrics and pulling the folds into circles or semicircles (*see the Round Cushion facing page 49 and the Black Bag facing page 112*). For a circle, it is not easy to make a neat join if all the folds meet in the middle. Therefore an extra circle needs to be inserted (*see the Round Cushion facing page 49*).

Picking up the dots

The dots are placed on the wrong side of the fabric and picked up from one to another. Use a suitable thread in a contrasting colour (*see page 35*). Starting with a firm knot on the right, pick up each dot across the fabric (*see diagram 5*).

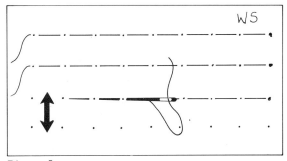

Diagram 5

Remember that one extra dot is required for a given number of folds on the right side, i.e. 21 dots should be picked up on the wrong side to produce 20 folds on the right side.

It is useful to cut the required number of threads in readiness for using. Cut each length approximately 10cm (4in) longer than the row of dots and leave threads hanging at the end.

Dots can be worked by running in and out of the dots. This gives only half the number of folds and the folds are very deep.

Pulling up the gathering threads

Pull up the threads to estimated width. This will depend upon the tension to which the embroiderer works, i.e. loosely or tightly. Do not pull the folds too close together. Leave enough room to work comfortably between the folds with a needle and thread. Keep the folds even and straight *(see diagram 6)*.

Tying off the gathering threads

Tie off the threads in pairs and then tie these in pairs again. This makes the threads extra secure. This is important as the foundation for the smocking must be strong. If a gathering thread comes out, it must be replaced *(see diagram 6)*.

It is difficult to estimate the length at which the gathering is tied. Only by working a small sample can one judge the tension required and the result.

Removing the dots

Take a clean plastic bucket and add ½ cup of biological washing powder (biodegradable detergent). Dissolve with 575ml (1 pint) of hot water (just off boiling). Add cold water, about 2 litres (3-4 pints), until the solution is at hand temperature. Test a sample piece which has dots on it and watch carefully. By rubbing the dots very gently with finger tips (not fabric against fabric) the dots will ease off the fabric. Be quick with this process. Do not leave in the water longer than is necessary. Rinse well in several changes of tepid water. Press sample piece of fabric over a clean dry towel with correct iron temperature whilst still damp. If the result shows that the dots have been removed and the colour of the fabric has not changed, it is safe to go ahead with the smocked pieces. For pressing place a clean folded thick towel on ironing board or table. Place smocked piece, wrong side upwards on this towel. Fold towel over the smocked piece to absorb excess water. Unfold the towel. Selecting the correct temperature for pressing, gently press the area surrounding the smocking. Do not press the smocked area. Turn the smocked piece on to the right side, and leaving on the towel gently pat into shape. Adjust folds and staighten the sides. Do not use pins as they may rust. Leave until absolutely dry.

Finishing

When the piece has been smocked, the work may be steam pressed to hold the folds in place. To do this, place finished smocked piece, wrong side upwards on to an ironing board or table. Set the iron to steam and hold it above the smocking. Never place an iron on smocking as this flattens the folds and detracts from the textured effect. Leave to dry, then remove gathering threads. The piece is now ready for making-up.

If the sides of the smocked piece need straightening, work pin tucks by hand on the wrong side close to the edge of the smocking on either side. This helps to give a very neat finish to a piece of work.

For making-up the garment, the extra row of gathers at the top of the smocking is useful when seaming.

STITCHES

The basic stitches of smocking are few and have been in use for a very long time. For present-day smocking, the common names for stitches are used.

Stitches give different effects. Some are straight such as stem, outline and chain; others give a wave or zig-zag effect such as wave, diamond (chevron) with repeats of these forming a trellis. Other effects are created by crossed-over stitches such as crossed-over diamond.

Using one stitch only can give a very rich effect. Many of the projects in this book use just one stitch, such as the Honeycomb Cushion worked in honeycomb only *(see illustration facing page 49)*; and the Formal Dress which was worked in diamond stitch only *(see illustration facing page 89)*.

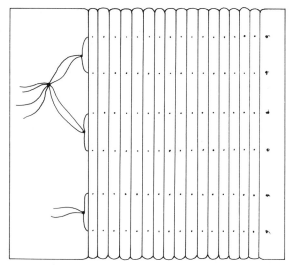

Diagram 6

Several stitches can be combined such as in the Gingham Dress which shows wave and diamond stitch *(see illustrations between pages 88 and 89)*; and the Round Cushion which shows vandyke stitch with cable flowerettes *(see illustration facing page 49)*.

Patterns can be made from stitches. These can be used as a repeat just as in any form of embroidery *(see Sampler facing page 48 for repeating border patterns at the bottom righthand corner)*. Any stitch or combination of stitches can be worked together to make a pattern.

The stitches used in traditional smocking can be enhanced by adding embroidered stitches *(see Sampler facing page 48)*. The basket of flowers contains bullion knots (bouillion stitches), French knots and lazy daisy stitch, which are all embroidery stitches.

Colour is an important factor in smocking. The choice of colour is very personal and most people have favourite colour schemes. Each project in this book has colour suggestions which might help to give further ideas. The texture of smocking gives light and shadow and is most effective when worked in self-colour, as this highlights the texture. A plain fabric smocked in tones of the colour of the fabric always enhances it; and working just one colour on a contrasting plain background always looks attractive.

Nature is the most marvellous lesson in colour. For inspiration look at a summer flower, an autumn leaf, a winter landscape or the fresh colours of spring. Look at stones with moss, an old tree trunk, a shell, and see the wonderful subtle colourings.

Points to remember when smocking
- Smocking is worked on the right side of the fabric; most stitches are started on the lefthand side except vandyke stitch which starts on the right; for most stitches, the needle is kept parallel to the gathering row.
- When working the stitches, pick up the top of each fold to a depth of approximately one third for normal gathering on a smock-gathering machine. Do not work too deeply as it will not look attractive.
- The stitches are worked with the thread either below the needle, or above the needle, or for some of the embroidery stitches, around the needle.
- Tension is an important factor in smocking. Work to an even tension, not too tightly, nor too loosely.
- When working a repeating pattern, or one that is equal on both sides, the pattern can be started in the centre and worked to the righthand side. Then come back to the lefthand side and work across to join the pattern.
- Start stitches on the left in the following way. Turn work on to the wrong side and with a knot in the thread, make one stitch on the end fold on the gathering row to be worked, which is now on the right. Take needle across fold and through to right side of fabric where the needle will emerge on the lefthand side of the first fold.
- At the end of a gathering row, finish a stitch by taking needle through to the wrong side beside the last fold and end with two small stitches on the nearest fold. Cut off, leaving 5mm (¼in) thread.
- If thread is not sufficient to finish row, take needle through to wrong side and finish off. Start new thread in the normal way, bringing the needle out so that the stitch is continuous.

Various terms are used throughout the book which must be understood clearly. They are:
- *Fold*. This refers to the fold so formed by the gathers. They are numbered from the left to right or in the order of working to help guide the working of the stitch pattern. Folds are sometimes called also pleats, reeds or tubes. Country people working smocking call the folds and spaces in between 'hills and valleys' which is most expressive.
- *Row*. This refers to the 'gathering row' which runs from right to left across the work. The row numbers are shown at the sides of the diagrams.
- To 'set the folds'. This means to work one row of stem stitch at the top of a piece of work which helps to even the folds ready for working. It can also be described as to 'set the gathers'.
- *Counting*. The numbered vertical lines show the folds and how the stitch is worked over the fold and the numbered horizontal lines show the gathering rows for working the stitches.

SMOCKING STITCHES

The smocking stitches in the following glossary are illustrated in the Sampler *(see illustration facing page 48)*. The row numbers after the heading for each stitch refer to the numbered vertical lines in the Sampler.

LEFT SIDE OF SAMPLER

Stem stitch *(see diagram 7; row 1)*
This stitch is a foundation stitch, as many stitches in smocking use this stitch in one form or another. It is a tight stitch and is useful for working at the top of a piece of smocking which has to be joined on to a yoke, as it helps to set the folds. It is an attractive stitch worked on its own.

Work as follows:
1. Start at position 1 on lefthand side of fold 1 and bring needle to the surface.
2. With thread below needle pick up top of fold 2 from 2-3, keeping the needle parallel to the gathering row.
3. Repeat across the row.

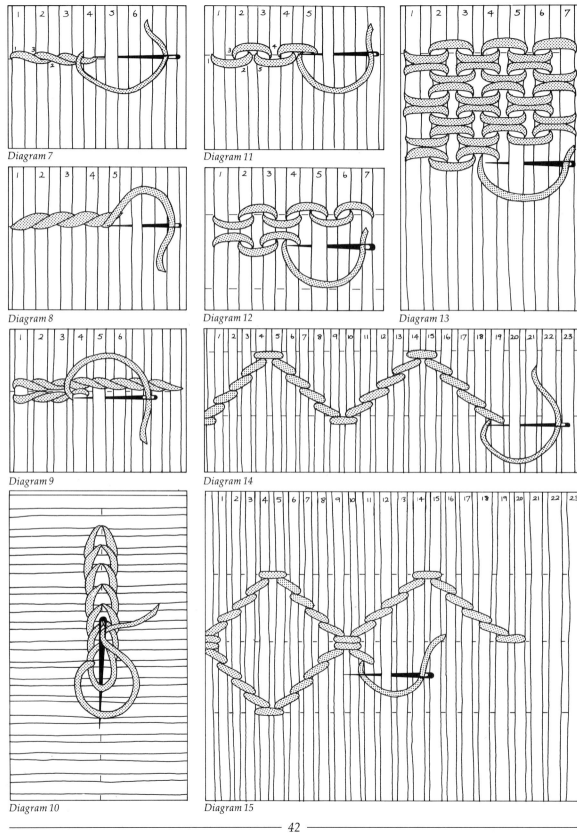

Diagram 7

Diagram 8

Diagram 9

Diagram 10

Diagram 11

Diagram 12

Diagram 13

Diagram 14

Diagram 15

Outline stitch *(see diagram 8; row 1½)*
This is the same as stem stitch except that the stitch is worked with the thread above the needle. It is sometimes called rope stitch and is used in the same way as stem stitch. It is a tight stitch.

Work as for stem stitch except that the thread is kept above the needle. Keep the needle parallel to the gathering row.

Mock chain stitch *(see diagram 9; row 2)*
This stitch comprises both stem stitch and outline stitch which form a chain effect, and is very decorative. It is sometimes called wheat stitch. It is a tight stitch.
Work as follows:
1. Work one row of stem stitch *(see diagram 7)*.
2. Work one row of outline stitch *(see diagram 8)* immediately below and adjacent to stem stitch.

Chain stitch *(see diagram 10)*
This is the same stitch as used in embroidery, but is worked across each fold. It is a tight stitch. It is useful for working designs, either in straight lines or curves, and also for tiny flower decorations *(see Floral Dress between pages 88 and 89)*.
Work as follows:
1. Turn work and work towards you.
2. Bring needle up between two folds.
3. Hold thread with left thumb. Take needle and insert it forwards through the top of the closest fold. With thread under the needle bring needle through, forming a loop by releasing the thumb.
4. To work the next stitch, insert needle into loop at top of first fold and take across to the second fold to complete the stitch.
5. Repeat across the row, watching the length of the stitch and keeping the tension even. Do not pull too tightly.

Cable stitch *(see diagram 11; row 3)*
This is a combination of working one stitch with the thread under the needle as in stem stitch, sometimes called a 'down' cable, and working the next stitch with the thread above the needle, as in outline stitch, sometimes called an 'up' cable. This is repeated across a row, alternating stem with outline. It is a tight stitch.
Work as follows:
1. Start at position 1 on left side of fold 1 and bring needle to surface.
2. With thread below needle pick up top of fold 2 from positions 2-3.
3. With thread above needle pick up top of fold 3 from positions 4-5.
4. Repeat across the row.

Double cable stitch *(see diagram 12; row 4)*
This comprises two rows of cable stitches worked close together to produce a cable effect. This is a tight stitch. Note how the stitches are placed together with the bottom cable of one row against the top cable of the next row.

Basket stitch *(see diagram 13; right side rows 20-21)*
This consists of several rows of double cable which when worked give the effect of a basket weave. It therefore gives a tight effect suitable for geometric or animal shapes.

Wave stitches *(see diagram 14; rows 5-6)*
Wave stitch which gives a zig-zag effect is used extensively in smocking. As it is elastic it can be used on little girls' dresses as well as for other items. The stitch can be worked to any height and can zig-zag in long and short waves. Work between two rows.
Work as follows:
1. Starting on row 2, come out at the left side of fold 1 at position 1.
2. Take needle straight across and pick up the top of fold 2 from positions 2-3.
3. With thread under the needle, start to ascend the wave by working across each fold at one third the depth between the rows; then two-thirds the depth between the rows and then reaching the top line, row 1, for three-thirds, coming out at position 9.
4. With thread over the needle, take needle across, picking up fold 6 and coming out at position 11.
5. Now begin to descend with thread over the needle, in the same way as ascending until row 2 is reached at position 17. Repeat across row.
6. Remember when ascending that the thread is under the needle, and when descending the thread is over the needle. Check the number of folds between the tops of each wave for accuracy. Working from this diagram there will be six folds in between.

Close wave stitch *(see row 7)*
This is when another row of wave stitch is worked close to the first wave stitch. It is attractive worked in another tone of the colour.

Spaced wave stitch *(see rows 8-10)*
This stitch comprises three rows of wave stitch.
Work as follows:
1. Work wave stitch across row 1.
2. Work wave stitch across row 2.
3. Work a row of wave stitch in between both rows.

Trellis stitch *(see diagram 15; rows 11-14)*
This is a very popular stitch which is formed by working one row of wave, then reversing the wave to

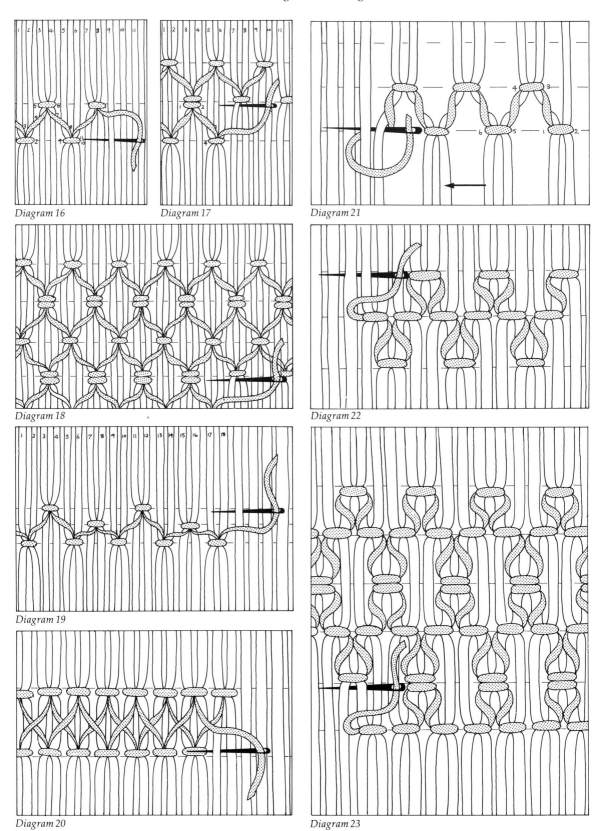

Diagram 16

Diagram 17

Diagram 21

Diagram 18

Diagram 22

Diagram 19

Diagram 20

Diagram 23

form a diamond, which in turn when repeated forms a trellis. The trellis can be worked in any way to form a zig-zag, with long and short waves. This is also called 'wave trellis stitch'. It is very effective worked on little girls' dresses (*see the Gingham Dress between pages 88 and 89*).

Work as follows:

1. Work one row of wave stitch.
2. Starting on row 2 with thread above needle, work one outline stitch from positions 1-2, come out at position 3. This stitch must be close to the row above.
3. Continue to work wave stitch to row 3 and repeat the wave across the row.
4. Keep repeating the pattern made by these two rows, for a trellis effect.

Diamond stitch: 1 (*see diagram 16; rows 15-16*)
This is a zig-zag stitch which when worked gives a loose effect and is therefore very elastic. Also called 'chevron' stitch.

Work as follows:

1. Starting on row 2, commence by bringing needle out at position 1, beside fold 1.
2. Pick up fold 2 from positions 2-3.
3. Take needle up to top line, over fold 3 and pick up top of fold 3 working from positions 4-5.
4. Take needle across folds 3 and 4, coming out at position 7 which is between these folds.
5. Take stitch over fold 5 to position 8 which is between fold 5 and fold 6, picking up fold 5 and coming out at position 9.
6. Continue across row.
7. Two rows of diamond stitch form a diamond in pattern.

Diamond stitch: 2 (*see diagram 17; rows 17-19*)
This is when diamond stitch is worked across two rows. For the second row, diamond is worked in reverse thus forming a true diamond. This is an elastic stitch. Also called 'chevron diamonds'.

Diamond trellis stitch (*see diagram 18*)
This is formed by working one row of diamond and then when the second row is worked close to it, and in reverse, the pattern forms a diamond. Many rows of diamond form a trellis. This stitch was used in the Formal Dress (*see facing page 89*).

Long and short diamond stitch (*see diagram 19, rows 20-21*)
This is, as the name suggests, one long diamond stitch followed by one short diamond stitch. Also called 'chevron' stitch. It is an interesting stitch which can be reversed to form diamonds, or when several rows are worked, it becomes a trellis.

Crossed diamond stitch (*see diagram 20; rows 22-23*)
This is formed by working one row of diamond stitch between two rows and then working another row of diamond in the spaces. It is very effective when worked in two colours.

Also, the stitch is attractive when diamond is worked between two rows and then the crossed-over diamond is worked in diamonds to half way only. Also called 'crossover chevrons'.

RIGHT SIDE OF SAMPLER

Vandyke stitch (*see diagram 21; rows 1-2*)
This is an attractive stitch which gives a crenellated effect. It is very elastic. It is the only stitch worked from the righthand side and is worked by inserting the needle through two folds at a time. It is best worked small to half way between two rows (*see Round Cushion facing page 49*).

Work as follows:

1. Starting on row 2, bring needle up at position 1 on lefthand side of fold 2.
2. Take needle across and pick up fold 1 and at the same time fold 2, coming out at position 1.
3. Take needle up the same fold, fold 2, and take fold 2 and fold 3 together, working from positions 3-4.
4. Work another stitch over the top from positions 4-3, and back to position 4.
5. Take needle down to row 2 at position 5 and take through to position 6. Work stitch over from positions 6-5 and back to position 6.
6. Continue working across the row.

Vandyke wave stitch (*see diagram 22; rows 3-4*)
This is worked in the same way as vandyke, but it is worked between two rows and is stepped.

Work as follows:

1. Work from row 1 to halfway between row 1 and row 2.
2. Continue down another step to row 2.
3. Repeat for other side of wave, working upwards.
4. Repeat across the row.

Vandyke trellis stitch (*see diagram 23*)
This consists of working several rows of vandyke wave to form a trellis. This can be very effective, but is quite loose.

Honeycomb stitch (*see diagram 24, rows 10-11*)
This stitch is worked between two rows only. It is a very elastic stitch and is worked at the bottom of a piece of work on a child's dress, or sometimes as one row to draw in gathers on a sleeve wrist or dress neckline.

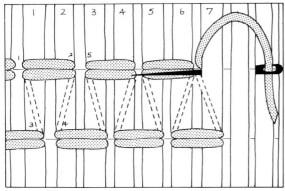

Diagram 24

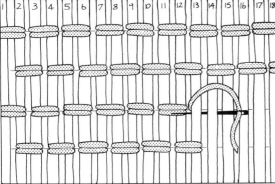

Diagram 25

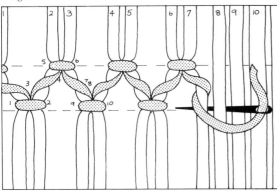

Diagram 26

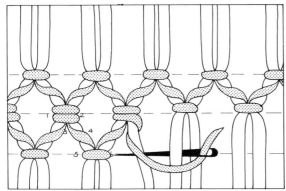

Diagram 27

Work between two rows as follows:

1. Bring needle to surface at lefthand side of fold 1 at position 1.

2. Take needle across to position 2. Come back to position 1 through the tops of both folds.

3. Take needle across to position 2 again but this time swing the needle downwards through the channel of fold 2 to position 3.

4. Take needle across to position 4 and back to position 3 through the tops of both folds.

5. Take needle across to position 4 and turn needle upwards to row 1, fold 3, at position 5.

6. Repeat the stitches, working up and down across the row.

Honeycombing *(see diagram 25; rows 12-15)*

Honeycombing has been in existence a very long time. *The Workwoman's Guide* published in 1838 describes 'honey-combing' in the following way: 'This sort of work is much used for the inside of the tops of work-boxes, and sometimes for the tops of heads of beds; it is usually done with silk, satin, or velvet, for the former; and highly-glazed chintz or calico, for the latter. Crease your material in even folds, taking care to have them very regular, and of a proper depth to suit the purpose for which it is intended; with a strong thread, tack the folds together with long stitches, so as to make them lie compactly one against another; then, with sewing silk of the proper colour, stitch firmly together, at moderate equal distances, the first and second folds; afterwards, stitch the second and third folds, at equal distances, taking your stitches, in the intermediate intervals. The third and fourth folds are only repetitions of the first and second, and by continuing your work in this way, the stitches of the alternate rows will accord with each other. When the piece is completed, and the tacking thread drawn out, pull your work open, and it will form puffings, in the shape of diamonds, on the right side.' Honeycombing gives deep texture and is also very elastic.

Work as follows:

1. Work honeycomb stitch across the first two rows as in diagram 24.

2. Then repeat the stitch on the next two rows, 3 and 4. Check to see that the spaces form diamond-shaped cells.

3. Alternatively, another effect can be produced by starting on row 3 but this time at fold 2.

Surface honeycomb *(see diagram 26, rows 5-6)*

This is really not like honeycomb as the thread lies on the surface and it is not worked in the same way. It is similar to diamond, but not so spread out. It is an attractive stitch and is elastic.

Work as follows:

1. Bring needle out at position 1 on lefthand side of fold 1.

2. With thread under needle, take needle across to position 2 and through fold 2, coming out at position 3.

3. Take needle up to position 4 and pick up fold 2, coming out at position 5.

4. Repeat across the row.

Surface honeycombing *(see diagram 27; rows 7-9)*

This is when several rows of surface honeycomb are worked. The effect is very attractive and is very elastic.

Work by starting on row 2 immediately under row 1, and work across in the same way as surface honeycomb stitch *(see diagram 26).* A small diamond-shaped pattern will emerge.

EMBROIDERY STITCHES

The row numbers after the heading for each stitch refer to the numbered vertical lines in the Sampler *(see illustration facing page 48).*

Bullion (bouillion) rosebuds *(see diagram 28; rows 19-20)*

Work as follows:

1. It is easier to work these by turning the work so that the folds are horizontal as shown in the diagram.

2. Come up at position 1 and take needle across two folds to position 2 and back through the two folds to position 1.

3. Loosely wrap thread around needle for the length of the space over the two folds.

4. Keeping thumb on wrapped needle, push needle through and pull all thread through, still keeping thumb on wrapped thread.

5. Release thumb and swing bullion (bouillion) into position.

6. Work two bullions (bouillions) side by side, leaving enough space for two satin stitch spots in the middle or a French knot for the centre.

French knots *(see diagram 29; rows 19-20)*

Work as follows:

1. Bring needle up in the top of a fold.

2. Place work down on a table.

3. With left hand, hold thread near fabric approximately 3cm (1¼in) away.

4. Hold needle behind thread and near fabric.

5. Holding needle firmly, twist thread once around the needle, or several times for a thicker effect.

6. Still holding thread with thumb and finger, swing the needle around and go down in the same place where the needle came up.

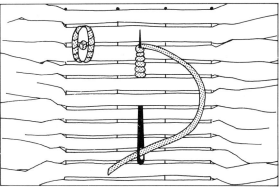

Diagram 28

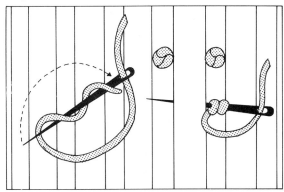

Diagram 29

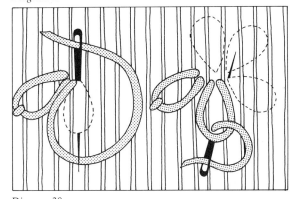

Diagram 30

Lazy daisy leaves *(see diagram 30; rows 19-20)*

Leaves can be worked singly or in pairs and are often used to decorate bullion (bouillion) rosebuds.

Work as follows:

1. Work with the thread under the needle.

2. Follow the second stage of finishing the leaf as shown in the diagram. Work on the tops of the folds.

Lazy daisy flowers *(see diagram 30)*

These are worked as for leaves and can have any number of petals. Work through the tops of the folds if possible, otherwise the stitches disappear.

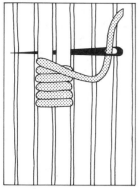

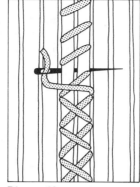

Diagram 31　　　*Diagram 32*

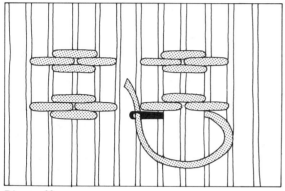

Diagram 33

Satin stitch spots *(see diagram 31; central column)*
The needle is taken across two folds and pulled together. Usually two stitches make a decorative spot.

Satin stitch *(see diagram 31; central column)*
This is worked across two folds at an even tension.

Whipping *(see diagram 32; central column)*
This is used to decorate two folds.
　Work as follows:
1. Using one colour, whip in one direction over two folds.
2. Cross the original stitches by whipping in another colour in the opposite direction.

Cable flowerettes *(see diagram 33; rows 22-23)*
　Work as follows:
1. Come up at the side of fold 1 at position 1.
2. With thread under the needle, take needle across to position 2 and come out at position 3.
3. With thread above needle, take needle across to position 4 and come out at position 5.
4. With thread above needle, take thread across to position 6 and come out at position 7.
5. Take needle straight across to position 8 and go down between fold 1 and 2.

Introduction to Projects

This book is about smocking. It is not a text book on dressmaking. However, smocking is usually adapted to clothing, so the projects have both elements included.

　The projects which follow are aimed at the home dressmaker who wants to have clear step-by-step instructions to guide her. The experience required varies from project to project and all are clearly indicated.

● When a project has been selected, read through the text carefully before deciding upon requirements.
● Drafting the pattern before buying the fabric is also advised. Follow the graphs for drafting the pattern pieces. There is no need to draft oblong shapes as they can be marked out directly on to the fabric. Use special dressmaking paper sold for drafting patterns, but as it can be expensive, new wrapping paper, or lining paper can be used also. Use a long ruler (1 metre long or a yardstick) and a pencil and eraser. Plot the pattern from the graph directly on to the pattern paper. If in doubt go by the measurements given on the graph.
● The measurements given are for average sizes, but as figures vary, it is strongly recommended that extra care is taken to ensure that the pattern is adapted to your measurements. This can be done by cutting out an extra pattern in tissue paper, or better still, making a 'toile' which is a pattern made out of cheap cotton fabric, usually calico. Washed cotton fabric can also be used. It is well worth the extra time spent. While every care has been taken with the patterns, it is sometimes not easy to get accuracy on such a small scale, especially on collars and yokes.
● For adjusting paper pattern to a smaller size: check sleeve and skirt length and adjust. Check width of bodice front and yoke back. Adjust with a small tuck or pleat placed at centre shoulder line, and running the length of the bodiced front and the depth of the yoke back. Check lengths of bodice front and bodice back. Likewise, enlarge the pattern by adding to sleeve and skirt length; enlarging the bodice front and yoke back by adding along a line taken from centre shoulder seam to bodice front waist, and centre shoulder seam on yoke back; check lengths of bodice front and bodice back yoke.
● Seam allowances, unless otherwise stated, are 2cm (¾in) which is generous.
● When cutting out, fold fabric with right sides together. (If the fabric is creased press well beforehand.) Follow the layout for pinning the pattern pieces to the fabric and mark any oblong shapes

Opposite Project 1: Sampler *(see page 52).* The numbers in the margins refer to the row numbers used in the text.

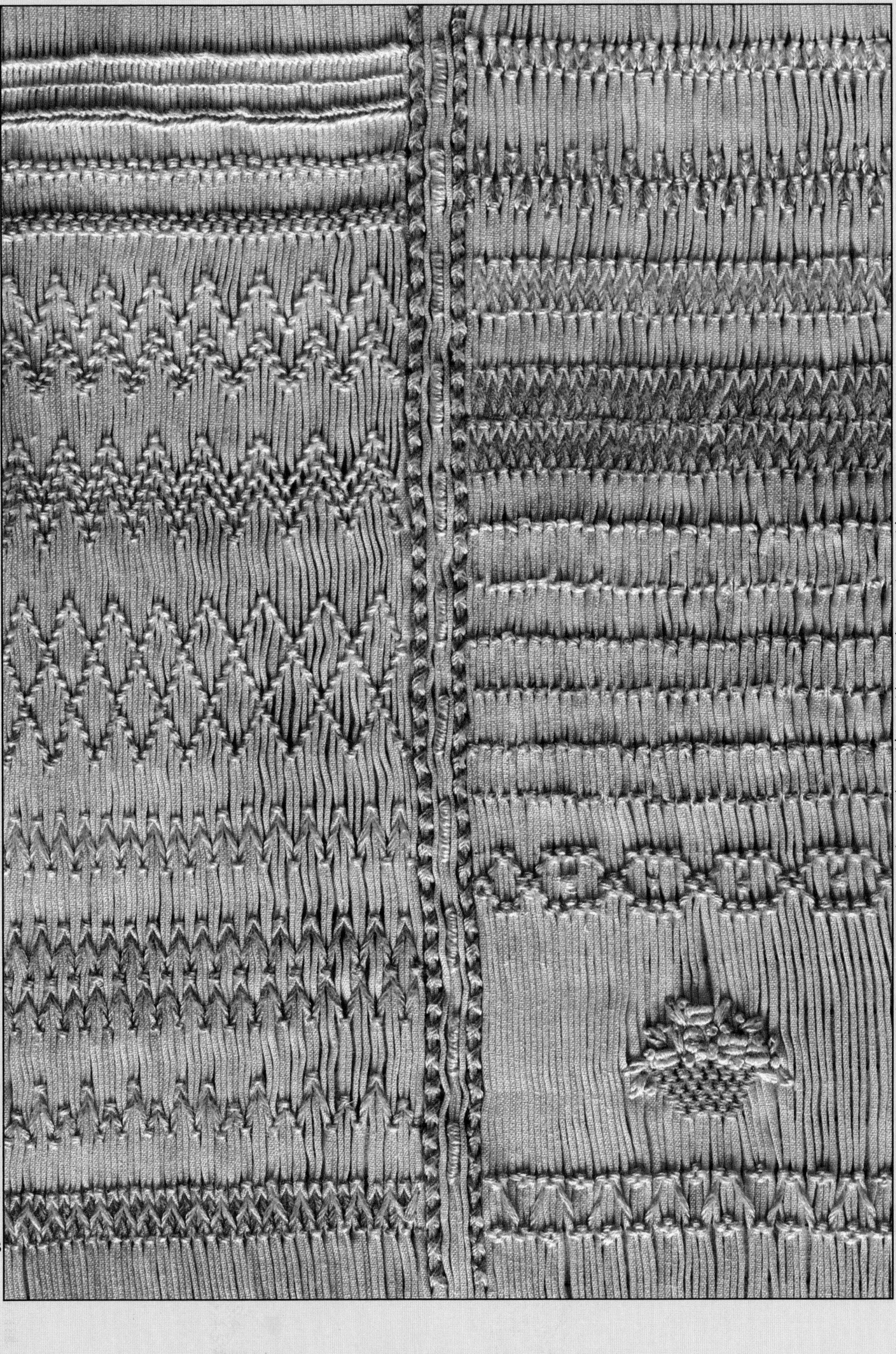

before cutting out. Take note of the 'fold' and 'selvedge' on the pattern.

● Make sure you have the following to hand: Sharp cutting-out scissors; sharp embroidery scissors; reliable tape measure; needles as specified in the text, usually Crewel embroidery needles which have a long eye for easy threading and a sharp point; thimble; fine pins (if working with fine fabrics do not use coarse pins – if fine pins are not available use fine needles if possible); tacking (basting) thread.

● Use tailor's chalk to mark the pattern pieces. For other markings a water-erasable pen can be used. This is like a coloured felt pen which makes a blue mark, but disappears when cold water is applied. Do not put heat near it, or iron over it, as this will set the mark. Never use felt pens or biros of any kind on your work. A soft pencil, lightly used, is very handy also. Do not press hard as it may be difficult to remove.

● The thread used for stitching your project is very important. Mercerised cotton sewing thread is very versatile. Synthetics can be difficult to use as they slip. Advice should be sought from the shop where the fabric is bought. Do not buy cheap thread as it is not worth using.

● Good handbooks are provided with sewing machines. Consult your handbook for advice about the type of machine needle suited to your machine and purpose. Keep your machine in good working order. Use it for all your stitching and for finishing seams with a zig-zag.

● Keep your iron and ironing board nearby and press your work as you go. Be careful with synthetic fabrics and test the temperature of the iron on a spare piece of the fabric first.

● Work tidily and neatly and finish off as you go along. Tie off threads as you work, and take out used tacking (basting) threads as you proceed. Keep a small wastepaper basket or bin beside you for the clippings.

● Try on the garment as you progress to make sure the fit is correct. When finishing the garment, it must be tried on for adjusting the hem length. Wear the shoes which will be worn with the garment and ask a friend to help measure the length from a level floor to hem edge. It must be the same the whole way round.

BASIC TERMS USED IN THE TEXT

Back stitch for zips *(see diagram 34)*

This is a useful method of inserting a zip, as some zips can be difficult to manipulate by machine. Tack (baste) the zip so that the edges of the seam, which must be pressed beforehand, meet centrally over the

Opposite Project 2: Honeycomb Cushion *(see page 55)* and Project 8: Round Cushion *(see page 91)*

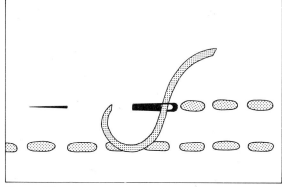

Diagram 34

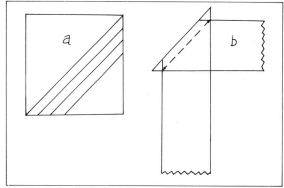

Diagram 35

teeth of the zip. Work the stitch near to both sides of the zip stitching, through all thicknesses. Space the stitches apart so that they are not joined as this leaves a harsh line.

Bias *(see diagram 35)*

This is used for binding and for covering piping cord as used for cushions. As it is cut diagonally across the weave of the fabric, it can stretch very slightly and therefore can be used where other finishes would not be suitable.

To cut bias strips: Find the true diagonal on a square by folding fabric from corner to corner. Mark this fold with tailor's chalk and a ruler, or by pressing. This diagonal must be accurate. Cut the strips all the same width. *(See diagram 35a.)*

To join bias strips: Join the strips by stitching the short slanting ends together. Tie off stitching threads and trim projecting ends. Press seam flat. Seam so that the joins lie in the same direction. Be careful to match right sides together. *(See diagram 35b.)*

Blind stitch *(see diagram 36)*

This is very useful for finishing hems, as it helps the hem to lie flat and when well worked is almost invisible. To work blind stitch, zig-zag edges of hem; turn

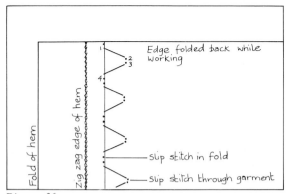

Edge folded back while working

Zig zag edge of hem

Fold of hem

slip stitch in fold

slip stitch through garment

Diagram 36

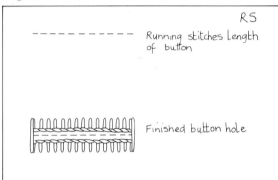

RS

Running stitches length of button

Finished button hole

Diagram 37

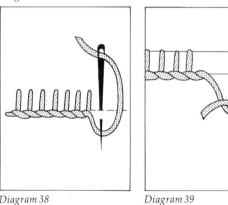

Diagram 38

Diagram 39

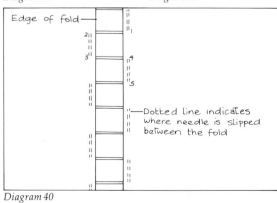

Edge of fold

Dotted line indicates where needle is slipped between the fold

Diagram 40

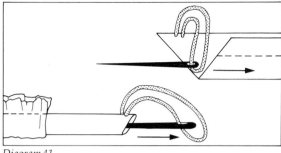

Diagram 41

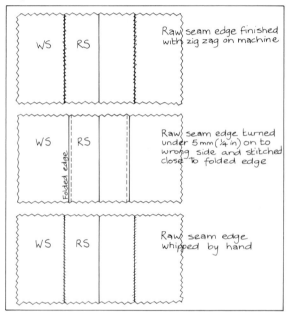

WS RS

Raw seam edge finished with zig zag on machine

WS RS

Folded edge

Raw seam edge turned under 5mm (¼ in) on to wrong side and stitched close to folded edge

WS RS

Raw seam edge whipped by hand

Diagram 42

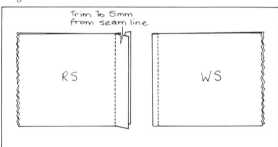

Trim to 5mm from seam line

RS

WS

Diagram 43

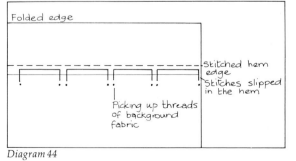

Folded edge

Stitched hem edge

Stitches slipped in the hem

Picking up threads of background fabric

Diagram 44

up hem; fold back approximately 2.5mm (⅛in) of zig-zag edge on to hem; stitch with small stitches, using fine thread and a fine needle. Work so that the stitches hardly show on the right side.

Buttonholes *(see diagrams 37 and 38)*
These are quick to make and give a very neat finish. Use fine thread and a fine needle, and work button-hole stitches close together. Note that the buttonhole is not cut until after it has been worked.
Work as follows:
1. Work tiny running stitches the length of the button.
2. Work close buttonhole stitches closely around running stitches.
3. Work several satin stitches at the ends.
4. Lastly, slit the running stitches with a sharp pointed pair of scissors or a tool for unpicking and ripping seams.

Buttonhole loop *(see diagram 39)*
This is used for fastening buttons. Make a bar with straight stitches and work buttonhole stitches over the thread of the bar only. Work with the eye of the needle downwards.

Ladder stitch *(see diagram 40)*
This is a most useful stitch for lacing two folded edges together. The stitch is always worked straight across from one fold to the other, working as shown in the diagram. After working a few stitches, pull on the thread and the two edges will meet edge to edge.

Rouleau (Bias-strip tubes) *(see diagram 41)*
This is made from a strip of bias approximately 2cm (¾in) wide by folding it over lengthways and, with right sides together, stitching about 5mm (¼in) from folded edge. The bias is then turned inside out in the following way:
1. Using a needle with strong thread, attach the thread to the end of the bias by stitching securely.
2. Insert needle, eye first, through the bias until the needle emerges at the other end of the bias. Pull through thread, which is attached to the bias, and keep pulling until the strip is turned inside out.

Seams *(see diagrams 42 and 43)*
Several types of seams are used in the projects, mostly 'flat' *(42)* and 'French' *(43)*.
Flat seams: These are stitched together with right sides facing, 2cm (¾in) from the edge. The edges are then neatened by trimming, and one of the finishes shown in diagram 42 applied. Do not leave raw edges as the garment will deteriorate with washing. Always press seams as you work, on the wrong side, and finally on the right side of the fabric.

French seams: This is a seam which is seamed twice in the following way. The first seam is stitched on the seam line with wrong sides together. Trim back to within 5mm (¼in) of the seam line. Turn on to wrong side with right sides together. Tack (baste) and press. Stitch just a fraction beneath the double thickness.

Slip stitch *(see diagram 44)*
This is applied to hems which already have had the edges prepared by turning under approximately 5mm (¼in) and stitching approximately 2.5mm (⅛in) away from the edge. In working this stitch pick up a few threads of the background fabric and then the needle enters the fold between the stitched line and the edge where the needle 'slips' along the fold approximately 1cm (½in). Push the needle into the fabric background and pick up another few threads.

Stab stitch
This is either worked to anchor several thicknesses, or it can be decorative. Bring the needle to the surface and go down a few threads away to the wrong side. Come up to the surface the distance required away from the first stitch and continue. It is worked straight up and down into the fabric, in two movements.

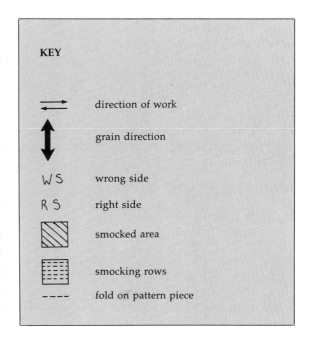

KEY

⟶ direction of work

↕ grain direction

W S wrong side

R S right side

▨ smocked area

▤ smocking rows

- - - - fold on pattern piece

Sampler

Size: 17.5 × 22.5cm (6¾ × 8in) actual size of smocked area before releasing gathers.

General description: This sampler shows the basic stitches used in traditional English smocking. It is worked in shades of pink and green on a fine ivory cotton. As well as using a wide selection of stitches, there are two border patterns and an attractive basket which complete the sampler.

Alternative suggestions: This sampler would look attractive in any colour. If working in a different colour scheme, substitute one colour for the pink and another colour for the green. For those with experience who wish to make a more decorative sampler, consider the following: using different thicknesses of white thread together with a metal thread on black fabric; using threads in creams, together with a gold metal thread, on sand-coloured fabric; using green and blue threads on a sludge green colour; orange and pink threads on yellow. For those with experience, dupion or silk fabric could be used instead of cotton.

Smocking stitches: There are sixteen stitches in the sampler: stem; mock chain; cable; double cable; basket; wave; close wave; spaced wave; trellis; diamond; long and short diamond; crossed diamond; vandyke; vandyke wave; surface honeycomb and honeycomb.

The following embroidery stitches are also used: cable flowerettes; bullion (bouillion) rosebuds; French knot forget-me-nots; lazy daisy leaves; satin stitch bars; satin stitch dots and whipped folds.

Also included on the sampler are two border patterns using the above stitches as well as a basket decoration.

System for preparing smocking: Smocking dot transfers.

Experience required: This sampler has been designed as a comprehensive sampler for beginners, as well as for those who have some experience. It is large enough for beginners to practise on.

Notes
● Use fine cotton fabric or a fine polycotton in a plain colour.
● A smock-gathering machine may be used, as the transfer dot is the same size.

● If wished, beginners may make half the sampler at a time. The centre section could be practised separately.
● When finished, the sampler can be framed. Consult the picture framer about framing the sampler in a deep frame.

MATERIALS

Fabric: 30 × 90cm (12 × 36in) wide ivory fine cotton lawn or fine polycotton.

Needles: Crewel embroidery needles, No. 8, 9, or 10.

Thread for gathering: 1 reel (spool) mercerised blue sewing cotton No. 50.

Thread for smocking: 1 skein each of stranded cotton in three shades of pink; two shades of green; 1 length pale blue stranded cotton and 1 length yellow stranded cotton.

Smocking dots: 2 sheets size 6.5 × 9.5mm (¼ × ⅜in) – Deighton's size H.

Usual workbox equipment.

GENERAL INSTRUCTIONS

1. Prepare fabric.
2. Prepare for smocking.
3. Smock sampler *(see diagrams 1-3)*. For detailed stitch instructions see Chapter 2: 'Basic English Smocking', pages 35-51.
4. Finish the sampler.

Preparation of fabric
1. Cut off selvedges.
2. If possible, withdraw a thread across the top and bottom to even the fabric. If this is not possible, cut a straight edge.
3. Protect edges of sampler by either whipping by hand, or by using a zig-zag on a machine.
4. Press fabric flat.
5. Make a tacking (basting) line down the centre of the fabric.

SMOCKING

Preparing and transferring the dots
1. The smocking dots are approximately 90cm (36in) wide and 17cm (6¾in) deep, giving 19 rows of dots. The sampler will require one complete sheet, plus 11 rows from the second sheet, making a total of 30 rows. Cut off all details, such as size etc. surrounding the dots. Count 141 dots along the top and cut. Mark centre of each sheet.
2. Working on the wrong side, and starting approximately 1cm (½in) down from the top edge, pin the full sheet of dots, wax side down, with centre aligned with

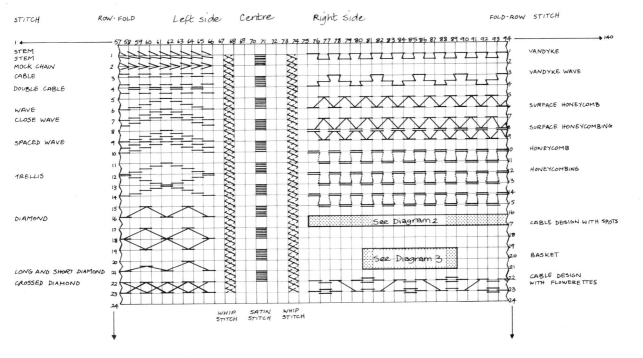

STITCH ROW-FOLD Left side Centre Right side FOLD-ROW STITCH

STEM		VANDYKE
STEM		
MOCK CHAIN		VANDYKE WAVE
CABLE		
DOUBLE CABLE		
		SURFACE HONEYCOMB
WAVE		
CLOSE WAVE		SURFACE HONEYCOMBING
SPACED WAVE		HONEYCOMB
		HONEYCOMBING
TRELLIS		
DIAMOND		CABLE DESIGN WITH SPOTS
	See Diagram 2	
		BASKET
	See Diagram 3	
LONG AND SHORT DIAMOND		CABLE DESIGN
CROSSED DIAMOND		WITH FLOWERETTES

WHIP STITCH SATIN STITCH WHIP STITCH

Diagram 1

centre tacking (basting). Keep top line of dots parallel to the top edge. Use only a few pins.

3. Test the iron temperature on a scrap of the fabric, using the extra details cut off from the transfer sheets.

4. Quickly iron the dots on to the sampler by pressing the iron down repeatedly. Do not press as for clothes back and forth as this may blur the dots. Unpin quickly and lift off the paper.

5. Take the second sheet of dots (11 rows) and carefully align with the transferred dots. Pin in position using only a few pins. Iron the dots on quickly. Unpin and lift off the paper.

Picking up the dots

1. Check that there are 141 dots. This will give 140 folds. Check that the centre line is between fold 70 and 71 (see diagram 1).

2. Check that there are 30 rows.

3. Working on the wrong side and starting with a very firm knot on the right, pick up each dot across the sampler (see page 39). It saves time to cut 30 lengths of thread in readiness for the work. Cut each length approximately 10cm (4in) longer than the row.

Pulling up the gathering threads

Working on the wrong side, pull up the gathering threads to approximately 17.5cm (7in) and tie off in pairs (see page 40). Make sure there is enough space between the folds to insert a needle.

Smocking the sampler

1. Work on the right side.

2. Leave the first three rows and start on the 4th row from the top. Note that this now becomes row No. 1 on the sampler (see diagram 1). Follow the smocking graph for the sampler on diagram 1. This shows all the details, except those for the cable design with spots (see diagram 2) and for the basket (see diagram 3).

3. For detailed stitch instruction, follow stitches in Chapter 2: 'Basic English Smocking', (see pages 35-51).

4. Note that all stitches for the sampler start on the left, except vandyke stitch which starts on the right (see rows 1-4 right side).

5. The sampler is referred to as 'left', 'right', 'centre' and 'basket'. Colours are referred to as 'L' for light; 'M' for medium; 'D' for dark; 'P' for pink and 'G' for green. e.g. 'LP' stands for light pink.

6. Use stranded cotton throughout, using 2, 3, 4, or 6 strands at a time. Four strands are generally used. Two shades can be threaded in the needle at the same time (see row 21 left side for 'long and short diamond'). Two strands of light green together with two strands of dark green were used in the needle. For 'crossed diamond', rows 22 and 23 (left side) diamond was worked in dark green from row 23 up to row 22. Then using light green, diamond was worked in the spaces from row 22 down to row 23.

Working the sampler

LEFT SIDE *(The numbers given are the row numbers)*

1   *Stem* (LP).
1½   *Stem* (LP).
2   *Mock chain* (MP).
3   *Cable* (LG).
4   *Double cable:* Top cable (DG); bottom cable (LG).
5   *(See row 6)*
6   *Wave:* Work up to row 5 (LP).
7   *Closed wave:* Work wave up to row 6 (LP); work another row of wave close to this (DP).
8   *(See row 9)*
9   *Spaced wave:* Work wave up to row 8 (LP).
9½   *Spaced wave:* Work wave up to row 8½ (MP).
10   *Spaced wave:* Work wave up to row 9 (DP).
11   *(See row 12)*
12   *Trellis:* Work wave up to row 11 (LP); return to row 12 and work wave down to row 13 (MP).
13   *(See row 12)*
14   Work wave up to row 13 (DP).
15   *(See row 16)*
16   *Diamond:* Work up to row 15 (LG).
17   *(See row 18)*
18   *Diamond:* Work up to row 17 (DG); return to row 18 and work down to row 19 (DG).
19   *(See row 18)*
20   *(See row 21)*
20½ *(See row 21)*
21   *Long and short diamond:* Work short diamond to row 20½ and complete on row 21; work long diamond up to row 20 and complete on row 21. Repeat across row. (LG and DG together).
22   *(See row 23)*
23   *Crossed diamond:* Work diamond to row 22 (DG); work diamond in spaces in another colour (LG).

RIGHT SIDE

1   *(See row 1½)*
1½   *Vandyke:* Start on the righthand side to work this stitch. Work up to row 1 (LP).
2   *(Leave blank)*
3   *Vandyke wave:* When working this stitch start on the righthand side. Work down to row 4 (DP).
4   *(See row 3)*
5   *(See row 6)*
6   *Surface honeycomb:* Continue working from left-hand side as usual. Work up to row 5 (LG).
7   *(See row 8)*

8   *Surface honeycomb:* Work up to row 7 (DG); return to row 8 and work down to row 9 (DG).
9   *(See row 8)*
10   *Honeycombing:* Work down to row 11 (LG).
11   *(See row 10)*
12   *Honeycombing:* Work down to row 13 (DG).
13   *(See row 12)*
14   *Honeycombing:* Work down to row 15 (DG).
15   *(See row 14)*
16   *(See row 16½)*
16½ *Cable design with spots:* Work cable up to row 16 (DP) *(see diagram 2)*. Come back to row 16½. Work cable. Work up to row 16 and work cables, following smocking graph. Continue across sampler repeating the pattern with the larger number of cables on the top line, and ending with the smaller number of cables on the top line. Work second row of pattern down to row 17 in the same way to form 'boxes'. Note that there are small 'boxes' at each end of the pattern and a total of four larger ones in the middle. Work satin stitch spots in the centres of each (PG).
17   *(See row 16½)*

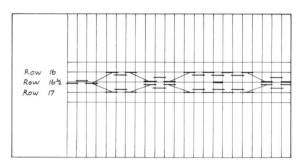

Diagram 2

18   *(Leave blank)*
19, 20, 21 *Basket:* The basket with flowers is placed in the centre between rows 19 and 21 *(see diagram 3)*. There are four rows of cable to work between row 20 and 21 for the basket (DG). Starting on

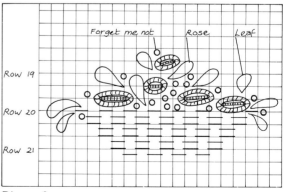

Diagram 3

row 20, work 8 cables across for the top of the basket, counting the top bar as one cable. Work three more rows. Work roses in bullion (bouillion) stitch in two tones of pink. Work satin stitches for the centre of the rose (DP). Work bullions (bouillions) each side (LP). Work leaves in lazy daisy stitch (LG and DG). Work forget-me-nots in French knots (B and Y).

22 *Cable design with flowerettes:* Work cable (DP). Work down to row 23. Work cable. Work up to row 22. Continue working across the sampler. Work cable flowerettes (LG and DG).

23 *(See row 22)*

Working the sampler – the centre

1. Take the two centre folds, 70 and 71, and working between row 1 and row 2, work satin stitch in green.
2. Work satin stitch in pink between rows 3 and 4.
3. Continue alternating the colours down the centre of the sampler, down to the bottom.
4. Turn the sampler sideways, and taking folds 67 and 68 together, whip over the folds in pink.
5. Using green, whip in the opposite direction, making a cross stitch.
6. Taking folds 73 and 74 together, repeat 4 and 5.

FINISHING THE SAMPLER

1. If framing the sampler, finish in the following way. Working on the wrong side, work stem stitch in one strand of stranded cotton or mercerised cotton sewing thread to match fabric, across the top, on rows 1, 2 and 3. Also work across the bottom on rows 27, 28, 29 and 30. This will help to give a flat finish for framing. Do not pull the gathering threads out.
2. If using as a workbox sampler, work on the wrong side on rows 3 and 27, working stem stitch as above. This will help to keep the shape of the sampler. Take out the gathering threads. The sampler will stretch considerably, Alternatively, the gathering threads may be left in.

Honeycomb Cushion

Size: Approximately 37.5cm (14¾in) square.

General description: The cushion is made in a heavy cream raw silk noil fabric and the front is simply smocked in widely spaced honeycomb stitch, in thick cream thread. The back of the cushion is plain. The cushion is finished with piping cord in the same fabric. The finished cover is slip-stitched. A bought cushion pad is used.

Alternative suggestions: Although the cushion was made in silk, any firm fabric can be used. If the fabric is not firm, the large honeycomb cells will not hold their shape. Furnishing fabrics are also suitable. This is a most attractive cushion when made in other colourways such as: any plain colour can be smocked in a matching coloured thread; a tone of one colour can be used for smocking, such as pale pink on a darker pink, or dark green on a pale green; also contrasting colours such as cerise on violet, rust on blue, black on white.

Those with experience may wish to experiment further by lacing narrow ribbon through the honeycomb spots either diagonally or in waves across the cushion; by working different coloured satin stitch spots in the cells (the flat areas) of the honeycomb; by dripping fabric dye into the cells; or by working honeycomb in either variegated thread, or changing the colour for a random spot effect.

Smocking stitches: Only one stitch, honeycomb stitch, spaced 2.5cm (1in) apart, is used.

System for preparing smocking: As the dots are far apart, use a soft pencil to mark the dots lightly on the wrong side of the fabric.

Experience required: Suitable for a beginner.

Notes
● A beginner should practise on a spare piece of fabric such as calico, or any plain cotton, until familiar with the working of honeycomb stitch.
● It is more economical to use 90cm (36in) wide fabric than other widths.
● Press fabric before commencing.
● Wash and dry the piping cord before using to shrink it.
● Using a zipper foot on the machine gives the neatest finish, but it is possible to make it by hand.

● When you need to wash the cushion cover, undo the slip stitching and hand wash in warm soapy water. Rinse well. When almost dry, set iron to correct fabric temperature and iron the back of the cushion cover only. Slip cover back on to the cushion pad and slip stitch into place. If required, steam press the smocked front of the cushion, being careful not to let the iron rest on the smocking.

MATERIALS

Fabric: 90 × 90cm (1yd × 36in) wide heavy cream silk.

Needles: Chenille No. 22 if available. The needle must have a large eye to take Perle No. 3.

Thread for sewing: 1 reel (spool) mercerised cotton thread No. 50.

Thread for gathering: 1 reel (spool) strong thread in a contrasting colour. A fine synthetic thread is suitable.

Thread for smocking: 2 skeins Perle No. 3. If unobtainable 2 skeins of Perle No. 5 or stranded cotton can be used but these do not give the lustre of Perle No. 3.

Cotton cord for piping: 2 metres (2 yards) of No. 1 or No. 2, preshrunk.

Usual workbox equipment, plus soft pencil or water-erasable pen.

Cushion pad approximately 38cm (15in) square.

GENERAL INSTRUCTIONS

1. Cut out the cushion *(see diagram 1)*.
2. Smock cushion front *(see diagrams 2-3)*.
3. Make up the cushion *(see diagrams 4-8)*.

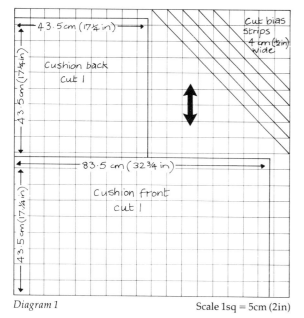

Diagram 1   Scale 1sq = 5cm (2in)

SMOCKING

Preparing the dots
1. Whip around the edges of the cushion front and cushion back to prevent fraying.
2. Mark seam line by tacking (basting) 2cm (¾in) in from edge around cushion front *(see diagram 1)*. Likewise, mark seam line on cushion back.
3. Place wrong side of cushion front (larger piece) on a table or smooth surface. Using a soft pencil or water-erasable pen, and a ruler or yardstick, mark dots for smocking, starting 3cm (1¼in) down from the top edge, and 3cm (1¼in) in from the side edge of the left hand corner *(see diagram 2)*. Mark every 2.5cm (1in) across the piece, working from left to right. There should be 32 dots across *(see diagram 32)*. Mark second row 2.5cm (1in) down from the top row and immediately under the top row of dots. Continue marking every row (total of 16 rows) down to the bottom.

Picking up the dots
Cut a contrasting colour of gathering thread about 10cm (4in) longer than the width of the fabric. Prepare 16 of these gathering threads. Starting on the right with a strong knot, pick up each dot across the fabric. Do not end off but leave the thread hanging. Work each row likewise until all dots have been picked up.

Pulling up the gathering threads
Taking the loose threads on the left, pull up until the work measures 18.5cm (7in). Tie off in pairs.

Working the smocking
Working on the right side of the fabric, use one strand of Perle No. 3 in the needle, or one strand of Perle No. 5 doubled, or all six strands of stranded cotton and start to work honeycomb stitch. This stitch is worked over the entire front of the cushion. Do not work the stitches loosely. When finished, take out the gathering threads and the front should expand to approximately 43.5cm (17¼in) from edge to edge.

MAKING-UP THE CUSHION

Step 1: Front
When the smocking is completed, there will be loose pleats at the top and at the bottom of the cushion. Hold these pleats in position by tacking (basting) them firmly in place on the seam line at the top and at the bottom of the cushion front *(see diagram 4)*. This will help to keep the seaming flat.

Step 2: Preparing the piping
1. Cut the bias strips. Note that these strips are cut on the true diagonal 4cm (1½in) wide *(see diagram 1)*.

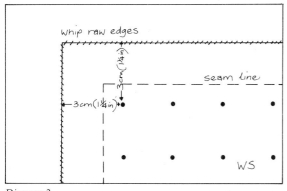
Diagram 2

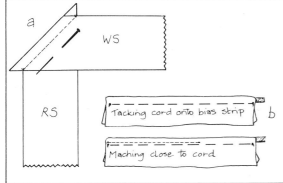
Diagram 3

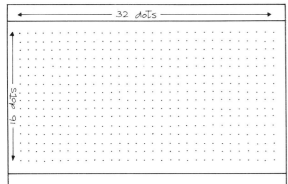
Diagram 4

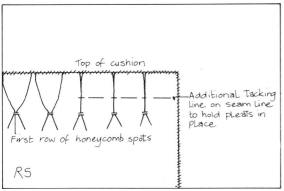
Diagram 5

2. Pin the strips together, right sides together and join by machine *(see diagram 5a)*. Make a strip long enough to go around the four sides of the cushion, plus 10cm (4in). Press seams flat. Trim joins level.

3. Place bias strips wrong side up and place pre-shrunk cord along the middle. Fold over. Tack (baste) near to the cord, leaving enough space to machine *(see diagram 5b)*. Starting approximately 5cm (2in) from the end of the piping, machine with a zipper foot, using a medium stitch length, very close to the cord *(see diagram 6)*. Stop machining approximately 5cm (2in) from the end. Leaving the ends free, ease the joining. Take out the tacking (basting) thread.

Step 3: Inserting the piping

1. Place smocked front, right side upwards, on a table. Start approximately 10cm (4in) from top righthand corner. Take the piping, and starting 5cm (2in) from the end of the piping (where the machining begins), pin in place on top of the smocked area, raw edges together. Be careful to place machine line of piping exactly over the tacked (basted) line of the cushion front seam line. Slightly round the corners and avoid seams on the corners *(see diagram 6)*.

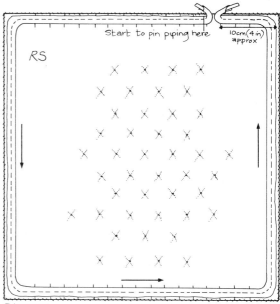
Diagram 6

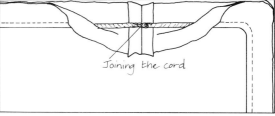
Diagram 7

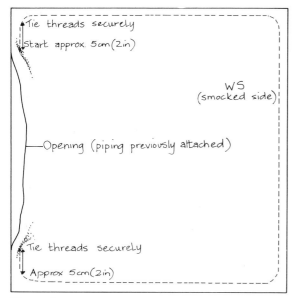

Tie threads securely

Start approx. 5cm(2in)

WS
(smocked side)

Opening (piping previously attached)

Tie threads securely

Approx. 5cm(2in)

Diagram 8

2. To join the bias of the piping neatly, this is better done by hand. Pin carefully and seam with back-stitches (*see diagram 7*).
3. Abut the cord and join with several stitches. Do not overlap the cord.
4. Place cord on the bias and continue line of machining, which is close to the rest of the cord, by hand. Place on top of smocked front. Pin in position.
5. Tack (Baste) all around the cushion on seam line.
6. Using a zipper foot, machine on the seam line close to the cord all around the cushion. Tie off securely. Take out tacking (basting).
7. Trim raw edges on the righthand side and zig-zag with machine, or whip by hand. This will be the opening for the cushion.

Step 4: Joining the cushion front to the cushion back
1. Place cushion back, right side upwards, on table.
2. Place smocked cushion front, right side downwards, on top of cushion back. Tack (Baste) approximately 5mm (¼in) away from machine line.
3. Starting on the lefthand side approximately 5cm (2in) below corner, machine stitch, using a zipper foot, on the machine line, all around the cushion, and ending approximately 5cm (2in) up from bottom left-hand corner. Leave the opening free (*see diagram 8*).
4. Tie ends off securely. Take out tacking (basting). Trim seams and zig-zag by machine, or whip by hand, on three sides of the cushion.
5. Turn cover inside out and pull corners into shape.
6. Insert cushion pad. Turn under seam allowance on the open side of the cushion back, and slip stitch in position.

PROJECT 3 (*See illustration facing page 64*)

Lampshade

Size: Diameter across the top: 17.5cm (7in); across the bottom 35cm (13¾in); depth 22cm (8¾in).

General description: This lampshade, which is mounted over an ivory lining, is covered in pale lemon georgette. At the top, it is simply smocked in honeycomb stitch on box pleats. These pleats are splayed out at the bottom and the shade is finished on the inside with a narrow ribbon.

Alternative suggestions: Any colour to suit individual furnishings can be used. Interesting colour combinations are: pale blue chiffon/georgette over pale pink lining; pale blue chiffon/georgette over yellow lining; and pale yellow chiffon/georgette over pale pink lining. Try samples of fabric, with a light behind, to show the different colour effects, bearing in mind that when smocked and pleated on to a frame, there will be various tones of colour. Jap (China) silk, which is fine, is another suitable fabric to use.

Any size of lampshade can be made. Those which have straight sides and are drum-shaped are easier to handle and are strongly recommended.

For a smocked effect which is not too deep, two rows of honeycomb could be worked over three rows, instead of over four rows. This is very suitable for a drum shape as the pleats can be attached to the bottom, keeping the box pleats flat.

MATERIALS

Lampshade frame: Size approximately 17.5cm (7in) across the top; 35cm (13¾in) across the bottom; 22cm (8¾in) depth. Painted finish.

Fabric for covering: 1 metre × 115cm (1 yd × 45in) wide pale lemon nylon georgette or similar.

Fabric for lining: 50 × 115cm (½ yd × 45in) wide ivory polyester satin.

Tape for binding: 7 metres (7 yds) tape 5mm (¼in) wide.

Ribbon for finishing: 2 metres (2 yds) pale lemon ribbon 5mm (¼in) wide.

Needles: Betweens, No. 5 or 6; or Crewel embroidery needles, No. 8, 9 or 10.

Sewing thread: Small quantity of mercerised sewing thread No. 50 to match lining. Small quantity of pale lemon mercerised sewing thread No. 50 to match cover.

Embroidery thread: Small quantity of stranded cotton in pale lemon to match cover.

Usual workbox equipment plus short fine pins or Lillikin pins (Lills) if available, soft pencil and ruler.

Small pot of enamel paint and paint brush if frame is not prepared.

GENERAL INSTRUCTIONS

1. Paint the frame if not already painted.
2. Bind the frame *(see diagrams 1-2)*.
3. Line the frame *(see diagram 3)*.
4. Smock the cover *(see diagrams 4-6)*.
5. Finish the lampshade.

PREPARATION

Painting the frame
1. Use quick-drying enamel paint and paint frame to protect it from rust.
2. Leave frame to dry thoroughly.

Binding the frame
1. The binding must be firmly done otherwise the lining and covering will slip.
2. For binding, use tape approximately twice the length of the strut or ring.
3. Begin binding on a strut *(see diagram 1)*.
4. Cut tape to a point and place tape behind the top ring.
5. Bring the pointed end of the tape over the ring and tuck in behind the strut.
6. Begin to bind with long end of tape. Bind at an acute angle and try not to overlap as this will leave a ridge.
7. When the bottom ring is reached, finish as shown in diagram 2.
8. Bind top of frame in the same way. Stitch ends securely.
9. Bind bottom of frame by cutting off ends from binding the strut, and bind tightly over these ends. Stitch securely.

Lining the frame
1. Place fabric against shade, wrong side uppermost, with the grainline as shown in diagram 3.
2. Pin at positions 1, 2, 3, 4 *(see diagram 3)*.
3. Starting at position 1, pin every 2.5cm (1in) down to position 2.
4. Follow grainline from positions 1 to 5 on lower ring and tighten. Pin at position 5.
5. Start to pin on lower ring from position 5 to strut at position 2, tightening against the strut.
6. Pin from positions 3-4 on the strut.

7. Working on the bottom ring, start to pin from positions 5 to 4, pulling at the strut *(see diagram 3)*.
8. Pin the top ring.
9. Using a soft pencil, faintly mark the pin lines on the struts positions 1-2 and positions 3-4; faintly mark top and bottom rings.
10. Trim sides and top and bottom rings to 2.5cm (1in). Unpin. Remove from frame.
11. Matching grainline, and with right sides together, place the cut-out fabric pattern on the remainder of the lining fabric and cut out the second half of the shade.
12. Pin side seams and slip over the frame. Adjust if necessary. It must fit snugly.
13. Slip lining off frame and tack. Stitch by machine, using a small stitch and a fine needle. Stitch again approximately 2.5mm (⅛in) away. Trim close to this second line.
14. Turn lining inside out. Place over frame, aligning the seams with the two side struts.
15. Pin top and bottom rings, stretching the fabric so that it is taut.
16. With matching thread and working so that the top edge of the fabric is turned slightly over the frame, whip with close stitches to the binding, on the inside. Trim close to stitching.
17. Finish the bottom ring in the same way.

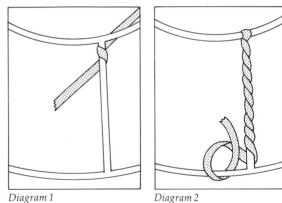

Diagram 1   *Diagram 2*

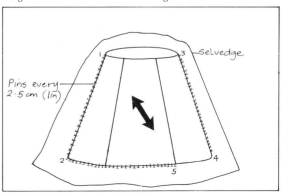

Diagram 3

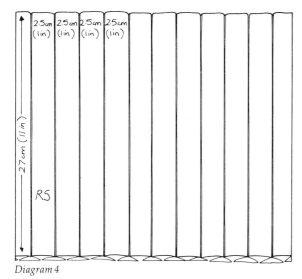

Diagram 4

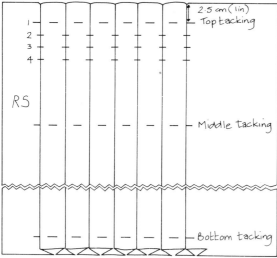

Diagram 5

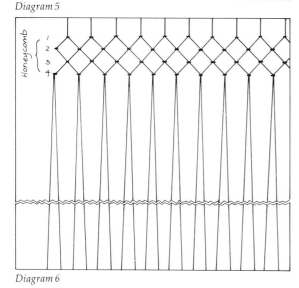

Diagram 6

SMOCKING

Preparing the cover for smocking

1. Cut two widths of georgette approximately 27cm (11in) deep. Join. Stitch again 2.5mm (⅛in) inside seam allowance. Trim to this line.

2. Place pins at intervals of 2.5cm (1in) along top edge of this strip.

3. Make into box pleats 2.5cm (1in) wide *(see diagram 4)*.

4. Starting 2.5cm (1in) down from the top edge, tack (baste) a line across the pleats. Tack (baste) another line at the bottom, and another line in the middle. Press pleats flat *(see diagram 5)*.

5. To prepare for the smocking, take a ruler and with a soft pencil mark lightly across pleat edges 2cm (¾in) down from tacking (basting) line. Mark two more lines each 2cm (¾in) apart in the same way *(see diagram 5)*.

6. Pin top to frame and mark top seam line. Remove pins. (This will not fit the bottom ring until the smocking is finished.) Stitch straight down. Stitch again 2.5mm (⅛in) inside seam allowance. Trim to this line. Turn to right side ready for smocking.

Smocking the cover

1. Using one or two strands of stranded cotton, depending on the thickness of the georgette, work honeycomb stitch between rows 1 and 2 *(see diagram 6)*.

2. Work second row of honeycomb stitch between rows 3 and 4, making sure that a cell is formed.

3. Take out tackings (bastings).

FINISHING THE LAMPSHADE

1. Pull smocked cover over frame, placing the seams as near as possible over the struts. Pin to the top of the frame.

2. Splay out the pleats on to the bottom ring and pin in place.

3. Closely whip the top and bottom edge to the lined frame. Try to whip on the inside of the frame, so that the stitches do not show.

4. Take ribbon, and working on the inside, neatly whip with tiny stitches over the raw edges, to finish.

3

Advanced English Smocking

Smocking in England has never been over elaborate. The basic stitches used have been worked in a restrained way. It is the repetition of basic stitches forming a richer pattern, or the combination of basic stitches which are used to form a more elaborate pattern that one can consider for advanced work.

Patterns can be built up in interesting ways, but the proportion of the area smocked, to the garment or article, as well as the scale of the stitch should always be taken into consideration.

The smocking for the Formal Dress *(see illustration facing page 89)* was worked using a motif of triangles which was repeated either side of the deep V. It was worked using one stitch only. Following this example, patterns can be built up in the following way:

Using triangles/diamonds

Using a triangle, a pattern can be worked out by placing two triangles together to form a diamond. Depending upon scale, the following are a few of the permutations which a triangle can give *(see diagram 1a)*.
1. Making the triangle into a diamond and repeating across the piece of work. The pattern can be worked in one colour and the spaces left free *(see diagram 1b)*. Alternatively, the spaces in between can be (1) worked in the same stitch using another colour; (2) the spaces can be decorated with a small motif.
2. Working the two triangles which make the diamond in different colours *(see diagram 1c)*.
3. Spreading the diamonds apart and working wave with cable stitch in the spaces *(see diagram 1d)*. Alternatively, a long and short wave stitch could link them.
4. Working two diamonds and linking them by a very deep wave, enclosing a diamond. This can be a starting point for a central motif *(see diagram 1e)*.
5. Working wave stitch either side of a line of triangles to form a border *(see diagram 1f)*.

Whilst the example is given for a triangle making a diamond, the idea can be adapted to wave stitch and other zig-zag stitches. Experiment on graph paper to see the possibilities, and then work a small sample. Consider using a stitch such as basket stitch for filled-in solid areas, as well as a small diamond stitch.

Using squares
Squares can make interesting patterns. Consider using squares in the following way:

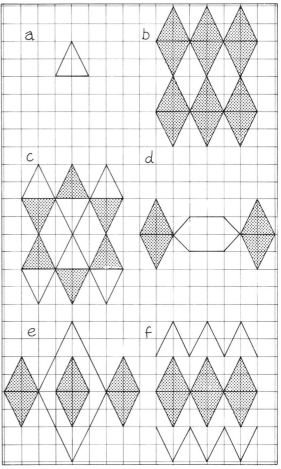

Diagram 1

1. Working squares in blocks of either basket stitch, diamond or stem stitch.

2. Alternating squares to make a chequer effect using diamond stitch. Link to form a pattern.

3. Joining two squares together to form an oblong.

Using trellis stitch

All zig-zag stitches will give a trellis effect. The shapes so formed can be filled in with embroidery stitches such as bullion (bouillion) roses or cable flowerettes depending upon the use to which the smocking is to be put. An attractive way to decorate ordinary trellis is to work out on graph paper another pattern over the trellis and work this over-pattern in bullion knots (bouillion stitches). It gives the effect of ribbon threaded through the pattern. Two bullion knots (bouillion stitches) worked one under the other can give a bold pattern *(see diagram 4)*.

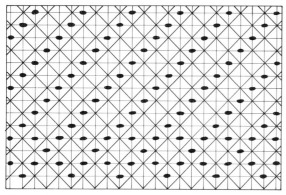

Diagram 2

Using other shapes

Interesting effects can be obtained by making shapes such as a basket, butterfly, animal or flower. Work a sample piece first by lightly pencilling the design on to the folds and working the shape in an appropriate stitch. Basket stitch makes distinctive shapes.

Using beads

Beads can be incorporated with smocking and make a most attractive decoration. Wedding dresses from the Victorian era were richly honeycombed using tiny pearl beads which were incorporated with the stitch. For today, the Christening Robe *(see facing page 88)* incorporates small pearl beads with the smocking stitches which has given a very unusual effect.

Beads can be added to most smocking patterns and incorporated with the smocking stitch. To do this, pick up the bead and then work the stitch. Use a beading needle and fine thread which matches the background. Wave stitch can be most attractive when worked in this way.

PROJECT 4 *(See illustration facing page 65)*

Smock

Size: Directions are given for a smock to fit size 89-97cm (35-38in) bust as well as for a small size 80-87cm (31½-34in) bust. The measurements vary only slightly as the smocking is elastic but the smocking is deeper in the larger size than in the smaller size.

The instructions for the larger size are given first and instructions follow only if there is a variation for the smaller size.

General description: This is a traditional 'round frock' cut from squares and rectangles. Both the back and the front are identical. The sleeves are long and fasten with a button and loop. There is a small neck opening which also fastens with a button and loop. The smock is made of beige cotton drill (a heavy cotton fabric with a pronounced weave) and is elaborately smocked and embroidered in dark brown twisted thread.

Alternative suggestions: Smocks are traditionally made in fairly heavy natural fabrics with self-coloured embroidery. Natural cottons and linens are suitable. The directions are given for a traditional smock worked in traditional colours. However, by varying the colours of the fabric and the colours used for smocking and embroidery, most interesting contemporary garments can be made. Suggestions for colours are: white smocking and embroidery on navy fabric; pale green smocking and embroidery on a darker green fabric; black smocking and embroidery on red fabric. Silk fabric can be used for exotic evening wear, with smocking and embroidery worked in a shiny thread.

Smocking stitches: Rope, wave, basket and feather are used.

Embroidery stitches: Feather and single feather stitch, together with French knots are used for the embroidery, the design being transferred by using a card template around which the outline is drawn with a soft pencil.

System for preparing smocking: Smocking dot transfers are used. The preparation can be done by eye also. This was the method used on traditional smocks.

Experience required: Some experience of smocking is advisable. The construction of the garment itself is simple.

Notes

- Decide which size you are making.
- Test measurements against figure before cutting out.
- Seam allowance of 1cm (½in) is included.
- Each piece is smocked and embroidered before making-up.
- Fabrics, if containing dressing or starch, should be washed and pressed well before cutting out.
- Press embroidery from the wrong side, face down on to a towel.

MATERIALS FOR BOTH SIZES

Fabric: 3.40 metres × 90cm (3¾ yds × 36in) wide cotton drill or heavy cotton fabric.

Needles: Crewel embroidery, No. 8.

Thread for sewing: 2 reels (spools) beige mercerised sewing thread No. 40.

Thread for gathering: 2 reels (spools) button thread or strong synthetic thread in a contrasting colour.

Thread for smocking and embroidery: 6 balls dark brown Perle No. 5.

Buttons: 4 small buttons size 5mm (¼in).

Smocking dots: 3 sheets size 9.5 × 12.5mm (⅜ × ½in) – Deighton's size C.

Usual workbox equipment plus card for cutting template and soft pencil.

GENERAL INSTRUCTIONS

1. Cut out the smock *(see diagram 1)*.
2. Smock the pattern pieces *(see diagrams 2-6)*.
3. Embroider the pattern pieces *(see diagrams 7-11)*.
4. Make up the garment *(see diagrams 12-14)*.

Diagram 1 Pieces to cut

Large size
Front (1): 115 × 90cm (45 × 36in)
Back (1): 115 × 90cm (45 × 36in)
Sleeves (2): 46 × 51cm (18 × 20in)
Shoulder straps (2): 37.5 × 17.5cm (14¾ × 7in)
Collars (2): 25 × 25cm (9¾ × 9¾in)
Cuffs (2): 25 × 17.5cm (9¾ × 7in)
Gussets (2): 15 × 15cm (6 × 6in)

Small size
Front (1): 115 × 90cm (45 × 36in)
Back (1): 115 × 90cm (45 × 36in)
Sleeves (2): 46 × 51cm (18 × 20in)
Shoulder straps (2): 35 × 15cm (13¾ × 6in)
Collars (2): 25 × 22cm (9¾ × 8¾in)
Cuffs (2): 23 × 17.5cm (9 × 7in)
Gussets (2): 12.5 × 12.5cm (5 × 5in)

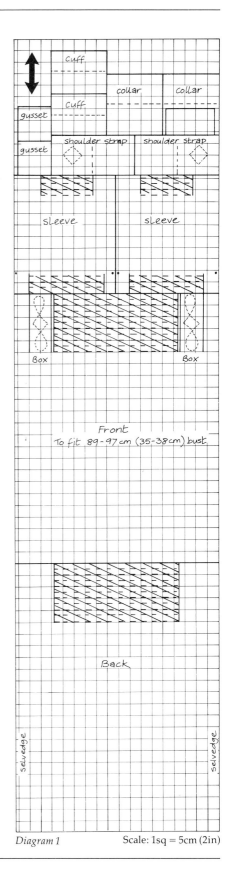

Diagram 1   Scale: 1sq = 5cm (2in)

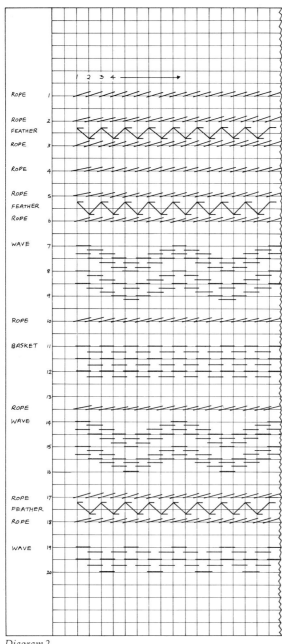

ROPE 1
ROPE 2
FEATHER
ROPE 3
ROPE 4
ROPE 5
FEATHER
ROPE 6
WAVE 7
8
9
ROPE 10
BASKET 11
12
13
ROPE
WAVE 14
15
16
ROPE 17
FEATHER
ROPE 18
WAVE 19
20

Diagram 2

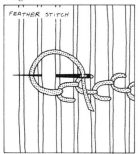

FEATHER STITCH

Diagram 3

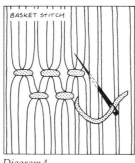

BASKET STITCH

Diagram 4

PREPARATION

Cutting out the smock
1. No pattern is required. Pin or mark out the measurements on to the fabric *(see diagram 1)*. Cut out.
● *For the small size:* Note the small size measurements given on page 63, and place in the same way as diagram 1 and cut out.
2. Whip all edges of pattern pieces to prevent fraying, or zig-zag on a machine.
3. Mark the centre of each piece and tack (baste). Mark 1cm (½in) seam allowance.

SMOCKING

Preparing the dots

Front: Prepare smocking dots, size 56 × 25cm (22 × 10in). Working on the wrong side, place smocking dots on front piece by aligning the first row of dots on the seam line, and matching centre of dots with centre tacking (basting) line. Iron dots and quickly remove paper.
● *For the small size:* Cut dot transfer to the size of 56 × 17.5cm (22 × 7in).

Back: Prepare the back using the same directions as for the front.

Sleeves: Prepare smocking dots for sleeve top 23 × 9cm (9 × 3½in) and for sleeve wrists 33 × 9cm (13 × 3½in). Iron dots on to both sleeves, matching centre of dots to centre tacking (basting) line of sleeve. Iron dots and quickly remove paper.

Picking up the dots
1. Before picking up the dots on the front and back pieces, cut a neck opening 5cm (2in) long on the centre tacking (basting) line. Make a small hem 5mm (¼in) wide.
2. On each piece, pick up each dot across the row, starting with a firm knot. Leave ends free. For the first few rows at the neck opening, stop and start at the neck edge.

Pulling up the gathering threads
Pull up each piece and tie securely. Do not pull up too tightly. There must be space for a needle between the folds.

Working the smocking
Note: All stitches are worked on the right side in one colour; after smocking remove all gathering threads;

Opposite Project 3: Lampshade *(see page 58)*

basket stitch for this smock is worked differently to 'basket' stitch on page 43. In this smock, the needle travels a short distance inside the fold, like honey-comb *(see diagram 4)*.

Front and back
Follow instructions in diagram 2. For row 7, to make the row symmetrical, it is advisable to start in the centre of the smocked panel and work to the right edge. Then begin again on the left and join up.
For rope stitch: *(see 'outline', page 43)*
For feather stitch: *(see diagram 3)*
For wave stitch: *(see page 43)*
For basket stitch: *(see diagram 4)*
● *For the small size:* Smock to and including row 13½. For rows 14 and 14½, follow rows 19 and 18½ in diagram 2.

Sleeves
Smock in the following way:
For the top of the sleeve *(see diagram 5)*.
For the wrist end of the sleeve *(see diagram 6)*. Turn sleeve upside down and start on row 1, rope.

EMBROIDERY

Note: All embroidery is worked in one colour.

Front and back
1. Make a card template from the diamond and pear shapes which are actual size *(see diagrams 7 and 8)*. Mark frame on 'box' of smock.
2. Place template on 'box' so that it is close to the smocked edge and almost level with the bottom row of smocking *(see diagram 1)*.
3. Using a soft pencil, trace around the outline of the template.
4. Work the embroidery following diagram 8. *(See diagrams 9 and 10)*.
● *For the small size:* Make template *(see diagram 7)*, but using the measurements in diagram 8.

Sleeve
Work a line of feather stitch close to each end of smocking on both the top and the wrist end of the sleeve.

Shoulder straps
Using the diamond shape from the box pattern *(see diagram 7)*, transfer to centre of shoulder strap *(see diagram 1)*. Embroider through one thickness only, using diagram 11 as a guide.
● *For the small size:* Follow diagram 11.

Opposite Project 4: Smock *(see page 62)*

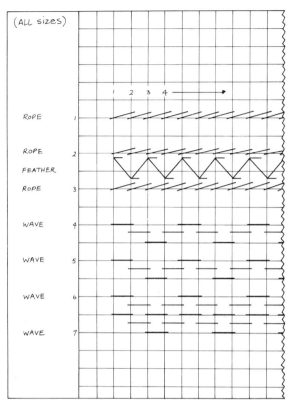

Diagram 5

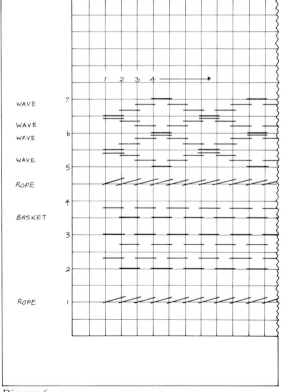

Diagram 6

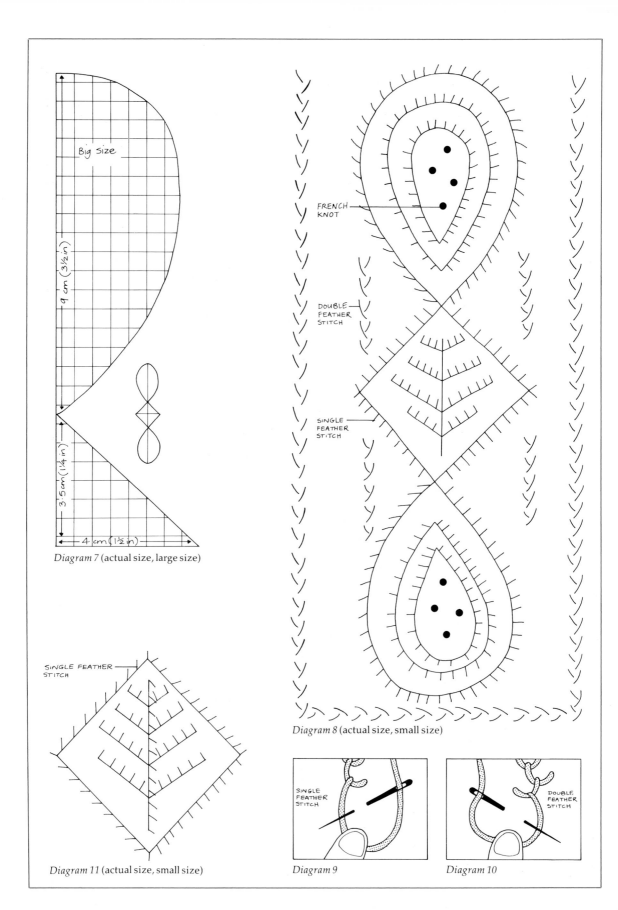

Big size

9 cm (3½ in)

3·5 cm (1¼ in)

4 cm (1½ in)

Diagram 7 (actual size, large size)

FRENCH
KNOT

DOUBLE
FEATHER
STITCH

SINGLE
FEATHER
STITCH

Diagram 8 (actual size, small size)

SINGLE FEATHER
STITCH

Diagram 11 (actual size, small size)

SINGLE
FEATHER
STITCH

Diagram 9

DOUBLE
FEATHER
STITCH

Diagram 10

Collar

1. On one half of the collar, right side, draw a line in soft pencil 2.5cm (1in) from edge, around two ends and in from the fold *(see diagram 1)*. Draw another line 5mm (¼in) in from the first line.

2. Working on single thickness of the collar, embroider outside line in double feather stitch *(see diagram 10)*.

3. Embroider the inside line in single feather stitch.

MAKING-UP THE SMOCK

Note: All pieces are now smocked and embroidered. Keep seam allowances of 1cm (½in) trimmed.

Step 1: Sleeve

At the wrist end of the sleeve, make a 1cm (½in) hem on either side of the smocking, starting at the spot marked on the pattern. This will be the opening for the sleeve.

Step 2: Cuff

Try cuff to see if it needs adjusting. (The pattern is generous.) Fold in half lengthways and stitch ends. Turn inside out and press. With right sides together, pin, tack (baste) and stitch cuff to sleeve, wrist end. Hem to inside.

Step 3: Collar

Stitch ends of each collar. Turn, tack (baste) and press.

Step 4: Joining front and back to shoulder straps

With right sides together, join front and back to shoulder straps, placing folded edge of shoulder strap at sleeve edge. Trim and neaten edges. Zig-zag by machine or closely whip by hand. Press seams upwards towards shoulder line *(see diagram 12)*.

Step 5: Joining collar to front, shoulder strap and back

With right sides together, join single collar edge to front shoulder strap and back, easing around corners. Turn over seam allowance and neatly hem on to stitching line *(see diagram 13)*. Join second collar in the same way.

Step 6: Joining sleeve to garment

With right sides together, join sleeve to the garment, matching centre of smocked panel at top of sleeve with centre of shoulder strap *(see diagram 14)*.

Step 7: The gussets

1. Take gusset and pin the corner of the gusset to the corner of the garment *(see diagram 0)*. Pin the gusset along the seam line of the sleeve down to ▲ and mark. Unpin.

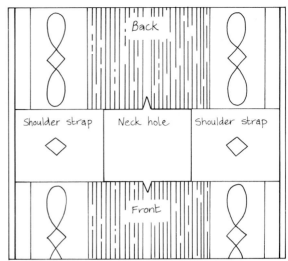

Diagram 12

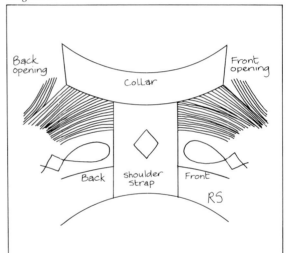

Diagram 13

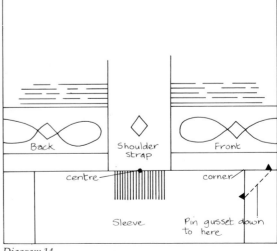

Diagram 14

2. Likewise, pin gusset along seam line on garment front and mark at ▲. Unpin.

3. The marks at ▲ will be the points from where the sleeve seam and the side seam will start.

4. Seam sleeves from ▲ to opening at wrist at the spot. Press seam flat. Trim. Finish edges with a zig-zag.

5. Seam sides, front to back from ▲ to hem edge. Press seam flat. Trim. Finish edges with a zig-zag.

Step 8: Inserting the gussets

1. Turn garment inside out.

2. Take gusset and pin at the four corners on seam lines of sides and sleeves, as well as the two opposite corners. Tack (baste) in place. Back stitch with small stitches, along seam lines, making sure that the corners are accurate. It is difficult to machine the gusset in place accurately.

3. Turn the garment on to the right side and tack (baste) the gusset flat. Press well. For a neat finish, machine top-stitch close to the edge.

4. Turn to the inside and trim seams. Zig-zag or whip by hand to neaten.

Step 9: Attaching buttons and buttonhole loops

1. Using brown embroidery thread, stitch buttons at neck front and neck back, on the opening and just under the collar.

2. Sew buttons on cuff.

3. Work buttonhole loops to fit all buttons.

Step 10: Finishings and hem

1. Turn garment inside out and check that all seams have been trimmed and neatly finished.

2. Even hem edge and zig-zag. Turn under 1cm (½in) and adjust length. Hem closely in place.

PROJECT 5 *(See illustration facing page 88)*

Christening Robe and Bonnet

Size of robe: Chest: 43cm (17in); length from shoulder to hem: 92cm (36in); yoke depth: 10cm (4in); sleeve depth with frill: 13cm (5in); sleeve band: 18cm (7in).
Size of bonnet: Baby size.

General description: This most attractive christening robe is made and lined in white polycotton and is trimmed in cotton broderie anglaise as well as in narrow satin ribbon. Pin tucks, sprays of simple embroidery and smocking incorporating small pearl beads add further to the richness of this practical garment. The robe has an attached slip. A bonnet completes the outfit.

The robe has a lined yoke which is pintucked with simple white embroidered sprays worked in shiny and dull threads between the tucks. It is edged with a broderie anglaise trimming which is 2.5cm (1in) wide. The neck is round with a back opening which fastens with three tiny buttons and loops.

The sleeves are short and puffed with pin tucks and embroidery decoration in between the tucks, as on the yoke. The bottom of the sleeve is gathered into a trimmed band which is edged with narrow satin ribbon with a bow in the centre of the band.

The skirt has a band of smocking 11.5 × 3.5cm (4½ × 1¼in) where the skirt joins the yoke. The smocking is worked in stranded cotton and shiny thread with tiny pearl beads decorating part of the smocking. Narrow satin ribbon outlines the smocking at the top and falls down in streamers at either side of the smocking.

At the bottom of the skirt there are four deep tucks, three of which are edged with a blanket stitch incorporating a tiny pearl bead. Narrow satin ribbon edges the bottom tuck. Above the top tuck is a narrow satin ribbon with small bows tied at intervals. Below the tucks is a smocked frill edged with trimming as well as narrow satin ribbon. The back of the skirt is gathered at the top edge and joins the yoke leaving a centre back opening.

The slip is gathered at the top of the skirt and is joined to the yoke lining leaving a centre back opening. The bottom edge of the slip is edged with trimming and narrow satin ribbon.

The bonnet matches the robe having a smocked band across the front and is trimmed with the same edging as well as in narrow satin ribbon. Embroidery decorates the back of the bonnet and two 2.5cm (1in) satin ribbons tie the bonnet.

Alternative suggestions: The robe and bonnet can be made also in a shorter length, shortening between smocked area and tucks on skirt, and altering the slip correspondingly.

Suitable fabrics are white cotton lawn, batiste, fine handkerchief linen, fine silk or crêpe de Chine. This robe and bonnet can be made in the best fabric available and trimmed with the best trimming or lace available. Whatever the fabric, if well made, it will become an heirloom. Embroidery transfers may be used instead of the design provided.

Smocking stitches: Two stitches, cable and wave are used throughout on both the dress and the bonnet.

System for preparing smocking: A smock-gathering machine is used.

Experience required: Some experience in smocking is required for working the dress and bonnet. As they are both very detailed, and the areas to stitch are small to handle, dressmaking experience is necessary for constructing the robe and the bonnet.

Notes
● A smock-gathering machine saves time. Smocking dots can be used, but the areas are very long.
● If possible, trimming should be bought already pleated or gathered. Ordinary flat trimming can be used, but it needs to be gathered allowing twice the finished length.
● Follow the detailed directions step by step. Press each seam as it is stitched.
● Work a sample piece of smocking to test graph, threads and beads. Test small needles and beading needles to see if they will take thread for embroidery as well as a bead.
● The embroidery design is simply worked. Practise the stitches so that they are familiar.
● The design can be lightly marked on the fabric with a soft pencil. Draw the design on to paper and place under the fabric. Transfer by lightly marking flowers and leaves with dots and lightly pencil the trailing stem.
● If smocking dots are used, they may show through. Follow directions on page 36 for their removal.
● This christening robe is washable. Wash by hand in warm soapy water. Rinse well. If possible drip-dry on a plastic coat hanger in the open air. Press while still damp. Test iron for temperature. Do not press over smocking. Be careful to test temperature for ribbons.
● Embroider the date inside the robe and bonnet together with initials of maker. Tie a label on to each garment giving all available information such as maker and date and relationship; name, address, date

and church where baby was christened. Wrap in acid-free white tissue paper and store in a large cardboard box. Label the box carefully.

MATERIALS

Dressmaker's Pattern Guide Paper ruled in 1cm (½in) and 5cm (2in) squares or similar. If this is not available use large-sized paper ruled into squares.

Fabric: 4 metres × 115cm (5 yds × 45in) wide white polycotton.

Needles: Crewel embroidery needles, Nos. 8, 9 or 10. Beading needle, No. 10 preferably.

Thread for sewing: 2 reels (spools) white mercerised sewing thread No. 50.

Thread for gathering: 1 reel (spool) any colour mercerised sewing thread No. 50.

Thread for embroidery: 1 skein white stranded cotton, 1 skein embroidery thread with a silky finish or Perle No. 5.

Smocking dots: 2 sheets size 6.5 × 9.5mm (¼ × ⅜in) – Deighton's size H.

Trimming: 9 metres × 2.5cm (10 yds × 1in) pregathered 2.5cm (1in) broderie anglaise (eyelit trim). (For ungathered trimming, double the quantity.)

Ribbon: 15 metres × 5mm (17 yds × ¼in) white satin ribbon. 1 metre × 2.5cm (1 yd × 1in) white satin ribbon.

Bias binding: 4 metres × 1cm (4 yds × ½in) wide.

Buttons: 3 tiny buttons to fasten at back.

Beads: Small white pearl – approximately 500.

Usual workbox equipment plus paper for drawing small designs and soft pencil.

GENERAL INSTRUCTIONS

1. Draft pattern for robe and bonnet. A 1.5cm (⅓in) seam allowance has been included *(see diagram 1)*.
2. Cut out robe and bonnet *(see diagram 1)*.
3. Smock robe front *(see diagram 2)*.
4. Smock robe frill *(see diagram 2)*.
5. Smock bonnet *(see diagram 2)*.
6. Practise embroidery stitches *(see diagrams 3-5)*.
7. Embroider robe yoke *(see diagram 6)*.
8. Embroider robe sleeve *(see diagram 7)*.
9. Embroider bonnet *(see diagram 8)*.
10. Make up the robe *(see diagrams 9-31)*.
11. Make up the bonnet *(see diagram 32)*.

Drafting pattern for robe and bonnet
Draft pattern pieces *(see diagram 1)*.

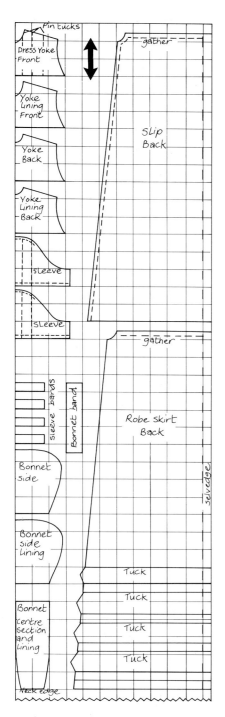

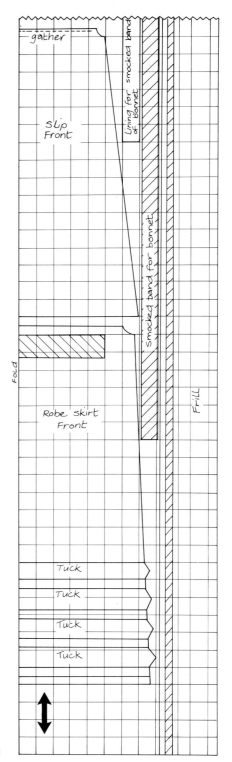

Diagram 1   Scale 1sq = 5cm (2in)

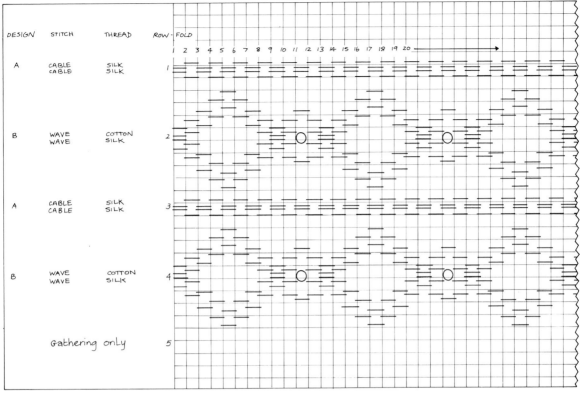

Diagram 2

Cutting out the robe and bonnet

1. Cut out robe and bonnet (*see diagram 1*).
2. Mark all seam allowances; mark tucks on skirts; mark pin tucks; mark centres of pattern pieces.

SMOCKING

THE ROBE

Preparing the smocking

Take robe skirt front and prepare 5 rows of gathering on smock-gathering machine, starting 1.5cm (just over ½in) down from top edge. Start and stop 6.5cm (2½in) at either side. If using dots iron 5 rows on to wrong side.

Pulling up the gathering threads

1. Pull up gathering threads to approximately a quarter of the width, to 12.5cm (5in).
2. Check that there are 80 folds on the right side.
3. Tie off gathering threads.

Working the smocking

1. The smocking is worked mainly in shiny thread or Perle No. 5. Stranded cotton, using three strands, is used for the outside of the large and small diamonds.

The bead is incorporated with the smocking. Use a fine needle.
2. Following diagram 2, work pattern A, B, A, B. The finished pattern consists of 7 large diamonds and 6 small diamonds with a bead added across each row.

THE FRILL

Preparing the smocking

Test smock-gathering machine to see if it will gather over a seam. If it will gather, join the short ends of the frill, trim and press seams flat. If the smock-gathering machine will not gather over a seam, each frill section will have to be gathered separately and then carefully joined. Prepare 4 rows only on the smock-gathering machine, the first row being used as a gathering line for attaching frill and the fourth row is for gathering only to help while smocking. If using transfer dots, seam frill and place 4 rows around the whole of the frill, being careful to align the rows.

Pulling up the gathering threads

1. Pull up the threads to fit around bottom of robe skirt – approximately 150cm (59in).
2. Tie off securely.

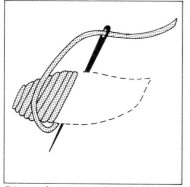

Diagram 3

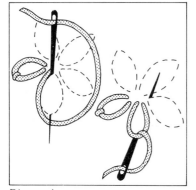

Diagram 4

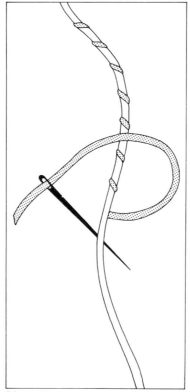

Diagram 5

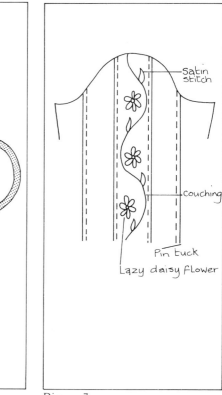

Satin stitch

Couching

Pin tuck

Lazy daisy flower

Diagram 7

Couching

Pin tuck

Satin stitch

Small pearl beads

Lazy daisy

Diagram 6

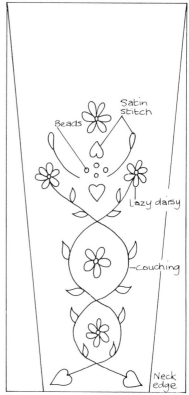

Satin stitch

Beads

Lazy daisy

Couching

Neck edge

Diagram 8

Working the smocking

Smock sections A and B on rows 2 and 3, using the same threads as for robe front *(see diagram 2).*

THE BONNET

Preparing the smocking

Prepare 5 rows only on the smock-gathering machine, the first and fifth row being used as gathering rows.

Pulling up the gathering threads

1. Pull up to 34cm (13½in) and tie off securely.

Smocking the bonnet

Smock sections A, B, A on rows 2, 3 and 4, using the same threads as for robe front *(see diagram 2).*

EMBROIDERY

Practising embroidery stitches

1. Satin stitch leaves: Work using three strands of stranded cotton *(see diagram 3).*
2. Lazy daisy flowers: Work using three strands of stranded cotton *(see diagram 4).* Add small pearl bead for centre of flower using same thread if possible. If the bead has a very small hole, end off flower and come back and attach bead using a beading needle with fine thread.
3. Couching: Work using shiny thread *(see diagram 5).*

Embroidering robe yoke front

1. Take robe yoke front. Working on the right side press along dotted lines. Make pin tucks by stitching just in from edge. Press tucks towards centre of yoke *(see diagram 6).*
2. Using white paper, draw design to fit between pin tucks. This is a simple design and can be changed.
3. Place design under the fabric and very lightly trace with a soft pencil by marking the stem and then using dots for flowers and leaves.
4. Work embroidery *(see diagram 6).*

Embroidering robe sleeve

1. Working on the right side of the sleeve, press along dotted lines. Make pin tucks by stitching just in from edge. Press tucks *(see diagram 7).*
2. Draw design on paper following diagram 7. Trace lightly on to fabric.
3. Work embroidery.

Embroidering bonnet

1. Take centre section of bonnet. Lightly mark the design, which is approximately 12.5cm (5in) in depth, to fit this section of the bonnet *(see diagram 8).*
2. Work embroidery.

MAKING-UP THE ROBE

Note: Broderie anglaise edging, whether bought gathered or ungathered, will be referred to as 'trimming' which has already been gathered.

Step 1: Yoke

1. Stitch yoke backs to yoke front at shoulder seams. Press seams flat *(see diagram 9a).*
2. Stitch yoke back linings to yoke front lining at shoulder seams. Press seams flat *(see diagram 9b).*
3. With right sides together, pin trimming along seam lines on yoke *(see diagram 9c).*

Step 2: Skirt

1. Gather top of each skirt back with two rows of gathering *(see diagram 10).*
2. Take smocked skirt front and join to skirt backs at sides, using a French seam *(see diagram 11).*

Step 3: Frill

1. Take smocked frill *(see diagram 12a)* and with right sides together, stitch trimming to bottom of frill *(see diagram 12b).*
2. Press trimming down *(see diagram 13a).*
3. On wrong side, turn skirt edge and stitch hem *(see diagram 13b).*

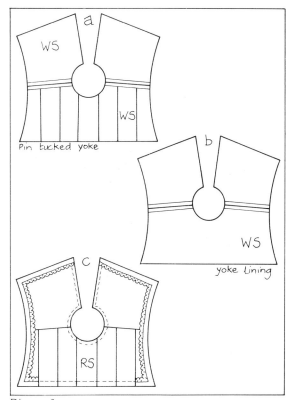

Diagram 9

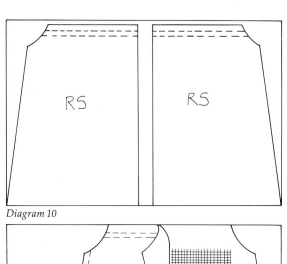

Diagram 10

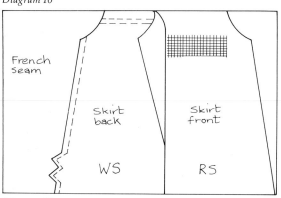

Diagram 11

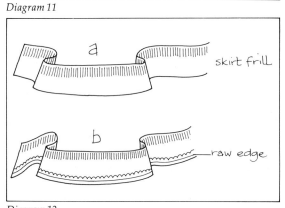

Diagram 12

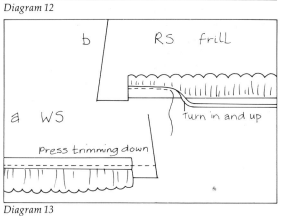

Diagram 13

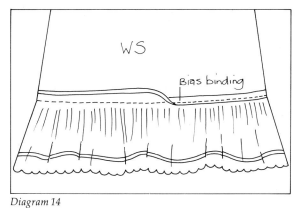

Diagram 14

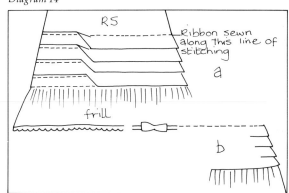

Diagram 15

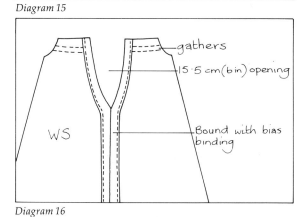

Diagram 16

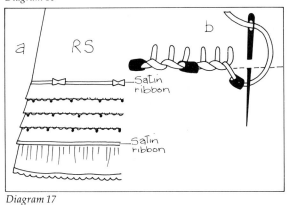

Diagram 17

4. On right side, finish frill edge by placing bottom edge of narrow ribbon on seam line. Stitch. Stitch again along top of ribbon.

5. Release gathers from smocked frill.

6. With right sides together, join smocked edge of frill to bottom of skirt. Trim *(see diagram 14)*.

7. Take bias binding and fold in half lengthways. Place over trimmed seam. Pin and tack (baste). Stitch *(see diagram 14)*.

Step 4: Tucks on skirt

1. Press lines for tucks around skirt back, skirt front and skirt back. Tack (baste) in place, making sure bottom tuck covers the seam line where the skirt joins the frill *(see diagram 15a)*.

2. Stitch tucks *(see diagram 15a)*.

3. Stitch ribbon along top row of stitching. Tie small bows at intervals, without cutting the ribbon *(see diagram 15b)*.

Step 5: Seaming skirt backs

1. With right sides together, pin skirt backs together down centre back seam, allowing 2.5cm (1in) seam allowance. Leave an opening 15.5cm (6in) at the top. Match tucks carefully. Tack (baste). Stitch and press seam flat *(see diagram 16)*.

2. Trim edges and finish with bias binding. To do this, press bias binding in half lengthways. Fold over seam. Tack (baste) and stitch.

Step 6: Trimming the tucks

1. Sew ribbon along the bottom edge of the last tuck by stitching on both sides of the ribbon *(see diagram 17a)*.

2. Work blanket stitch along the three tuck edges, adding a bead every third stitch *(see diagram 17b)*.

Step 7: Joining yoke to skirt

1. Take out gathering threads from smocking on skirt front.

2. With right sides together, pin yoke front only to skirt front aligning the edge of the smocking which is on the right side, with seam line. Ease gathers. Tack (baste). Stitch carefully as this is an important seam.

3. Pull up gathers on skirt back to fit yoke back. Pin in place. Tack (baste). Stitch *(see diagram 18)*.

Step 8: Yoke ribbons

1. Tack (baste) narrow ribbon across yoke front and down sides of smocking, making a neat corner by folding at right angles, and allowing the ribbon to fall from either side *(see diagram 18)*.

2. Stitch both sides of narrow ribbon in place *(see diagram 18)*.

3. Unravel ends of ribbon and tie knot.

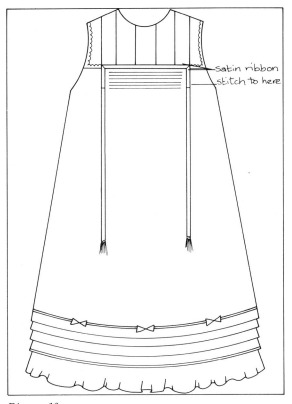

Diagram 18

Step 9: Slip

1. Gather front slip skirt at top edge and pull up to fit yoke lining.

2. Gather slip skirt, back, at top edge and pull up to fit back yokes.

3. Join side seams with a French seam *(see diagram 19a)*.

4. Pin centre seam, allowing 4cm (1½in) seam allowance. Tack (baste) and stitch. Turn under 2.5mm (⅛in) and stitch edges to neaten *(see diagram 19b)*.

5. Apply trimming to edge of skirt *(see diagram 20)*.

6. Working on the right side, with bottom edge of narrow ribbon on seam line, pin top edge of ribbon. Tack (baste) in place. Stitch on top line only.

7. Pin right side of yoke lining to wrong side of slip skirt, easing gathers. Tack (baste) and stitch.

8. With right sides together pin, tack and stitch around neck edge and back opening of yoke and yoke lining *(see diagram 21)*.

9. Snip around neck edge. Turn to right side and press *(see diagrams 22a and 22b)*.

Step 10: Sleeve

1. Gather upper edge of sleeve and lower edge of sleeve *(see diagram 23)*.

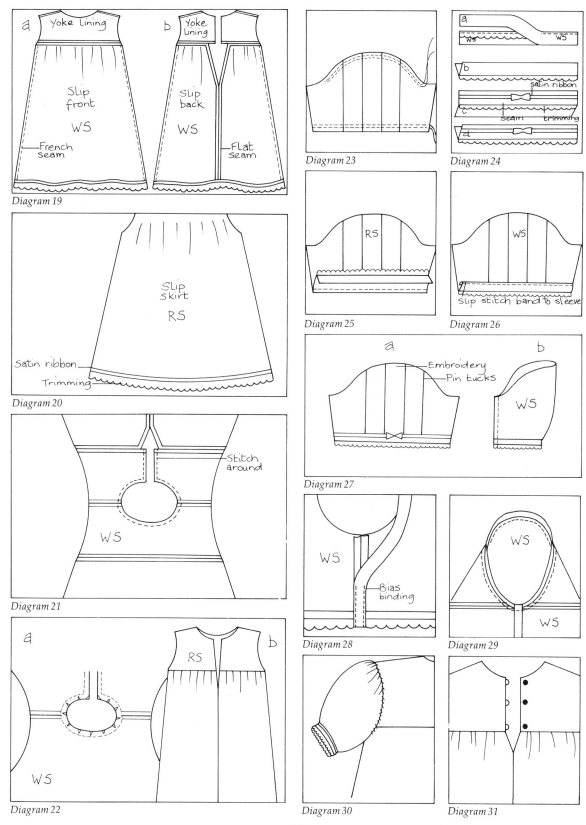

a

Yoke Lining

Slip
front

WS

French
seam

Diagram 19

b

Yoke
Lining

Slip
back

WS

Flat
seam

Slip
skirt

RS

Satin ribbon

Trimming

Diagram 20

Stitch
around

WS

Diagram 21

a

WS

RS

b

Diagram 22

Diagram 23

a

WS

b

WS

satin ribbon

seam   trimming

Diagram 24

RS

Diagram 25

WS

slip stitch band to sleeve

Diagram 26

a

Embroidery

Pin tucks

b

WS

Diagram 27

WS

Bias
binding

Diagram 28

WS

WS

Diagram 29

Diagram 30

Diagram 31

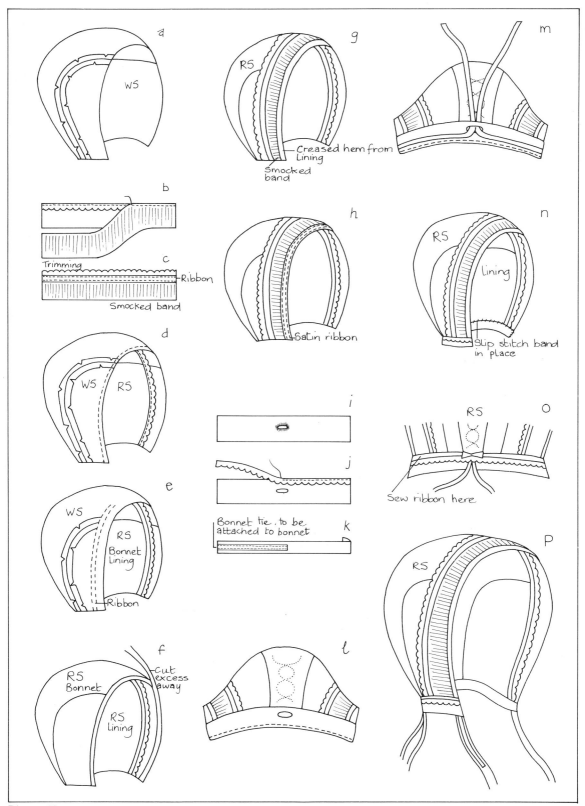

a

WS

b

c

Trimming

Ribbon

Smocked band

d

WS RS

e

WS

RS
Bonnet
Lining

Ribbon

f

RS
Bonnet

RS
Lining

Cut
excess
away

g

RS

Creased hem from
Lining

Smocked
band

h

Satin ribbon

i

j

Bonnet tie, to be
attached to bonnet

k

l

m

n

RS

Lining

Slip stitch band
in place

o

RS

Sew ribbon here

P

RS

Diagram 32

77

2. Stitch trimming between two sleeve bands. Press open *(see diagrams 24a and 24b)*.

3. Stitch satin ribbon, with bow tied in centre, along one sleeve band. Press *(see diagrams 24c and 24d)*.

4. With right sides together, pin sleeve band with ribbon on to bottom of sleeve, adjusting gathers on sleeve to fit band. Tack (baste) and stitch. Press *(see diagram 25)*.

5. Turn under hem on to wrong side and slip stitch band to sleeve *(see diagram 26)*.

6. Join sleeve with a flat seam. Pin seam together. Tack (baste). Stitch down sleeve and across bands. Press seam flat *(see diagram 27)*.

7. Trim excess fabric from seam. Place bias binding over seam and stitch on each side, thus covering all raw edges completely *(see diagram 28)*.

Step 11: Joining sleeve to robe

1. With right sides together, pin sleeve to robe. Do not catch in lining. Adjust gathers to fit armhole. Tack (baste) and stitch. Trim edges *(see diagram 29)*.

2. Turn in seam allowance on slip at armholes and slip stitch to robe *(see diagram 30)*.

Step 12: Attaching buttons and loops

1. Sew three small buttons to right side of bodice *(see diagram 31)*.

2. Work buttonhole loops to fasten.

MAKING-UP THE BONNET

Step 1: Joining bonnet pieces and adding trimming

1. Pin side sections of bonnet to centre section of bonnet which has already been embroidered. Tack (baste) and stitch. Press seams first, snipping around curves *(see diagram 32a)*.

2. Join lining in the same way.

3. Pin trimming to smocked band lining. Tack (baste) and stitch *(see diagram 32b)*.

4. Remove gathering threads from smocked band and with right sides together, pin smocked band to band lining *(see diagram 32b)*.

5. Open seam and press flat. Stitch narrow ribbon edge to edge with smocked band seam line *(see diagram 32c)*.

6. With right sides together, pin trimming to bonnet lining 2.5cm (1in) from face edge. Tack (baste) and stitch *(see diagram 32d)*.

7. Cover raw edges of trimming with narrow ribbon. Stitch both sides of ribbon *(see diagram 32e)*.

8. Press face edge of bonnet lining, making a 1.5cm (½in) hem.

Step 2: Placing outer bonnet over lining

1. Place bonnet over lining, wrong sides together. Trim face edge of outer bonnet away so that it just meets creased edge of lining *(see diagram 32f)*.

2. Pin lined smocked band around face edge of band and turn creased hem from lining over face edge *(see diagram 32g)*.

3. Stitch narrow ribbon along edge of creased hem to hold in place *(see diagram 32h)*.

4. Make a small eyelet hole in the centre of bonnet band by piercing a small hole with a stiletto or sharp pointed scissors or tool. Either whip over the edge very closely, or blanket stitch with small stitches. The finished hole must be large enough for the narrow ribbon to be threaded through *(see diagram 32i)*.

5. With wrong side of trimming to right side of band, stitch along edge *(see diagram 32j)*.

6. To make the bonnet ties, cut 2.5cm (1in) ribbon in half and sew narrow ribbon along half the length of each piece. Hem the end of the wider ribbon *(see diagram 32k)*.

7. Pin and stitch band to neck edge of bonnet *(see diagram 32l)*.

8. Cut two lengths of narrow ribbon each 30cm (12in) long. Pin end of ribbon to edges of band and thread other ends of ribbon through eyelet *(see diagram 32m)*.

9. Turn in band and slip stitch along its length, attaching it to the bonnet lining and making small hems at band edge *(see diagram 32n)*.

Step 3: Finishing the bonnet

1. By hand, stitch a narrow ribbon with a bow at centre back on to seam line where band and trimming is joined to outer bonnet *(see diagram 32o)*.

2. Stitch 2.5cm (1in) satin ribbon ties into place on neck band at face edge to complete the bonnet *(see diagram 32p)*.

Floral Dress

Size: This dress fits an eight-year-old child. The measurements are: chest 70cm (27½in) and finished length from neck edge at shoulder back 77cm (30½in). Instructions are also given for a smaller dress to fit a five-year-old. The depth of the smocking in the smaller size is not so great. Instructions for the smaller size are given only if there is a variation from the larger size.

General description: The dress is made in an attractive floral wool and cotton mixture in shades of blue, green and pink. These colours are used for the smocking. The yokes are lined and join the skirts, which are smocked to a depth of 13cm (5in), at both front and back. The sleeves are long and full and finish with a frill at the wrist edge. A frill also decorates the neckline where it is attached with a bias strip. A zip is used for the back opening. Two tie belts, which tie at the back, complete the garment.

Alternative suggestions: This classic style can be used to make a dress in most washable fabrics which are suitable for children. It is attractive in both floral and plain fabrics. It can be smocked in many colours, or just one or two colours. Consider: dark blue polycotton fabric smocked in white with flowers in red; green and white pin spot fabric smocked in white and green; lemon and white striped fabric smocked in a deeper lemon; or a cream polycotton smocked in coffee, ivory and white.

Smocking stitches: Stem, crossed diamond and wave are worked, using three strands of stranded cotton.

System for preparing smocking: A smock-gathering machine is used.

Experience required: Those who have some smocking and dressmaking experience would find this a very rewarding garment to make. The smocking is not complicated but it is a large piece to work. The making up of the garment is straightforward, except for the frill at the cuff, the directions for which need to be followed, step by step.

Notes
• If a smock-gathering machine is not available, smocking dot transfers can be used. As dots are sometimes difficult to see on a floral fabric, test before using them on the garment.

• Check all measurements and adjust before cutting out.
• Hand wash this garment in warm soapy water and rinse well. Press, avoiding the large smocked area. Do not stretch the smocking.

MATERIALS

Dressmaker's Pattern Guide Paper ruled in 1cm (½in) and 5cm (2in) squares or similar. If this is not available use large size plain paper, ruled into the appropriate squares.

Fabric: 3.20 metres × 90cm (3½ yds × 36in) wide floral wool and cotton mixture. For the small size: 2.40 metres × 90cm (2¾ yds × 36in).

Thread for sewing: 1 reel (spool) mercerised sewing thread No. 40 to match.

Thread for gathering: 1 reel (spool) mercerised sewing thread No. 40 in a contrasting colour.

Thread for smocking: 1 skein each of stranded embroidery cotton in white, pink, green or to match.

Buttons: 2 small buttons to fasten cuffs.

Smocking dots: 2 sheets size 6.5 × 9.5mm (¼ × ⅜in) – Deighton's size H.

Zip: Size 38cm (15in). For the small size: 35cm (14in).

Usual workbox equipment plus pencil, eraser and ruler.

GENERAL INSTRUCTIONS

1. Draft pattern. A 2cm (¾in) seam allowance has been included in pattern *(see diagram 1 or 8 according to size)*.
2. Cut out dress *(see diagram 1 or 8 according to size)*.
3. Smock dress *(see diagrams 2-3)*.
4. Make up dress *(see diagrams 4-7)*.

PREPARATION

Drafting the pattern
Follow diagram 1 or 8 according to size. As some of the pattern pieces are oblongs, these can be cut in newspaper. Pieces to be drafted are: Sleeve, yoke front and yoke back.

Cutting out the dress
1. Check all measurements and adjust before cutting out *(see diagram 1)*. If making the small size see diagram 8.
2. Place pattern pieces on fabric *(see diagram 1 or 8)*. Note that the cuff needs four pieces.
3. Mark all seam allowances, notches and centres of pattern pieces. Note the position of the sleeve opening on both sleeves.

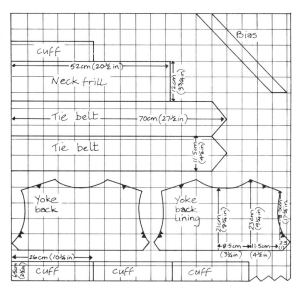

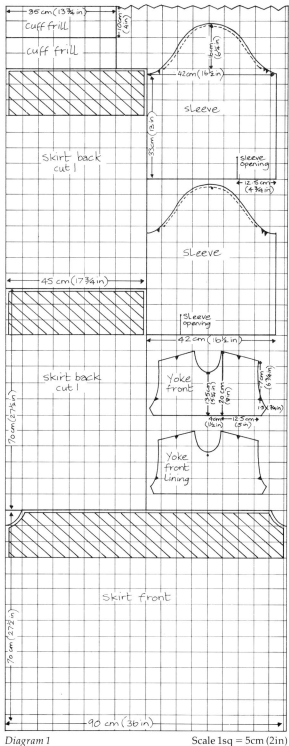

SMOCKING

Preparing the smocking

1. The smocking on the dress requires 16 rows of gathering which is the depth of the standard smock-gathering machine.

2. Prepare one skirt front piece by starting the gathering on the seam line.

3. Prepare two skirt back pieces by starting the gathering on the seam line.

● *For the small size:* Prepare 15 rows of gathering only. Row 1 is the seam line and row 15 a gathering row only.

Pulling up the gathering threads

1. Pull up skirt front to the width of the yoke less 2.5cm (1in).

2. Pull up each skirt back to the width of the yoke less 2cm (¾in).

3. Tie off securely on the wrong side.

Working the smocking

1. Use three strands of stranded embroidery cotton (*see diagram 2*).

2. Leave row 1 for seaming to yoke. Start and end each row just outside seam allowance on side seams and centre back seam.

3. Work stem stitch on rows 2, 3; 7, 8; and 12, 13. Note that these are not drawn in the diagram.

4. Work crossed diamond stitch inside each pair of lines worked in stem stitch.

5. Work remaining pattern following smocking graph. Note that there are two big diamonds, followed by one small diamond.

Diagram 1   Scale 1sq = 5cm (2in)
Pattern and layout for dress for eight-year-old child

Note: For the version for a five-year-old child follow diagram 8 on page 83.

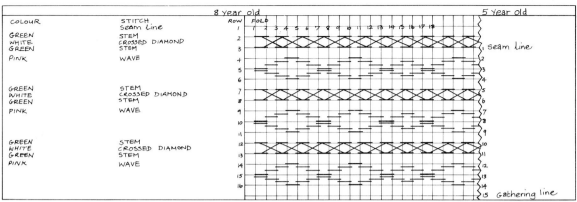

Diagram 2

6. Chain stitch flowers *(see diagram 3)* are worked in the centre of each big diamond, using white for the French knot in the centre. Using green, work 6 chain stitches around the knot to form a circle for the flower.
7. When the smocking is entirely finished, steam press each finished piece. Work on the right side by holding an iron set to 'steam' just above the folds. Do not press. Leave to dry.
8. Take out all gathering threads, except the top row of each piece. This row will be used for seaming to the yoke.

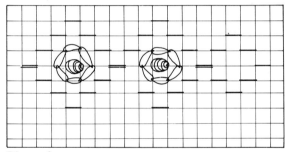

Diagram 3

MAKING-UP THE DRESS

Step 1: Joining yoke back to skirt back
1. With right sides together, pin yoke back to skirt back. Tack (baste) and stitch. Press seam upwards.
2. Join other yoke back to skirt back.

Step 2: Joining yoke front to skirt front
1. With right sides together, pin yoke front to skirt front. Tack (baste) and stitch. Press seam upwards.

Step 3: Making the ties
1. With right sides together, fold tie lengthways. Pin. Tack (baste) and stitch.
2. Turn inside out and tack (baste). Press well.

Step 4: Attaching ties to skirt back
1. Working on the right side, place tie to skirt back on seam line with top of tie in line with last row of stem stitch smocking *(see diagram 4)*.
2. Stitch down seam. Stitch again.

Step 5: Joining dress front to dress back
1. With right sides together, pin shoulder seams. Pin side seams, carefully matching smocking. Pin skirt, centre back seam, starting approximately 23cm (9in) down from yoke seam. Tack (baste) and stitch.
● *For the small size:* The seam on the centre back starts approximately 21cm (8¼in) below yoke seam.
2. Trim edges. Zig-zag side seam edges and centre back seam edges. Press flat. Press shoulder seams flat.

Step 6: Inserting the zip
1. Turn under seam allowance on opening edges of dress back. Place zip behind and on the right side pin in place, starting at seamline at neck edge.
2. Tack (Baste), making sure that the turned-in edges meet at the centre of zip.
3. Stitch 5mm (¼in) each side of centre and across end, using a zipper foot. Alternatively, the zip can be inserted by hand with a back stitch.

Step 7: Sleeve opening, seam and gathering
1. To strengthen sleeve opening, stitch either side of opening, starting 2.5mm (⅛in) away and tapering to 1 stitch across, at the top.
2. Slash opening *(see diagram 5a)*.
3. Cut strip 14 × 3cm (5½ × 1¼in).
4. Pin slashed opening edges to one side of strip with wrong side of sleeve to right side of strip. Tack (baste) and stitch on stitching line *(see diagram 4b)*.
5. Trim edges. Turn under 2.5mm (⅛in) of strip and pin on to stitching line on right side of sleeve. The finished strip should be 1cm (½in) wide. Stitch.
6. Turn finished strip to inside and press. Using a few

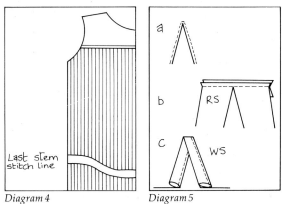

Last stem stitch line

Diagram 4   *Diagram 5*

a

b   RS

c   WS

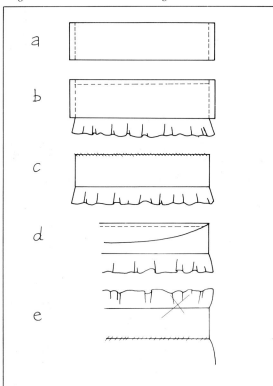

a

b

c

d

e

Diagram 6

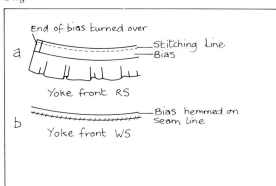

End of bias turned over

a   Stitching Line
           Bias

Yoke front RS

b   Bias hemmed on seam line

Yoke front WS

Diagram 7

stitches, stitch strip in place at sleeve *(see diagram 5c)*.
7. With right sides together, pin underarm seam together. Tack (baste) and stitch. Trim. Zig-zag edges. Press flat.
8. Gather at bottom edge of sleeve by stitching gathering line on seam line. Stitch another gathering line 5mm (¼in) away and within seam allowance.

Step 8: Sleeve frill
1. Take cuff frill and with right sides together fold lengthways. Seam ends. Turn and press.
2. Gather along seam line at raw edges. Stitch another gathering line 5mm (¼in) away and within seam allowance *(see diagram 6a)*.

Step 9: Joining cuff to frill and sleeve
1. Take two cuffs and with right sides together, seam ends together on seam line. Trim back to 5mm (¼in) *(see diagram 6b)*.
2. Take sleeve frill and gather up to fit cuff.
3. Insert frill between the two cuffs, with raw edges at the top. Pin. Tack (baste). Stitch on seam line along top through all four thicknesses *(see diagram 6b)*.
4. Turn on to right side *(see diagram 6c)*.
5. Take sleeve and join one cuff only by placing right side of sleeve to right side of one cuff. Ease gathers to fit, turning cuff seams towards centre. Pin starting at one edge of sleeve opening and finishing at other edge of opening. Tack (baste) and stitch *(see diagram 6d)*.
6. On wrong side, hem loose cuff to seam line *(see diagram 6e)*.

Step 10: Yoke lining
With right sides together, and matching notches, pin, tack (baste) and stitch shoulder seams. Trim seams back. Press flat.

Step 11: Attaching yoke lining to dress
1. Working on the inside of the garment and with wrong sides together, pin yoke lining along shoulder seams.
2. Pin and tack (baste) around neck edge.
3. Pin and tack (baste) around armholes.
4. Turn under seam allowance at zip-opening edge and bottom edge of yoke back and yoke front.
5. Slip stitch lining to stitching line of zip.
6. Slip stitch yoke edge to stitching line where yoke joins skirt on both the backs and the front.
7. Press lining to make sure it fits exactly.

Step 12: Joining sleeves to dress
1. Gather top of sleeve between small ● on seam line. Stitch another gathering line 5mm (¼in) away and within seam allowance.

2. Join sleeve to dress with a French seam. With wrong sides together, pin sleeve into armhole of dress, matching large ● to shoulder seam, matching notches and matching underarm sleeve seam to side seam of dress. Adjust gathers so that they are evenly distributed. Tack (baste). Stitch through all thicknesses. Trim seam to 5mm (¼in).

3. Turn work so that right sides are together. Pin. Tack (baste), making sure that the seams are carefully trimmed. Stitch through all layers.

Step 13: Attaching neck frill

1. Take neck frill and with right sides together, seam ends. Turn on to right side. Tack (baste) and press.

2. Stitch gathering line on seam line of frill. Stitch another gathering line 5mm (¼in) away and within seam allowance.

3. Pull up frill to fit neck line.

4. With right sides together, pin frill to neckline, matching centre of frill with centre front of yoke. Tack (baste) in place on seamline. Trim edge to 5mm (¼in).

5. Cut bias strip 3cm (1¼in) wide, the length of the neckline plus 2cm (¾in).

6. Pin bias, right side down, on top of the frill. Tack (baste). Stitch on seam line of neck, turning over 1cm (½in) at each end *(see diagram 7a).*

7. Turn bias on to wrong side and hem to seam line making a finished binding approximately 5mm (¼in) wide *(see diagram 7b).*

Step 14: Finishing the dress

1. Sew button in position on the cuff.

2. Work buttonhole to fit button.

3. Adjust hem length. Turn under 5mm (¼in) on hem edge. Stitch and press. Slip stitch hem in place.

4. If required, a hook and eye may be sewn to neck edge back to fasten.

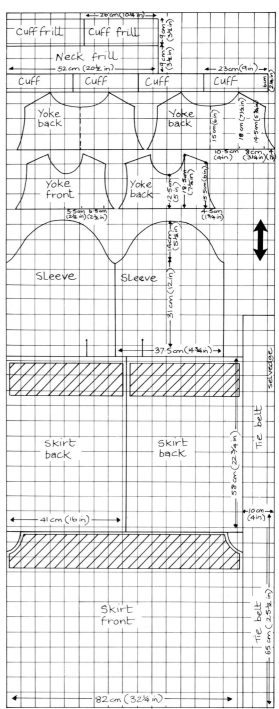

Diagram 8   Scale 1sq = 5cm (2in)
Pattern and layout for dress for five-year-old child

PROJECT 7 *(See illustration facing page 89)*

Formal Dress

Size: The pattern fits size 92cm (36in) bust. As the dress is full it will also be suitable for a 89cm (35in) bust or a 94cm (37in) bust.

General description: The dress is made in very fine polyester crêpe de Chine in bright pink and is richly smocked in teal green. The bodice front and yoke back are lined. It is a very full garment. Smocking decorates the full sleeves at the wrist as well as the full bodice back which is densely smocked beneath a yoke. The plain bodice opens down the front and joins a full gathered skirt at the waistline which has a side opening. A frill edges the neckline and a long sash, which can be used as a cummerbund, completes the outfit.

Alternative suggestions: As this dress is very full, a fine fabric is essential. Any fine silk or synthetic in a plain colour is attractive. While the smocking can be worked in several colours, it is more striking when worked in one colour only. Consider: a white silk dress smocked in black; ivory silk dress smocked in light tan; mid-blue silk smocked in white; navy silk dress smocked in navy; yellow silk smocked in ivory; or pale green silk smocked in darker green.

Smocking stitches: Only one stitch, diamond stitch is used for decoration. Stem stitch is used for preparation on the wrong side.

System for preparing smocking: Smocking dots.

Experience required: This dress is very full and as the fabric is very fine, it requires careful handling by an experienced person. The smocked areas are large and careful attention to the smocking graph is essential. There is a lot of preparation as well as smocking work. An experienced person would enjoy working the unusual smocking design of triangles.

Notes
● Fine crêpe de Chine, whether natural or synthetic, can be difficult to handle and might be awkward to sew by machine. Trial tests should be worked on scraps of fabric, using the machine to make sure the tension and stitch length, as well as the thread, are correct. White tissue paper placed under the fabric when stitching sometimes helps. It is easy to tear the tissue paper away afterwards.
● Use fine pins which do not mark the fabric, and if they are not available use fine needles.

● Before cutting out the fabric, it is essential to check your measurements against pattern pieces. It is strongly advised to cut a separate bodice front in tissue paper or old sheeting or fabric to test for fit.
● Note that pattern pieces to be smocked, back bodice and sleeves, are cut in oblong form to begin with. These pieces are not cut to the shape of the pattern until the smocking is finished and the piece ready for making up.
● Fine fabrics need careful hand washing and they should be washed separately. Wash a small scrap of the fabric to test before washing the whole garment.
● Always test the iron temperature on a scrap of the fabric. Synthetic fabrics require very low settings.
● When smocking pieces are finished, if the dots show through the fabric, they may be removed by washing before making-up.

MATERIALS

Dressmaker's Pattern Guide Paper ruled in 1cm (½in) and 5cm (2in) squares or similar. If this is not available use large size plain paper, ruled into the appropriate squares. White tissue paper for extra pattern if needed.

Fabric: 5.20 metres × 115cm (5¾ yds × 45in) wide silk or polyester crêpe de Chine.

Lining: 60 × 115cm (¾ yd × 45in) fine polycotton lawn to match.

Needles: Crewel embroidery needles, No. 8, 9 or 10.

Thread for sewing: 2 reels (spools) No. 50 to match fabric.

Thread for gathering: 2 reels (spools) mercerised sewing thread No. 50 in a contrasting colour.

Thread for smocking: 5 skeins stranded cotton.

Buttons: 2 small buttons to fasten cuffs.

Smocking dots: 4 sheets size 5 × 5mm (³⁄₁₆ × ³⁄₁₆in) – Deighton's size K.

Snap fasteners: 4 small snaps (clear plastic if available).

Zip: 35cm (14in) to match fabric.

Tape: 1 metre × 1cm (1 yd × ½in) wide cotton tape.

Usual workbox equipment plus fine pins, 2 hooks and eyes, tailor's chalk, pencil, eraser and ruler.

GENERAL INSTRUCTIONS

1. Draft pattern. A 2cm (¾in) seam allowance has been included in pattern *(see diagram 1)*.
2. Cut out dress *(see diagram 1)*.
3. Cut out lining for dress *(see diagram 2)*.
4. Smock bodice back *(see diagrams 3-6)*.
5. Smock sleeves *(see diagrams 7-9)*.
6. Make up dress.

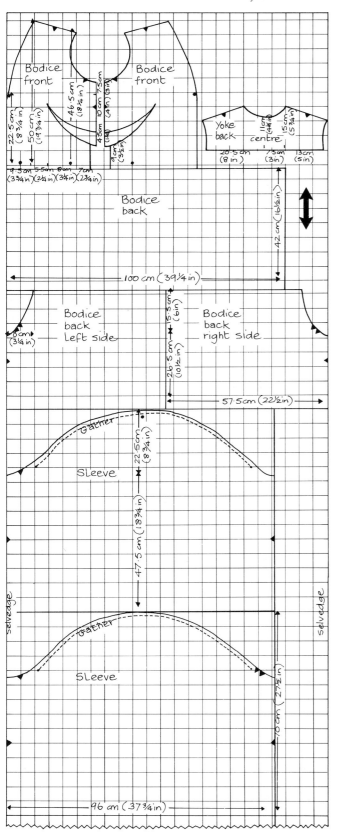

Diagram 1
Scale 1sq = 5cm (2in)

Bodice front

Bodice front

22.5cm (8¾ in)

50cm (19¾ in)

46.5cm (18¼ in)

10cm (4 in)

7.5cm (3 in)

4.5cm (1¾ in)

9cm (3½ in)

9.5cm (3¾ in)

5.5cm (2¼ in)

8cm (3¼ in)

7cm (2¾ in)

Yoke back

centre

11cm (4¼ in)

15cm (5¾ in)

20.5cm (8 in)

7.5cm (3 in)

13cm (5 in)

Bodice back

42 cm (16½ in)

100 cm (39¼ in)

Bodice back Left side

Bodice back right side

15.5cm (6in)

8cm (3¼ in)

26.5cm (10½ in)

57.5cm (22½ in)

Gather

Sleeve

22.5cm (8¾ in)

47.5 cm (18¾ in)

selvedge

selvedge

Gather

Sleeve

70cm (27½ in)

96 cm (37¾in)

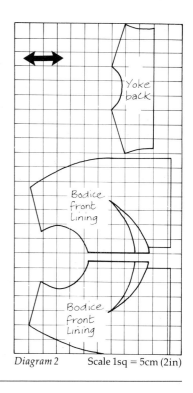

Yoke back

Bodice front Lining

Bodice front Lining

Diagram 2   Scale 1sq = 5cm (2in)

PREPARATION

Drafting the pattern
1. Draft the pattern *(see diagram 1)*.
2. Make adjustments if necessary.

Cutting out the dress
1. Cut the following off the fabric before placing pattern pieces: Frill: cut two widths each 8cm (3¼in); Skirt: cut two widths each 81cm (32in); Sash: cut two widths each 24cm (9½in).
2. Note that sleeves (2); bodice back right (1); bodice back left (1); bodice back centre (1) are cut in oblong shapes. Do not cut around these pattern pieces, but leave in oblong shape until they have been smocked and are ready for making-up.
3. Cut out dress as in layout *(see diagram 1)*.
4. Mark seam allowances with tailor's chalk; mark centre of sleeves, bodice front, yoke back, and skirts.

Cutting out the lining
1. Cut out the lining *(see diagram 2)*.
2. Mark seam allowances. Allow 2cm (¾in) on yoke and bodice front except for the neckline which is 1cm (½in). Mark centre yoke back. Mark dart.

SMOCKING

BODICE BACK

Smocking
1. With right sides together, and allowing 1cm (½in) seam allowance, pin bodice back left side to bodice back centre; and bodice back right side to bodice back centre. Tack (baste) and stitch. Zig-zag or whip edges. Press flat *(see diagram 3)*.
2. This oblong will measure approximately 211 × 42cm (82¾ × 16¾in) and is kept in this shape throughout all stages of smocking *(see diagram 3)*.
3. Place pattern on oblong and mark pattern outline. Tack (baste). Mark seam allowance across back and around armholes. Tack (baste) only. Do not cut out. Tack (baste) centre line.
4. Whip edge of oblong to stop fraying.

Preparing the dots
1. Two complete sheets of dots of 37 rows are required to cover the smocked area for the whole of the back. Be very careful to align dots at the join. Cut off all markings from the transfers. These can be used for testing.
2. Working on the wrong side, and with wax side down, place second row of dots on seam line. Pin at intervals across the entire width of the back, from armhole seam to armhole seam.
3. Test iron temperature on a scrap of the fabric, using the cut-off markings.
4. Iron dots on to bodice back, taking extra care at the join. Alternatively, one sheet of dots can be ironed on at a time, repeating for the second sheet.

Picking up the dots
1. This is a very long piece to prepare and takes time. Cut 37 threads the width of the back plus 10cm (4in).
2. Start with a very firm knot on the righthand side and pick up each dot right across the back from armhole seam line to armhole seam line.

Pulling up the gathering threads
1. Pull up to approximately 36cm (14½in).
2. There should be 392 folds on the right side. Adjust and tack (baste) centre line in contrasting colour between folds 196 and 197 *(see diagram 4)*.
3. When correct, tie very securely in pairs. Trim ends to approximately 2.5cm (1in).

Preparing for the smocking
1. As this is a large expanse of smocking with some of the gathers left blank to form the design, the wrong side needs to be prepared with stem stitch.
2. Working on the wrong side and using one thread of stranded cotton or fine sewing thread which exactly matches the fabric, work stem stitch using very tiny stitches, across the first 20 rows. To work the V, start to work stem stitch on row 21 at fold 164 and work across to the same position on the right of the centre. Work row 22 starting at fold 166 and repeat as row 21. Following the chart in diagram 4, decrease at each row down to row 37, which is the base and is worked over folds 196/197.

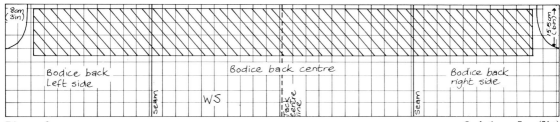

Diagram 3   Scale 1sq = 5cm (2in)

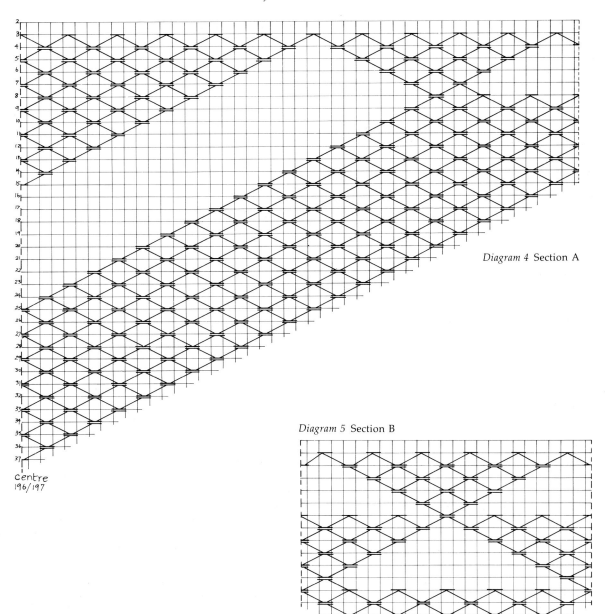

Diagram 4 Section A

Diagram 5 Section B

centre
196/197

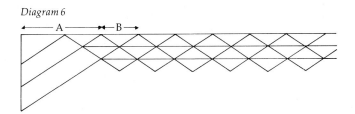

Diagram 6

A ←——→ ←►◄ B ——→

3. Turn the work on to the right side as it is now ready for smocking.

Working the smocking

1. The entire design is worked in diamond stitch (see page 45), using three strands of stranded cotton *(see diagram 6)*.

2. The smocking is worked from the centre to the right side of bodice back and then reversed for the left side as follows:

3. Start with diagram 4 (Section A); then work diagram 5 (Section B); then repeat diagram 5 five times. Check from the centre line, that the design consists of half the large diamond plus seven small diamonds along the top *(see diagram 6)*, then work two diamond stitches to the armhole seam line. Repeat for the left side, working in reverse and working right across to the centre. Alternatively, the graph may be copied on to graph paper and used to work across the whole back.

Releasing the gathering threads

1. When the entire design has been worked, the gathering threads are released.

2. Depending upon the tension, the gathers should release to approximately 37.5cm (14¾in) from armhole seam line on the left to armhole seamline on the right, to fit the yoke of the same measurement at seam line.

3. If the dots show, follow directions for removal *(see page 36)*.

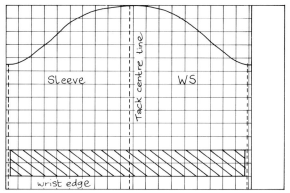

Diagram 7   Scale 1sq = 5cm (2in)

SLEEVE

Preparing the dots

1. Keep the sleeve in an oblong shape 96 × 70cm (37¾ × 27½in) until the dress is ready for making-up. Tack (baste) the shape of the sleeve top; tack (baste) seam allowances on sides of sleeve; tack (baste) centre line down sleeve; on the wrong side mark with tailor's chalk a line 5cm (2in) in from wrist edge *(see diagram 7)*.

2. Turn the sleeve so that the wrist edge becomes the top of the work.

3. Cut smocking dots the width from side seam to side seam by 23 rows deep. Cut off all markings from the transfers.

Note: Diagrams 8 and 9 are shown with the wrist edge at the top

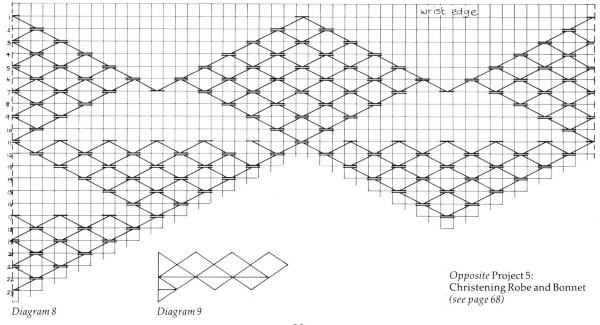

Diagram 8   *Diagram 9*

Opposite Project 5:
Christening Robe and Bonnet
(see page 68)

4. Working on the wrong side place first row of dots on the line which has been marked 5cm (2in) in from top and pin in place *(see diagram 8)*.
5. Test temperature of iron. Iron on dots and quickly remove paper.

Picking up the dots
Start with a very firm knot on the right and pick up each dot across each row, starting and stopping at the seam line, and working on the wrong side.

Pulling up the gathering threads
1. Pull up to wrist measurement, approximately 16cm (6½in) on this garment. Check that centre line is between folds 87 and 88 and adjust accordingly.
2. When correct, tie securely in pairs. Trim ends to approximately 2.5cm (1in).

Preparing for the smocking
1. Working on the wrong side, the sleeve is prepared in the same way as the bodice back, by working stem stitch. Start on row 7 and work a total of 11 rows. By starting on row 7, the wrist frill falls freely without restriction.
2. Turn the work on to the right side in readiness for smocking.

Working the smocking
1. The sleeve is worked in the same way as the bodice back, in diamond stitch using three strands of stranded cotton *(see diagram 8)*.
2. The smocking is worked from the centre to the right side of the sleeve and then reversed for the left side as follows:
3. Following diagram 8, start the design at centre on row 6 and work diamond stitch to row 7 continuing down to row 23; turn work upside down and work from row 5 to row 1; on rows 6 to 7 work half a diamond stitch to finish the pattern. Check from the centre line that the design consists of 3½ diamonds at wrist edge *(see diagram 9)*. Repeat for the left side, reversing the pattern.
4. Work the other sleeve in the same way.

Releasing the threads
1. When the smocked piece is finished, take out the gathering threads. This should release to approximately the same measurement, and should be elastic enough to fit over the hand and yet firm enough to stay in position.
2. If dots show follow directions for removing them.

Previous page Project 6: Floral Dress *(see page 79)* and Project 13: Gingham Dress *(see page 119)*
Opposite Project 7: Formal Dress *(see page 79)*

MAKING-UP THE DRESS

Step 1: Joining yoke lining to yoke
Pin lining to yoke, with right side of lining to wrong side of yoke. Tack (baste) together just inside seam line.

Step 2: Joining yoke with lining to bodice back
1. Take bodice back and cut out armholes adjusting so that the armhole seam line is close to the smocking *(see diagram 3)*.
2. With right sides together, pin yoke with lining to bodice back, matching centres and easing smocking to fit. The seam line will be on the second row of dots. Tack (baste), making sure that the gathers are even. Carefully stitch. This is an important join and care is needed as it must be absolutely straight. Trim. Zigzag or whip.

Step 3: Bodice front and bodice front lining
1. Working on wrong side of bodice front, pin dart. Tack (baste) and stitch from side seam to point. Carefully cut to within 1cm (½in) of this point. Press seam flat, snipping carefully where necessary.
2. Prepare bodice front lining in the same way. Whip edges of dart seam.
3. Pin lining to bodice front with right side of lining to wrong side of bodice front. Tack (baste) around bodice front just inside the seam line.
4. Prepare other bodice front in the same way.

Step 4: Joining bodice front to bodice back
1. With right sides together, pin bodice fronts to bodice back at shoulders and side seams, leaving left side seam open approximately 14cm (5½in) above waistline seam for zip. Tack (baste) and stitch. Trim seam edges. Zig-zag or whip edges. Press seams flat.
2. Gather bodice fronts between ●; gather bodice back between ●.
3. Try on bodice and adjust if necessary.
4. Pull up and tie off gathering to waist measurement.

Step 5: Frill
1. Note that seam allowance on frill and neckline is 1cm (½in).
2. Take both frill pieces and seam together at short end. Press flat.
3. With wrong sides together fold frill lengthways. Pin and tack (baste). Press.
4. Make a gathering line, 1cm (½in) in from raw edges. Make another gathering line 5mm (¼in) in from raw edges.
5. Gather the frill to fit all around the neckline, keeping the frill flat on bodice front, left side, from waistline to ● centre front.

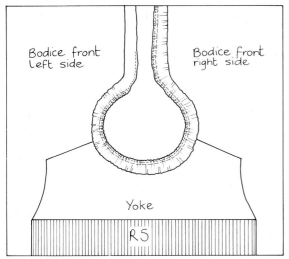

Diagram 10

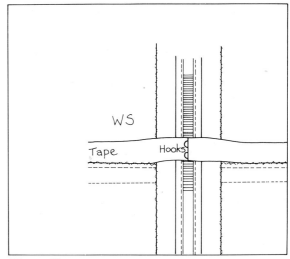

Diagram 12

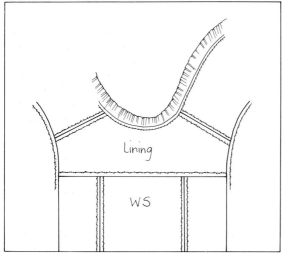

Diagram 11

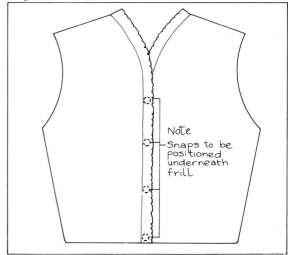

Diagram 13

6. With right sides together, pin frill all around neckline. Tack (baste) *(see diagram 10).*

Step 6: Joining frill to bodice neckline
1. From scraps of dress fabric cut bias strip approximately 120 × 4cm (47 × 1½in) wide. Join. Trim seams. Press all seams flat.
2. Place on top of frill, right sides together and ease on to seam line. Pin, tack (baste) and stitch 1cm (½in) from edge, on seam line.
3. Trim seam. Remove gathering threads which show.
4. Turn back bias on to lining. Turn under 5mm (¼in) and hem on to lining, making sure that the stitches do not show on the right side *(see diagram 11).*
5. Press carefully.
6. Overlap bodice fronts on centre seam line, right side over left side. Pin in place.

Step 7: Sleeve
1. Cut out the top of the sleeve *(see diagram 7).*
2. Pin side seams, aligning the smocking at wrist edge so that the smocking is continuous. Tack (baste) and stitch. Trim. Zig-zag or whip edges. Press seams flat.
3. Gather top of sleeve on seam line between small ●. Make another gathering line 5mm (¼in) inside this line. Pull up gathers to fit sleeve.
4. With right sides together match large ● to shoulder seam, and sleeve seam to bodice side seam. Pin. Tie off gathers. Tack (baste) and stitch. Trim seam. Zig-zag edges together or whip by hand. Press seam towards sleeve.

Step 8: Skirt
1. With right sides together, pin and tack (baste) side seams, leaving an opening on left side approximately

24cm (9½in) below waistline seam for zip. Stitch. Trim. Zig-zag edges or whip. Press flat.

2. Gather skirt front at top, starting and ending 6cm (2¼in) either side of seam line. Gather skirt back in the same way. Gather on seam line and place second line of gathering 5mm (¼in) inside this line.

3. Adjust measurements to waistline. Tie off gathering threads.

Step 9: Joining bodice to skirt

With right sides together, pin skirt and bodice together, matching centre of skirt front to bodice front centre, centre skirt back to centre bodice back and side seams of skirt to side seams of bodice. Adjust gathers. Tack (baste). Try on dress. Adjust if necessary. Stitch. Trim seam edges. Zig-zag or whip edges together. Press seam upwards towards bodice.

Step 10: Inserting zip

1. Turn under seam allowance on opening edges for zip and placing zip on the inside of the garment, pin in place. Tack (baste) carefully, making sure that the turned-in edges meet at the centre of zip.

2. Stitch 5mm (¼in) each side of centre and across end, using zipper foot. Alternatively, the zip can be inserted by hand with a back stitch.

Step 11: Attaching tape to waistline

1. Take waist measurement and add 5cm (2in). Cut tape to this measurement.

2. Turn back 2.5cm (1in) at each end and hem.

3. Stitch tape to waistline seam edges, stopping approximately 6cm (2¼in) either side of zip (*see diagram 12*).

4. Sew two hooks to one end and two eyes to the other end for fastening.

Step 12: Finishing the dress

1. Sew four snaps under the frill (*see diagram 13*).

2. Try on dress. Fasten snaps; fasten tape at waistline; zip the side opening. Adjust length.

3. As the fabric is fine, zig-zag edges of hem and slip stitch the hem in place with tiny stitches.

4. Finish sleeve edge by hemming back on to the smocking.

Step 13: Sash

1. The sash is cut with straight or pointed ends.

2. Take the two pieces for the sash and seam at short ends. Press.

3. With right sides together, pin and tack (baste). Stitch along whole length and across one end.

4. Remove tackings (bastings). Turn inside out. Tack (baste) along seam line. Press well. Slip stitch ends. Remove tackings (bastings).

PROJECT 8 (*See illustration facing page 49*)

Round Cushion

Size: Approximately 37cm (14½in) in diameter.

General description: This circular cushion is made in fine pale green polycotton lawn. The central area is a plain circle which is piped with cord. A band of smocking approximately 12cm (4¾in) in depth surrounds the circle. The cushion has a plain back and is finished with a piped cord edge.

Alternative suggestions: This cushion can be made in any fine fabric such as Jap (China) silk, silk crêpe de Chine, polyester crêpe de Chine or cotton lawn. It needs a very fine fabric to gather into the circle.

Any colour to suit individual requirements could be used. A plain colour for the cushion, trimmed with a tiny floral cord piping is attractive with the smocking picking up the colours in the trimming. A cream lawn cushion piped in a tiny stripe in red and blue looks effective when smocked in red and blue. A pale turquoise green fine silk can be used with the circle in ivory lace, using plain ivory silk for the piping and ivory threads for the smocking. Alternatively, a bright cushion can be made in red and smocked in white.

Smocking stitches: The smocking is worked in pale yellow in two stitches only – vandyke and tiny cable stitch flowerettes. On the wrong side cable stitch is used to hold the folds in place.

System for preparing smocking: A smock-gathering machine was used. Alternatively, smocking dot transfers can be used but it is a very long piece to gather up (4.60 metres × 16cm/5 yds × 5¾in).

Experience required: This is not suitable for beginners but anyone with some experience would find it a delight to work. It is not difficult but circles require extra care when making-up.

Notes

● Practise the smocking stitches on a spare piece of the fabric before commencing the project.

● Press fabric before commencing.

● Wash and dry the piping cord before using to preshrink it.

● A bought cushion pad is used, but one can be made by using a synthetic stuffing for the filling. Follow the measurements for the cushion back.

● If the cushion cover has to be washed, undo the slip stitching and wash by hand in warm soapy water.

Rinse well. When half dry, set iron to correct fabric temperature and iron the back of the cushion and the circle of the front of the cushion only. Slip the cover back on to the cushion pad and slip stitch in place. If required, steam press the smocking, being careful not to rest the iron on the smocking.

MATERIALS

Fabric: 1.10 metres × 115cm (1¼ yds × 45in) wide.

Needles: Crewel embroidery needles No. 8, 9 or 10.

Thread for sewing: 1 reel (spool) mercerised cotton sewing thread No. 50.

Thread for gathering: 2 reels (spools) strong fine sewing thread No. 40.

Thread for smocking: 3 skeins stranded cotton.

Cotton cord for piping: 2 metres (2 yards) No. 1, No. 2 or a fine cord.

Smocking dots: 5 sheets size 6.5 × 9.5mm (¼ × ⅜in) – Deighton's size H.

Cushion pad: 37cm (14½in) diameter.

Usual workbox equipment plus fine pins; scissors; soft pencil or water-erasable pen.

GENERAL INSTRUCTIONS

1. Cut out the cushion. A 2cm (¾in) seam allowance has been included in pattern *(see diagram 1)*.
2. Smock the band *(see diagrams 2-3)*.
3. Make up the cushion.

SMOCKING

Preparation by machine
Note: A smock-gathering machine will not go through seams, so each band has to be put through the machine separately.
1. Mark seam allowance on the top of each band by making a crease with an iron, or a soft pencil can be used lightly.
2. Thread 14 rows of the gathering machine with strong thread approximately 50cm (20in) long for each band, in a contrasting colour.
3. Feed each band through separately, aligning the first row with the creased line, or seam line.
4. Seam all four pieces together making sure that each line of gathering thread is in line. Make a flat seam. Trim to 5mm (¼in) and whip edges. Press well.
5. Cut a paper circle 12cm (4¾in) in diameter. Fold the circle in quarters. This will help as a guide when pulling up the threads.
6. Pull up the gathers very tightly on the top edge, splaying out the gathers for the edge of the cushion.

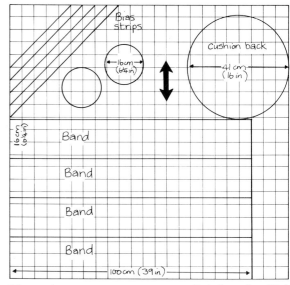

Diagram 1   Scale 1sq = 5cm (2in)

7. Working on the wrong side, place paper circle on the top of the gathering to act as a guide, by placing the edge of the circle on the first line of gathering threads. Pin each seam to the quarter mark on the paper. Pull up each section and when all gathering lies flat, making a large circle, and tie off each section very securely. Check that the seams are smooth and disguised *(see diagram 2)*. The whole process needs careful attention and cannot be rushed.
8. Unpin the paper circle ready for smocking.

Preparation by dots
1. This is a very time-consuming process but the end product will be worth the time taken. The length of a sheet of dots is 91cm (36in). The length of each band is 100cm (39in) and the depth 16cm (6¼in), therefore each band will need one length of smocking dots plus an additional piece. Keep one sheet of smocking dots for adding this additional piece.

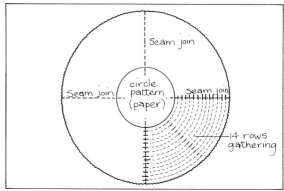

Diagram 2

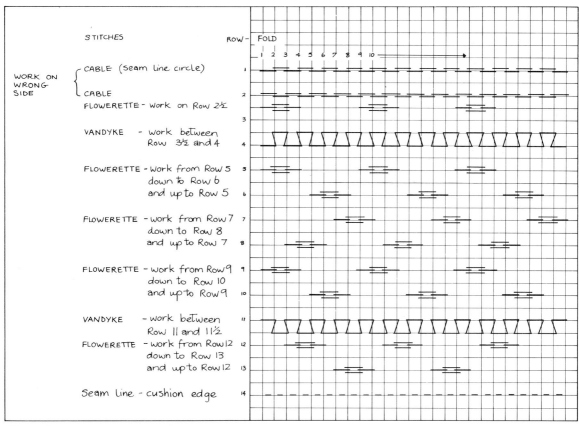

Diagram 3

2. Take a band and mark seam lines lightly on the wrong side with a soft pencil.

3. Prepare one sheet of smocking dots by cutting the strip 14 rows deep. Cut off all other information. This can be used for testing the iron temperature on a scrap of the fabric.

4. Place band, wrong side upwards, on ironing table. Place one sheet of prepared smocking dots, wax side downwards, on top by placing first row of dots over the top seam line. Pin in place. Test iron on spare piece of fabric. Iron dots and quickly remove pins and paper. Repeat for the additional piece approximately 24cm (9in), being very careful to align the rows.

5. Prepare each band in the same way.

Gathering the dots

1. Using strong thread and beginning with a strong knot, pick up each dot across the width of each band leaving the ends of the thread free.

2. Pin the bands together making four seams. Tack (baste) in place, being careful not to catch end threads in and making sure that the rows are aligned. Machine. Trim seams to 5mm (¼in). Whip raw edges. Press seams flat.

Pulling up the gathering threads

Follow the instructions for 'Preparation by machine' Nos. 5, 6, 7 and 8 on page 92.

Note: All the gathering threads are left in until the cushion is made up.

Working the smocking

The cushion is now ready for smocking. Note that the first two rows are worked on the wrong side in cable stitch. Work these two rows very tightly to set the gathers to fit the circle, then turn the cushion on to the right side and work down to and including row 13. Row 14 is the seam line for making-up. Two strands of thread are used to work cable (on the wrong side) *(see page 43)* and vandyke *(see page 45)*. The flowerettes are worked in four strands.

Note: One row only is worked around the cushion on row 2½. For the rest of the cushion, flowerettes are worked from row to row in a zig-zag. i.e. work one flowerette on row 5; take needle behind and come out on row 6; work one flowerette and take needle behind coming out on row 5. Repeat around the cushion and in rows 7 and 8 as well as rows 9 and 10.

MAKING-UP THE CUSHION

Step 1: Preparing the piping
1. Cut the bias strips. Note that these strips are cut on the true diagonal 4cm (1½in) wide *(see diagram 1)*.
2. Make one piece of piping approximately 46cm (18in) long for piping the circle. Make another piece of piping approximately 120cm (48in) long for piping the edge of the cushion. Follow directions for making the bias and the piping on page 49. Take out the tackings (bastings).

Step 2: Attaching the piping to the circle
1. With wrong sides together, tack (baste) both pieces of the circle together on the seam line. Make sure that this is a true circle.
2. Lightly fold the circle into quarters and tack (baste) across and down on the creases.
3. Place the smaller length of prepared piping on top of this circle, edges together. Pin, aligning seam line with machine line of piping. Carefully join ends of bias and ends of cord by hand. Tack (baste) in place. Using a zipper foot carefully machine around the circle. Tie off ends. Take out tackings (bastings) around the circle.

Step 3: Joining the circle to the smocked band
1. Place the circle with attached piping and smocked band, right sides together *(see diagram 0)*.
2. Match quarter tackings (bastings) on circle to seams on smocked band. Carefully pin and tack (baste) into place, making sure that the machine line of the piping aligns with the seam line of the smocked band which is the first gathering line. Using a zipper foot on the machine gently machine around the circle. This stage is most important. If the circle is not perfect, the whole effect will be spoilt.

Step 4: Attaching piping to the edge of the cushion
Place cushion right side up on table. Take long piece of prepared piping and with raw edges together, pin around the cushion, matching the machine line of the piping to the 14th row of gathering. Make sure that the gathers are evenly distributed around the cushion. Join piping as for the circle. Tack (Baste) in place. Using a zipper foot machine the piping to the cushion. Tie ends securely. Remove tackings (bastings).

Step 5: Joining cushion back to cushion front
1. Place cushion back and cushion front right sides together. Pin, leaving an opening of approximately 25cm (10in). Tack (baste) in place. With zipper foot, machine in place, leaving the opening free. Tie off securely. Take out all tackings (bastings). Trim edges.

Zig-zag the opening on each side separately. Zig-zag the remainder of the cushion with all edges together.
2. Take out all the gathering threads from the smocking.
3. Turn the cushion inside out.
4. Place the cushion pad inside the cushion cover. Working from the cushion cover back, turn under seam allowance and slip stitch on to the cushion cover front seam line.

4

Contemporary Smocking

At the present time the scope of smocking is being continually extended, for example to give textural effects to wall decorations and to clothing.

Several of Britain's leading designers are exploring the possibilities of smocking creatively. Polly Binns, who was selected for inclusion in the Craft Council Index in 1982, has exhibited wall hangings showing smocking in an exhibition in Boston, USA in 1984. As mentioned earlier in the book she says of her work that 'Each piece of work is an intuitive exploration into the depth and play of light on the surface fabric, often enhanced by the addition of stitches, ceramic discs, Japanese papers, dyed and printed marks.'

Fabrics to use

There are many fabrics on the market which are very suitable for contemporary smocking. They can be natural or synthetic; coarsely or thinly woven; shiny or dull. When choosing fabrics various points need to be considered. Plain fabrics can be smocked in self-colour or contrasting colours. Patterned fabrics, when gathered up, can give distorted effects to the fabric. Geometrical patterns as well as floral designs may be used in this way.

Thick fabrics such as velvet, panné velvet, needle-cord, woollen fabrics, hessian and furnishing fabrics are most effective as long as they drape well. Natural or synthetic suedes and leathers can give most unusual textural effects, as well as satins and shot taffeta.

Threads to use

Any thread which will thread in a needle may be used, either natural or synthetic as well as threads used in knitting or crochet; if the fabric is coarse, all kinds of strings or fine strips of leather are appropriate, depending upon the purpose of the smocking; two colours of thread may be used together, or a metal thread may be used with another type of thread in the same needle. Spontaneity and experimentation should be encouraged.

Preparation

All preparation for contemporary smocking is worked in the same way as for traditional work. When preparing for a large-scale piece, use a water-erasable pen and a metre ruler (yardstick). For working on a smaller scale, use the methods for traditional smocking.

Having prepared the fabric, an additional preparation on the back of the fabric can be very useful for contemporary work. This is called 'prepared smocking' or 'back smocking'.

Prepared smocking

This is an extra preparation worked across the back in either cable stitch or stem stitch, before decoration. By preparing in this way, the front can be freely smocked. Sometimes this extra preparation is worked after the decoration (see Cocktail Dress 'finishing the smocked collar' page 109). Always work this preparation in a fine thread, either sewing thread, or one strand of stranded cotton to match the background exactly, and use tiny stitches which are unobtrusive. For cable stitch, start to work the first row with thread under the needle, and work across the row. For starting the next row, start with thread above the needle.

The surface will now be ready for decorating freely. When the piece is finished, take out the gathering threads. If there is a harsh line from the preparation on the back, the cable stitching may be undone to the edge of the design to give a softer effect. If required, the gathering threads may be taken out after preparing the back and before decorating the surface. The finished smocking is firm but still elastic.

Scale

The scale of smocking can be varied. If working on a large scale, as for a wall hanging, the dots for preparation could be inches apart. But for a dress, they would only be the normal scale as used in traditional smocking. Usually thick fabrics are worked to a larger scale, and fine fabrics to a smaller scale.

DESIGNING

Inspiration for design

As smocking gives such a wonderful textured effect there is endless scope for interpreting from nature. Natural forms such as the following may be used as the basis of a design: bark on an old tree; mossy stones; textured leaves and flowers; mushrooms; encrusted shells along a seashore; waves; sand-dunes; deserts; landscapes. Inspiration can also come from a piece of fabric, which when drawn up suggests shapes which can be further decorated.

Designing for contemporary smocking

The inspiration for the bag right came from the underside of a mushroom. A drawing was made of the mushroom omitting the stalk, this area becoming part of the handle. The bag was then planned in sections and each section was freely smocked in honeycomb stitch with added beads. The sections were then mounted on to a stiffening, and finally assembled as a bag, the reverse side being plain, and the inside quilted in mushroom pink-coloured silk, taking inspiration from the gills of the mushroom for the design.

FURTHER IDEAS FOR CONTEMPORARY SMOCKING

Smocking can be worked in various ways, by working across or down the folds. It can also be worked leaving spaces parallel to the folds. These spaces can be further decorated with tucks, ribbons, lace or embroidery.

Using honeycombing

Free honeycombing: This is worked like honeycombing *(see page 46)* and although this is a very traditional stitch, it can be worked creatively in a most interesting way. In this stitch any number of folds can be held together, and the needle can slide down a fold for any length; the gathering rows, though necessary for the preparation, are disregarded as far as the working of the stitch is concerned. To work free honeycombing, see Cocktail Dress and directions for smocking *(page 107)*.

Threaded honeycombing: This is when a thicker thread is threaded through the honeycomb spots when worked freely. It is a very quick and effective way to decorate honeycombing. Narrow ribbons, preferably soft ribbons, can also give an unusual finish. Ordinary honeycombing can either be threaded across the work or down the work for unusual effects.

Mushroom bag by Diana Keay

Random honeycombing: In this stitch, the fabric is not prepared in any way. It is worked by picking up spots at random, and working honeycomb stitch in the usual way. Worked across a piece of work, an irregular pattern evolves giving interesting textural areas. These areas can be further embellished with beads, French knots or other stitches.

Vertical honeycombing: This is worked down two folds by working one honeycomb stitch, and then turning the work upside down to work the next stitch. Keep reversing the work until the end has been reached, and then start off at the top with two more folds. This stitch gives a linear effect. Beads worked in the slit which the honeycombing creates between the two folds, add interest. The stitch can be worked regularly or irregularly.

Stitched lines for honeycombing: The fabric is worked with lines, by machine in a contrasting thread, from top to bottom. Honeycombing is then worked drawing the lines together to make the cells.

Using embroidery stitches

Many stitches used in embroidery can be used for smocking. The stitches which follow are worked on a prepared foundation of cable stitches, unless otherwise mentioned.

Straight stem stitch: This can be worked making a braid effect by working each line close together. Use beads and contrasting threads such as a metal thread with dull cotton threads for variety.

Opposite Project 9: Blouse *(see page 101)*

This stitch has a tendency to pull out of shape, so work one row and then turn upside down to work the next row, which is worked close to the first row. Stem stitch can also be used to make blocks of colour. Try working each block in a variety of contrasting colours or in tones of one colour.

Curved stem stitch: In this sample *(see right)*, a curved line was tacked on the front of the prepared piece of work. Stem stitch was worked on this tacked line by gradually working around the curves. Chain stitch was also used. In the area created by the curve, free honeycomb was worked, with a few beads added. The prepared cable stitching on the back was undone to shadow the outer curve, thus giving a very soft edge to the design which was further decorated with beads. It was worked on a cotton and wool mixture, several types of thread were used, such as cotton, crewel wool and Perle. Simple curves can be very attractive when worked in the style of the above sample, when small satin stitch spots and added beads can soften the line.

Chain stitch worked across folds: This is worked as a basic smocking stitch. Again, tacking (basting) a curved line or using tailor's chalk to mark a line, chain stitch can be worked in a flowing line across a piece of work. It can be further decorated with other stitches, such as stem or satin, to shadow the line, and further decoration could be added by scattered lazy-daisy leaves on the folds together with a few scattered beads.

Chain stitch worked down the folds: Instead of working chain stitch across the folds, it can be worked down the folds in broken lines, using variegated cotton threads. If working for a wrist, lazy-daisy flowers or leaves could be worked below the gathers in a random way.

Interlacing chain stitch: This can be worked in two colours. One wavy row of chain is worked across a row in one colour, and then using a contrasting colour, chain is worked forming an interlace over the first row. Chain is attractive also worked in a scallop using two colours.

Satin stitch: This is an effective stitch when worked in tubes down two folds, by changing the colours at the top and bottom. This gives an added interest and softens the harshness of the straight lines. Work tiny tubes, touched with colour at both ends, in a free way on a prepared piece of work. The background can be filled in with honeycombing *(see right)*. Also, see

Opposite Project 10: Cocktail Dress *(see page 107)*

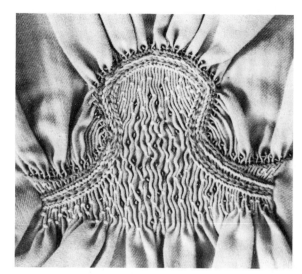

Curved stem stitch

Sampler central column for plain satin stitch tubes *(see illustration facing page 48)*.

Honeycombing using small satin stitch tubes, instead of the usual spots for honeycomb, can be very effective, especially if worked on stripes.

Buttonhole: Unusual decorations can be made using buttonhole stitch. See the interesting use of buttonhole to make circles, or wheels, decorating the blouse *(see illustration facing page 96)*. The stitch was worked across several folds.

Another use is to work small buttonhole loops to decorate a piece of prepared smocking. The loops are like needlepoint lace, and are worked across the folds;

Satin stitch with honeycombing

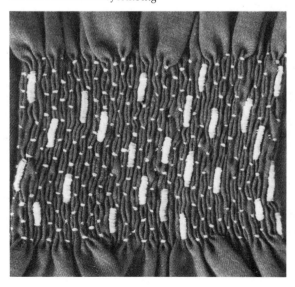

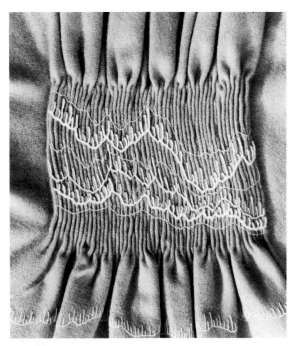

Blanket stitch

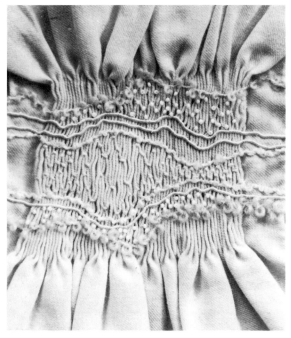

Couching

the idea can be carried further to edge a piece of work. If worked diagonally across a piece of work, the diagonals can be in different colours, or tones of colours. Beads added between the loops add to the overall effect. In the eighteenth century long button-hole loops were finely worked on baby bonnets (*see illustration on page 11*).

Blanket stitch: This stitch can be worked on a prepared foundation. If different weights of thread are used, the effect is very interesting. Work in a very free way across a piece of fabric, and if a sleeve is being made, the wavy design which the blanket stitch makes can be repeated on the wrist edge. The sample (*see above left*) was worked in sewing thread, Perle No. 8 and stranded cotton in whites on bright pink fine flannel.

Couching: This is quick to work and very decorative. In the sample (*see above right*) a textured cream wool thread which is dull, a fine shiny cord and a shiny textured yarn were couched down on to a cream cotton and wool mixture fabric. In between the couched lines scattered beads were added as well as honeycomb worked in a cream silk thread in the larger area. The couching is interesting because of the contrast between the shiny and dull threads, and between the textured and smooth threads. Couch with tiny stitches in a thin thread across each fold to hold securely in place.

Herringbone: This is another embroidery stitch adapted to smocking. It can be most attractive worked in a metal thread and incorporating a bead with each stitch. If worked large, the beads move and add another dimension to the work.

Using beads
Beads are most attractive when added in a free way. Honeycomb gives a very interesting effect (*see Cocktail Dress in illustration facing page 97*). Always use a beading needle and fine thread which matches the background fabric (*see directions for adding beads with free honeycomb on page 109*). Beads can be added to a smocked piece by using an ordinary stitch.

Using ribbons
Ribbons can be incorporated with smocking, by either applying or inserting them. Remove the gathering threads before using ribbon, as once the ribbon is used, the work will not stretch. While stiff ribbons are used for straight decoration, soft narrow ribbons are used for other forms of decoration.

For applying ribbons, consider the following ideas:
1. Using very narrow stiff ribbon in bands across a piece of work. Hold in place at regular intervals with tiny beads, or French knots. Smocking can decorate in between the bands.
2. Applying straight bands of ribbon with a slip stitch working over each fold. Rosette flowers, which can be made by working a running stitch along one edge of

the ribbon, and drawing up to make a tiny circle for the flower, can be applied to smocking. For the centre of the flowers, French knots or beads can be added and further decoration can be added with stitches to the piece.

3. Soft ribbon can be rucked by making small running stitches on both sides of the ribbon, then pulling up into either a straight, wavy or looped effect. This is then applied with tiny stitches across each fold. Depending on the purpose and the design, smocking stitches can further decorate the piece, or beads can be added with honeycombing.

4. Ribbon can be twisted, pleated and applied using a slip stitch. A bead or French knot added to each fold can add interest, and the piece can be further decorated with smocking.

5. If smocking is worked leaving several wide spaces between the folds, ribbon can be applied in these spaces. Consider applying a ribbon down the spaces and leaving the ends of the ribbon to hang freely *(see right)*.

Also consider using two ribbons of different widths and colours, pleating them together, and applying down the spaces.

For inserting ribbons, consider the following ideas:
1. Working honeycombing across a piece of work, then threading narrow ribbons down each line of cells. The ribbons will need to be further held in place with tiny stitches at the original honeycomb spots *(see right below)*.

2. Narrow ribbons can be threaded in and out of honeycomb *(see ideas for threaded honeycombing on page 55)*. It can also be threaded through ordinary smocking, but be careful to select stitches which will hold the ribbon in place securely. Working a design using diamond stitch, worked to a small scale to accommodate the ribbon, can be attractive.

3. Another way to insert ribbon is to work buttonhole loops or bullion (bouillion) knots parallel to the folds for inserting ribbon.

Using dyes

This is a fascinating way to enhance creative smocking. By dyeing in an uncontrolled way, most exciting effects can emerge. The cells of honeycomb can be decorated interestingly by dropping strong dye with a spoon into the cells. In this case remove the gathering threads first. Alternatively, the fabric can be dyed before smocking. Many interesting effects can be obtained by dyeing. Consult books from the library on the subject as it is a technique in itself.

Fabric dyes should be used and the maker's directions followed. Natural fabrics should be used as they absorb the dyes well. Synthetics can be dyed, but they will be paler and in some cases may not absorb the dye

Above Smocking with ribbons and beads added
Below Ribbons threaded through honeycombing

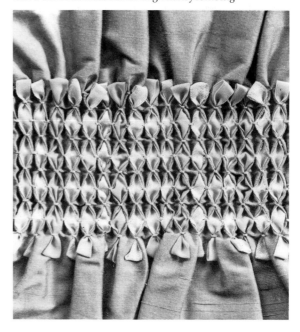

at all. The directions for the dye should be studied to see if it is suitable for synthetic fabrics. It is advisable to practise on samples first.

The following procedure should be followed when dyeing:

Prepare the white natural fabric in the usual way for smocking, but pull up the gathers as tightly as possible. Do not prepare the sample on the back. Smock the sample. The dye will absorb natural and synthetic threads in different degrees and thus add interest to the finished work. Do not take out the gathering threads. The sample can then be dip-dyed or tie-dyed.

To dip-dye: Hold part of the sample in the dye bath for the correct time. Then hold another part of the sample in another dye bath of a different colour for the appropriate time. Follow the directions for rinsing. Take out the gathering threads which will have prevented the dye from penetrating some of the folds. Also the dyes from the two dye baths will have 'bled' into one another, giving interesting effects.

Any number of colours can be used, remembering that over-dyeing will produce other colours. One colour can give several shades by varying the length of time the sample is left in each dye bath.

To tie-dye: The sample can be tie-dyed by dyeing in the above way, but instead of holding the sample in a dye bath, bind the sample and tie it in certain ways to resist the dye.

Pin tucks

Pin tucks can give a most unusual and attractive effect to smocking if worked in the following way.

Gather the fabric in the usual way, but tie off loosely, leaving enough room to work one pin tuck at a time. Do not prepare on the back of the work.

To make pin tucks down the folds: This is usually done by hand, though the tucks can be machined 2.5mm (⅛in) away from the edge, depending upon the fabric and the distance between each fold. Stitch pin tucks on every third fold, leaving the two folds in between to work vertical honeycomb *(see page 96)*. After working vertical honeycomb, beads can be added to the slit so made, by sewing the beads so that they are seen through the slit *(see right)*.

Smocking can be worked over prepared tucks of any small size. Honeycomb is most effective worked in this way, as every fold is tucked before smocking, and gathering is not required. The smocking is worked by eye. Tucks can also be threaded with thick wool before smocking for a padded and quilted effect.

Quilted effects

Quilted effects can be obtained with smocking. For padded quilting, this effect may be obtained by attaching a smocked piece to a background, such as

for a cuff of a jacket or other trimming. Wadding is inserted between the smocking and the background. Certain areas are then held in place with a few small stitches.

Another way to achieve a padded effect is to stuff only certain areas between the smocking and the background, and then hold in place with a few stitches. Further interesting effects can be obtained by using a transparent fabric for the smocking, and using coloured cottonwool balls for the stuffing.

Another interesting effect can be achieved by shadow quilting. To do this, delicately smock a strip of transparent fabric in free honeycombing, adding a few beads and sequins. Sandwich this strip between two layers of transparent fabric. This can be very effective on a sleeve.

Quilted tucks can be very decorative.

Using the sewing machine

The sewing machine can be used for smocking, by decorating the fabric before smocking, as in stitched lines, or in the preparation of tucks before smocking. Depending upon the fabric and the temperament of the machine, prepared gathers can be held in place by working across the surface, but not all machines will do this. Fine fabrics should be used and it is necessary to experiment with samples.

An interesting effect can be obtained by withdrawing threads, as for drawn work, and decorating the threads with a zig-zag. This can then form a band with smocking either side. Colour can be introduced behind the lacy effect by using fabric applied behind, or by pulling the fabric through to the surface.

Pin tucks with vertical honeycombing

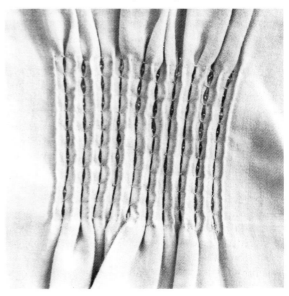

PROJECT 9 *(See illustration facing page 96)*

Blouse

Size: The pattern will fit bust sizes 92-102cm (36-40in) because it is so full. The length below the waist is 25cm (9¾in), which makes it also suitable for maternity wear.

General description: This blouse shows a very interesting and contemporary use of smocking. It is made in a synthetic, white, self-striped crêpe georgette, the self-stripes helping to guide the placing of the embroidery. It buttons down the front with 7 self-covered and embroidered buttons, and it is finished at the neck with a high-standing collar. The long sleeves, which are very full, finish in a frill as an extension of the smocking.

The smocking is in the form of buttonhole circles which fall freely across the folds of the smocking. The embroidery follows the same theme, together with feather stitching, and is an extension of the free design which delicately decorates the blouse. The smocking and the embroidery are worked in thin, variegated threads from white through to grey. The design theme was inspired by water lily leaves.

Alternative suggestions: This blouse can be made in any fine fabric which drapes well. Although the original has self-coloured stripes which act as a guide for the embroidery, plain fabric, such as a fine silk, cotton, or synthetic fabric can equally well be used, bearing in mind that synthetic fabrics are usually more difficult to handle than natural fibres. If using a plain fabric, plan the embroidery design on the drafted pattern. Using tissue paper and pencil, trace the design and sections of the blouse where the embroidery is to be placed. Place this tissue-paper tracing on to the right side of the fabric in the exact position. Using a contrasting colour to the fabric, tack the design through the paper and through the fabric, two thicknesses together. Use medium-sized stitches, and start and end securely. Once the whole design has been tacked, tear off the tissue paper. The fabric will be left with the original design and ready for embroidering.

The original design was worked in variegated threads, but any plain colour combination can be used to suit the wearer, e.g. any pale-coloured fabric could be worked in tones of that colour; black or a dark-coloured fabric could be worked in a silver or gold metal thread suitable for threading in a needle for embroidery; any plain colour could be worked in polychrome colours.

Smocking/embroidery stitches: Both are worked in buttonhole stitch and feather stitch.

System for preparing smocking: As the fabric is transparent, smocking dots are placed under the fabric and transferred with a soft pencil on to the wrong side.

Experience required: To make this blouse, reasonable dressmaking skills are necessary, together with a knowledge of collar construction. The smocking and embroidery would appeal to a person wishing to work in a more unusual way.

Notes
- It is essential to work a small sample piece of the smocking first. This will give a good idea of the tension required as well as the suitability of the fabric, design and colours envisaged.
- Check your own measurements against the pattern pieces before cutting out. This is a one-size pattern and may need slight adjustment.
- When pressing, care should be taken with all fabrics, especially synthetics. Always test the iron temperature on a scrap of the fabric to be used.
- The blouse requires careful laundering, which should be done by hand.

MATERIALS

Dressmaker's Pattern Guide Paper ruled in 1cm (½in) and 5cm (2in) squares or similar. If this is not available use large size plain paper, ruled into the appropriate squares.

Fabric: 2.80 metres × 115cm (3¼ yds × 45in) wide or 3.40 metres × 90cm (3¾ yds × 36in) wide.

Interfacing: Lightweight fusible 70 × 20cm (27½ × 7¾in).

Buttons: 7 self-covering approximately 5mm (¼in) in diameter.

Snap fasteners: 7 clear plastic or metal snaps.

Needles: Crewel embroidery, No. 8, 9 or 10.

Thread for sewing: 2 reels (spools) of suitable machine thread to match fabric and type. Ask advice when obtaining fabric.

Thread for embroidery: 'Titania 30' or similar fine lustrous rayon thread. If not available use D.M.C. variegated stranded cotton in white shaded to dark grey. Other variegated colours are available from D.M.C. and Coats.

Smocking dots: 1 sheet size 1 × 1cm (⅜ × ⅜in) – Deighton's size F.

Usual workbox equipment plus fine pins, sharp scissors, pencil, eraser and ruler.

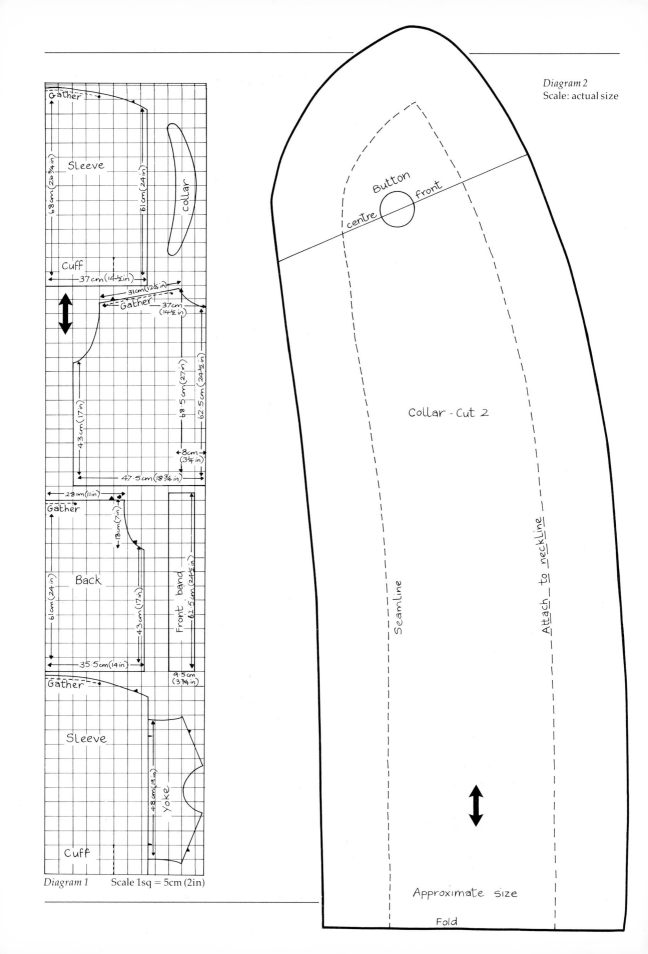

Diagram 2
Scale: actual size

Sleeve

collar

68cm(26¾in)

61cm(24in)

Cuff

37cm(14½in)

31cm(12¼in)

Gather

37cm (14½in)

43cm(17in)

68·5cm(27in)

62·5cm (24½in)

8cm (3¼in)

47·5cm(18¾in)

28cm(11in)

Gather

18cm(7in)

Back

61cm(24in)

43cm(17in)

Front band

62·5cm (24½in)

35·5cm(14in)

9·5cm (3¾in)

Gather

Sleeve

48cm(19in)

yoke

Cuff

Button

centre   front

Collar · Cut 2

Seamline

Attach to neckline

Approximate size

Fold

Diagram 1   Scale 1sq = 5cm (2in)

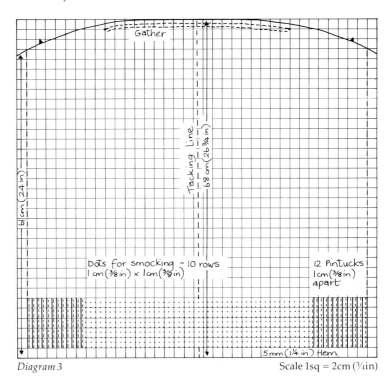

Diagram 3   Scale 1sq = 2cm (¾in)

GENERAL INSTRUCTIONS

1. Draft pattern. A 2cm (¾in) seam allowance has been included in pattern *(see diagram 1)*.

2. Place pattern pieces as in layout plan except collar and cut out *(see diagram 1)*.

3. Make a mock collar in cotton fabric (new or old), adjust and cut out *(see diagram 2)*.

4. Make a sample piece by gathering 10 rows, 1cm (½in) by 1cm (½in), work embroidery stitches *(see diagrams 3-6)*.

5. Work smocking and embroidery on sleeves, yoke, front, back and on buttons.

6. Make up the garment.

SMOCKING AND EMBROIDERY

Preparing the dots

If using a smocking-dot transfer the dots will be 1cm (⅜in) apart and the rows 1cm (⅜in) between. If marking by pencil 1cm (½in) measurement can be used. Smocking dots show through fine fabric, so carefully use a pencil to mark lightly on the wrong side of the fabric. If using a water-erasable pen, test first on a spare piece of fabric. Do *not* use heat on or near these pens, as this will set the mark. To eliminate dots showing, it is preferable to mark the first row only and then to work the remaining rows 'by eye'.

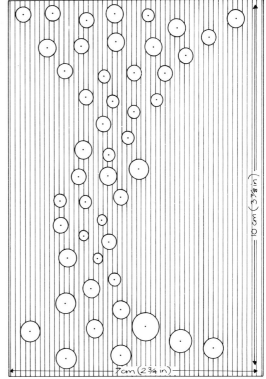

Diagram 4   Scale: actual size

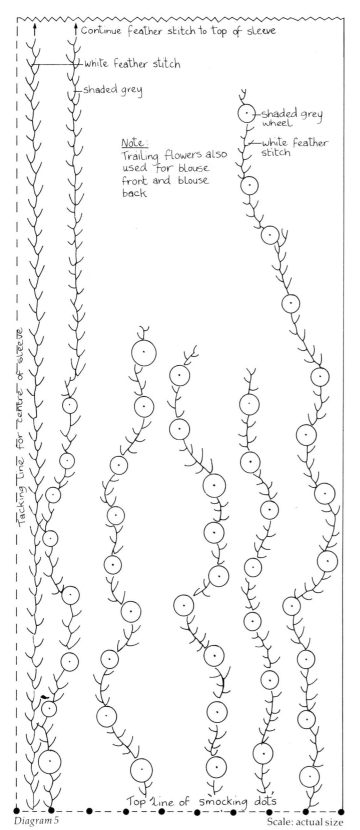

Continue feather stitch to top of sleeve

white feather stitch

shaded grey

shaded grey wheel

white feather stitch

Note:
Trailing flowers also used for blouse front and blouse back

Tacking line for centre of sleeve

Top line of smocking dots

Diagram 5

Scale: actual size

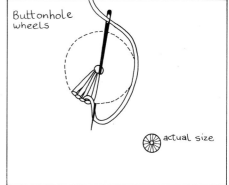

Buttonhole wheels

actual size

Diagram 6

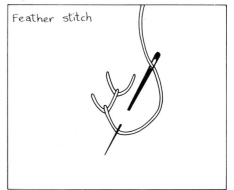

Feather stitch

Diagram 7

Sleeves

1. Make a 5mm (¼in) hem by hand along the wrist edge. Starting 1cm (½in) from this edge, mark at 1cm (½in) intervals across the sleeve (*see diagram 7*).
2. Make 12 pin tucks 10cm (4in) deep and 1cm (½in) apart at either side of the sleeve (*see diagram 7*).
3. Work 10 rows of gathering threads 1cm (½in) apart between the tucks. Do not draw up.
4. Run a tacking (basting) line down the centre length of the sleeve. Embroider a line of white feather stitch (*see diagram 6*) the length of the sleeve parallel to the tacking (basting) (*see diagram 6*).
5. Embroider wheels (*see diagram 3*) and feather stitch, reversing the design on either side of the centre tacking (basting) line (*see diagram 6*).
6. Draw gathering threads up to approximately 7cm (2¾in). Pin side seams together and check that you are able to get your hand through the cuff as there is no fastening. Adjust as required. Unpin and fasten off gathering threads securely as these are left in. Even out and gently steam press gathers. Do not let the iron touch the fabric. Embroider wheels (*see diagrams 5 and 6*).

Yoke

Embroider parallel lines of shaded-grey feather stitch across the back of the yoke 1cm (½in) apart.

Front

Embroider wheels on fronts, using sleeve embroidery diagram 0 turned upside down or design your own sprays. The first row is approximately 8cm (3¼in) from the front edge, and the complete embroidered panel measures approximately 20cm (7¾in) deep. Feather stitch on the front is worked after the attachment of the band.

Back

1. Tack (baste) line down centre.
2. Tack (baste) parallel lines 15cm (6in) either side of the centre. Embroider 4 lines of feather stitch, in shaded grey 1cm (½in) apart towards the sides of the blouse.
3. Embroider the central panel with sprays as on the front (*see diagram 7*).

Buttons

Cut double-thickness circles of the fabric 3cm (1¼in) in diameter and embroider a white buttonhole wheel in the centre of each. Make up seven buttons, six for the blouse and one spare.

MAKING-UP THE BLOUSE

Note:
2cm (¾in) seam allowances are allowed on the pattern. Sew French seams throughout, apart from setting in the sleeve into the armhole, which may require binding if the fabric frays.

Step 1: Front bands

1. Cut 2 interfacing strips 3cm (1¼in) wide and the length of the front band 62.5cm (24½in).
2. With one edge along fold line (*see diagram 8a position 4*), fuse interfacing to wrong side of front band.
3. With right sides together pin, tack (baste) and stitch band to blouse front (*see diagram 8a position 2*).
4. Trim seam (*see diagram 8a position 3*) and press towards interfacing.
5. Fold band on fold line (*see diagram 8a position 4*) with wrong sides together and tack (baste) near edge and press.
6. Turn under seam allowance (*see diagram 8b position 5*) and bring across the interfacing and hem on to seam join on the left at position 2.
7. Press well. On the right side (outer side), top stitch approximately 2.5mm (⅛in) on either side of the band (*see diagram 8c position 6*).
8. Repeat for the other side.

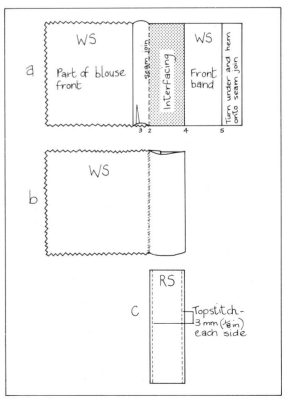

Diagram 8

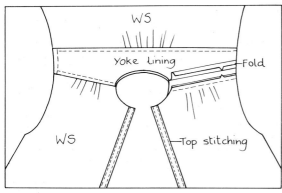

Diagram 9

Step 2: Back, yoke and yoke lining
1. Gather between the dots at the top of the back and ease to fit yoke back, using two rows of gathering threads, and tie off. With the right sides together, pin the yoke to the back. Tack (baste).
2. Pin the right side of the yoke facing to the wrong side of the back and tack (baste) in place. Stitch through all thicknesses.
3. Press the seam allowance towards the yoke.
4. Press under the 2cm (¾in) seam allowance on the front edge of the yoke facing.

Step 3: Attaching the fronts to the yoke
1. Gather each front at shoulder between dots to fit yoke front edge, using two rows of gathering threads *(see diagram 1)*. Tie off.
2. With the right sides together, pin the yoke to the front, matching notches and adjusting the gathers. Tack (baste). Stitch, keeping the yoke facing free. Press seam allowance towards the yoke.
3. Tack (baste) pressed-under edges of facing over seams and hem *(see diagram 9)*.
4. Tack (baste) raw edges at neck edge together.

Step 4: Sides of the blouse
Join sides of the blouse together using a French seam *(see diagram 43, page 51)*.

Step 5: Collar
1. Cut out collar interfacing.
2. Fuse interfacing to the wrong side of the collar.
3. Press under 2cm (¾in) on the neck edge of the collar.
4. Pin the collar facing to the collar, right sides together. Stitch around the curved edge. Trim the seam, snip, turn and tack (baste). Press.
5. Pin the collar to the neck edge of the blouse, right sides together. Tack (baste) and stitch. Clip the curve. Press the seam allowance towards the neck band. Hem the edge of the neck band over seam.

Step 6: Seam sleeve
1. Gather the top of the sleeve between the two dots with two rows of gathering threads to fit armhole.
2. With the right sides together, pin the sleeve into the armhole, adjusting the gathers to fit and matching the centre of the sleeve with the yoke shoulder line and underarm seam. Tack (baste). Stitch on seam line. Stitch again 5mm (¼in) from first stitching. Trim. Either use zig-zag on the machine or whip by hand.
3. To protect edges further, the seam can be finished with a bias binding.

Step 7: Attaching buttons
Stitch buttons to the front band and collar centre front, at approximately 9cm (3½in) intervals, making sure that the right front laps over the left front when worn. Sew on snap fasteners beneath the buttons as making buttonholes is difficult on a sheer fabric.

Step 8: Finishing
1. Embroider three rows of feather stitch 1cm (½in) apart parallel to the front band on both fronts.
2. Trim the bottom edge of the blouse. Turn up 5mm (¼in) and hem by hand.

PROJECT 10 *(See illustration facing page 97)*

Cocktail Dress

Size: To fit 89/92cm (35/36in) bust. This is not a fitted garment.

General description: The main part of this dress is made in dull red raw silk. It consists of a plain skirt which joins the bodice at the waistline with a casing through which elastic is threaded for a fitted effect. The V-neckline bodice has a falling collar on the front only. This is in dull green fine silk, and it is most interestingly and freely smocked with red and green beads, with added beads forming the trimming on the edge of the collar. The tie belt also has a smocked and beaded trim. The sleeves of the dress are short.

Alternative suggestions: This dress can be made in any colour combination, the beads picking up the colour of the dress. Alternatively, it can be made in one colour only, but in two different weights of fabric. The collar must be made in a fabric which will drape well. Metallic beads can look most effective. For example, metallic bronze beads on brown; metallic dark blue/green beads on dark blue or dark green fabric; metallic blue/green beads on navy fabric; or dull gold beads on black fabric.

Smocking stitches: Honeycomb stitch, with added beads, is used throughout. Stem stitch worked on the wrong side holds part of the smocked areas in place.

System for preparing smocking: A smock dot transfer is used to prepare the collar and the ties.

Experience required: Anyone with experience can make this simply constructed dress with smocked collar. The smocking, being freely worked, would appeal to those who wish to work in a creative way.

Notes
● Check your measurements against the pattern before cutting out the fabric.
● Make a sampler of smocking, working honeycomb freely. Then practise adding beads with a beading needle. Test beads for size and effect. Make sure enough beads are bought.
Make sure enough beads are bought.
● A smock-gathering machine can be used instead of dots, but it does not give such a fine gathering.

MATERIALS

Dressmaker's Pattern Guide Paper ruled in 1cm (½in) and 5cm (2in) squares or similar. If this is not available use large size plain paper, ruled into the appropriate squares.

Fabric for the dress: 3.20 metres × 90cm (3½ yds × 36in) wide red raw silk.

Fabric for the collar: 50 × 90cm (½ yd × 36in) wide of green Jap (China) silk.

Needles: Crewel embroidery needles, No. 8, 9 or 10. Beading needles, No. 10 preferably.

Thread for sewing: 1 reel (spool) red mercerised sewing cotton No. 50.

Thread for gathering: 1 reel (spool) mercerised sewing cotton No. 50 in a contrasting colour.

Thread for smocking: 1 skein dark green stranded cotton.

Elastic: 1 metre (1 yard) 5mm (¼in) wide.

Smocking dots: 2 sheets size 5 × 5mm (¼ × ¼in) – Deighton's size K.

Beads: 1 packet small red embroidery beads, ¼ packet small green embroidery beads.

Usual workbox equipment plus pencil, eraser and ruler.

GENERAL INSTRUCTIONS

1. Draft pattern for dress. A 2cm (¾in) seam allowance has been included in pattern *(see diagram 1)*.
2. Draft pattern for collar and tie-belt ends *(see diagram 2)*.
3. Cut out dress *(see diagram 1)*.
4. Cut out collar and tie-belt ends *(see diagram 2)*.
5. Smock the collar and tie-belt ends *(see diagrams 3-4)*.
6. Make up the dress *(see diagrams 5-7)*.

Drafting the patterns
1. Front and back pieces of the skirt are the same *(see diagram 1)*.
2. The bodice top front and back are similar except that the back V is higher than the front V. Note pattern for shape of armholes *(see diagram 1)*.
3. The facings for both front and back bodice are 8cm (3¼in) wide and can be cut from the bodice as a guide *(see diagram 1)*.
4. Draft a pattern for the smocked collar and tie-belt *(see diagram 2)*.
Cutting out the patterns
1. Follow the layout for the dress *(see diagram 1)*.
2. Follow the layout for the smocked collar and tie belt ends *(see diagram 2)*.
3. Mark all seam allowances and notches. Tack (baste) centres of all pieces.

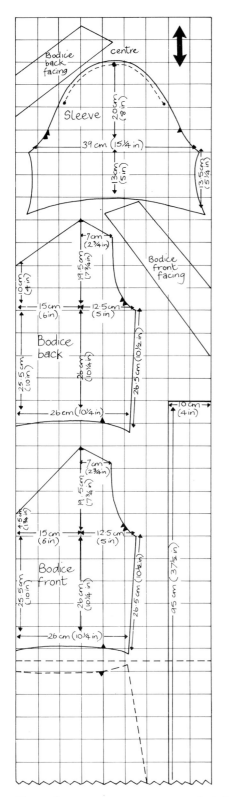

Bodice back facing

centre

Sleeve

2·0cm (8in)

39 cm (15¼ in)

13cm (5in)

13·5cm (5¼in)

7cm (2¾in)

19·5cm (7¾in)

Bodice front facing

10cm (4in)

15cm (6in)

12·5cm (5in)

Bodice back

26cm (10¼in)

26·5cm (10½in)

25·5cm (10in)

26cm (10¼in)

10cm (4in)

7cm (2¾in)

19·5cm (7¾in)

4·5cm (1¾in)

15cm (6in)

12·5cm (5in)

Bodice front

26cm (10¼in)

26·5cm (10½in)

95cm (37½in)

25·5cm (10in)

26cm (10¼in)

26·5cm (10½in)

Skirt front

95cm (37½in)

80cm (31½in)

79·5cm (31¼in)

10cm (4in)

39 cm (15¼ in)

26·5cm (10½in)

Skirt back

80cm (31½in)

79·5cm (31¼in)

39 cm (15¼ in)

Diagram 1　　　　　　　　Scale 1sq = 5cm (2in)

SMOCKING

THE COLLAR

Preparing the dots
1. Take cut-out collar piece and whip edges.
2. Tack (baste) a line down the centre in a contrasting colour.
3. Place smocking dots on the wrong side of the collar piece, wax side down, making sure that the lines are parallel as indicated by the dotted lines of the pattern *(see diagram 2)*. Note that these lines are used only to show the direction for placing the dots.
4. Pin the dots in position and trim back to the edge of the collar piece. As two sheets of dots are required, be careful to align the dots. Iron dots on to collar.

Picking up the dots
Starting on the right side with a firm knot, pick up each dot across the collar.

Pulling up the gathering threads
1. Pull up gathering threads using the collar guide *(see diagram 3)*. Make sure that the gathers are evenly distributed.
2. Tie off securely.

Smocking
1. Tack (baste) seam allowance around collar.
2. Use a beading needle and very fine thread, either sewing thread or one or two strands of stranded cotton, to match collar fabric exactly.
3. Avoid smocking near the seam line. Keep 5mm (¼in) in from it.
4. The honeycomb with beads is denser at the top of the collar and thins out towards the edge of the collar *(see diagram 6)*.

Working free honeycomb with beads
1. This is worked in the same way as ordinary honeycomb *(see page 46)* except that, instead of the stitch being worked in a regular way, it is worked in a random way.
2. Come up on left side of fold at position 1 *(see diagram 4a)*.
3. Take needle over three folds to position 2 and come back to position 1 as in ordinary honeycomb.
4. Thread one red, one green, then one red bead on to the needle and insert the needle in the fold at position 2. Slide down to position 3 *(see diagram 4a)*.
5. Any number of folds can be held together and the distance between positions 2 and 3 can be any length.
6. Work freely across the collar. Come back and work freely in areas which are not covered, thinning out towards the edge of the collar.

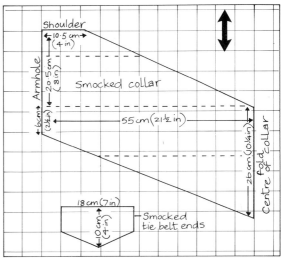

Diagram 2   Scale 1sq = 5cm (2in)

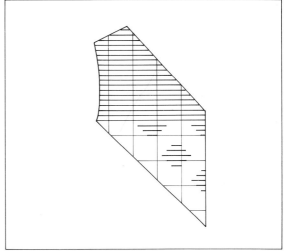

Diagram 3   Scale 1sq = 5cm (2in)

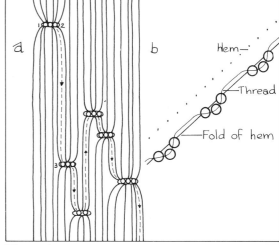

Diagram 4

Finishing the smocked collar

1. When the collar is smocked, turn it over on to the wrong side.

2. Working in a matching colour, and using fine thread, work stem stitch loosely from edge to edge, on every second line and across seam allowances. Follow smocked collar guide *(see diagram 3)*. Note that in the bottom part of the collar, only sections are held in place with stem stitch so as to give a softer effect.

3. When all the stem stitch has been worked, release the gathers.

4. With matching thread, make a 5mm (¼in) hem on the bottom edge of the collar. Press hem only.

5. Decorate the finished edge by adding three beads, one red, one green, one red, approx. every 5mm (¼in) by slipping along the edge of the hem. Work so that the beads fall over the edge. The way in which they fall is determined by the size of the beads *(see diagram 4b)*.

TIE-BELT ENDS

1. Use eight rows of dots and place at the straight edge of the tie.

2. Pick up the dots and pull up to the width of the tie-belt.

3. Smock in free honeycomb, like the collar, adding only one bead instead of three beads. Leave a V at the top for attaching the tie-belt *(see diagram 5)*.

4. On the back, hold gathers with stem stitch, like the collar. Work across all eight rows.

5. Make hem 5mm (¼in), like the collar, and edge with beads in the same way.

6. Scatter a few beads on the back of the smocking, as the belt will turn with movement.

MAKING-UP THE DRESS

Step 1: Bodice front
Take smocked collar and matching centre line of collar with centre line of bodice, pin in place. Pin the collar, matching V-neck, shoulders and armholes, matching large dots on seam line of armhole *(see diagram 6)*. Make sure the collar lies flat. Tack (baste) on seam line.

Step 2: Joining bodice front to bodice back
Place bodice front and bodice back, right sides together. Pin, tack (baste) and stitch seams at sides and shoulders. Zig-zag edges. Press flat.

Step 3: Sleeves
1. Gather sleeves between dots.

2. With right sides together seam sleeves and zig-zag edges. Press flat.

3. Turn under 5mm (¼in) on to the wrong side on sleeve edge. Stitch. Make 2cm (¾in) hem. Slip stitch.

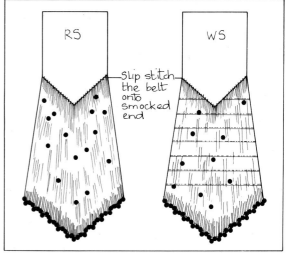

Diagram 5

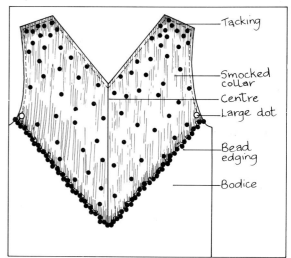

Diagram 6

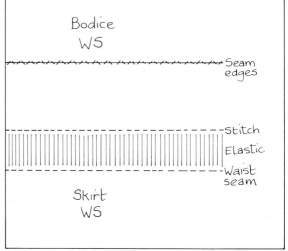

Diagram 7

Step 4: Attaching sleeves to bodice

1. Pin centre of sleeve to shoulder seam. Match notches and adjust gathers. Pin. Tack (baste) and stitch.
2. Trim edges and zig-zag edges.

Step 5: Facings for bodice

1. Take front facings for bodice and join at the centre. Press flat.
2. Take facings for bodice front and bodice back, right sides together, and join. Press flat.
3. Turn under 2cm (¾in) on outer edge and stitch 5mm (¼in) away. Trim and press.
4. Pin and tack (baste) facing, right sides together to the bodice, matching front facing to bodice front and back facing to bodice back. Stitch and trim edges. Turn facing on to inside. Snip carefully where necessary to enable the facing to lie flat. Tack (baste) in place. Slip stitch.

Step 6: Skirt

With right sides together, pin, tack (baste) and stitch side seams. Zig-zag edges. Press flat.

Step 7: Joining skirt to bodice

1. With right sides together, pin skirt to bodice. Tack (baste) and stitch. Press seam towards bodice.
2. Working on the inside stitch 5mm (¼in) away from seam line through seam allowances and bodice to form a casing for the elastic and leaving a space of 5cm (2in) for inserting elastic (*see diagram 7*).
3. Cut elastic to waist measurement plus 2.5cm (1in).
4. Insert elastic with a small safety pin. Overlap the ends by 2.5cm (1in). Fasten with a safety pin. Try on. Adjust if necessary. Stitch.
5. Stitch opening in casing which was left open for inserting elastic.

Step 8: Tie-belt

1. Join tie-belt pieces. Press flat.
2. Seam long edge only. Turn inside out. Tack (baste). Press well.
3. Cut ends of tie to a V point.
4. Insert smocked tie end to belt end. Turn under edge of tie-belt on to smocked tie-belt end and slip stitch very neatly. Work on one side and then on the other (*see diagram 6*). Attach smocked end to other end of tie-belt in the same way.

Step 9: Finishing

1. Try on dress and adjust hem length.
2. Turn under 5mm (¼in) and stitch. Turn up hem and slip stitch into place.

PROJECT 11 *(See illustration facing page 112)*

Green Bag

Size: The bag measures 11.5 × 21cm (4½ × 8¼in).

General description: The bag, which is made of dull polyester satin in jade green, is an elongated envelope shape with side gussets. The front flap is most unusually, but simply smocked in various shiny and dull threads, together with added beads. The handle is made of plaited rouleaux (braided bias-strip tubes) and the bag fastens with a tassel.

Alternative suggestions: This most interesting bag can be made in any colour to suit individual requirements: A black bag smocked in gold threads with added gold beads looks most attractive; and an ivory-coloured bag smocked in cream, with tiny pearls added, is interesting. A fabric with a tiny stripe can be considered, using the stripes as a guide for the gathering threads. A plaited handle can be made in three different colours, with the smocking worked to match. Alternatively, a gold chain necklace or a cord can be used for the handle. A bought tassel can be used also. The bag looks attractive also without the tassel. The wavy lines for the design need not be exactly as given, but can be made up individually. If metallic threads are not available, the lines can be smocked in an additional colour.

Smocking stitches: The bag is smocked entirely in one stitch, outline stitch, using three strands of stranded cotton. Beads are added with a beading needle.

System for preparing the dots: A template from graph paper was made and the dots were transferred using powdered chalk. A smocking-dot transfer or a smock-gathering machine can be used also.

Experience required: Some smocking experience is necessary and an understanding of construction is useful as the bag has to be neatly finished.

Notes

● Work a sampler in the fabric to test the fabric, colours selected and the tension of the smocking.
● Test that the beads are small enough to fit between the folds when worked.
● For transferring the design, in preparation for smocking, a test should be made on a scrap of the fabric to see whether a soft pencil, water-erasable pen or watercolour paint is suitable.
● A 1cm (½in) seam allowance is included.

MATERIALS

Fabric: ½ metre × 90cm (½ yd × 36in) wide dull polyester satin.

Needles: Crewel embroidery, No. 8, 9 or 10. Beading needle, preferably No. 10.

Thread for sewing: 1 reel (spool) polyester to match fabric.

Thread for gathering: 1 reel (spool) polyester in a contrasting colour.

Thread for smocking: 1 skein stranded cotton, black. 1 reel (spool) green metallic thread. If not available, use 1 skein green stranded cotton.

Beads: Small quantity of small embroidery beads which will fit between the folds (approximately 150 tiny beads). 1 large black bead for fastening.

Smocking dots: 2 sheets size 1 × 1cm (⅜ × ⅜in) – Deighton's size F.

Pelmet (drape valence) vilene or heavy vilene (pellon) for stiffening: 1 piece 60 × 10cm (23½ × 4in).

Wadding (batting), synthetic, lightweight: 1 piece 40 × 10cm (16 × 4in).

Stiff card for backing: 17 × 9cm (6¾ × 3½in).

Usual workbox equipment plus graph paper; stiletto or thick needle; powdered chalk or talcum powder; tracing paper; pencil; eraser.

GENERAL INSTRUCTIONS

1. Cut out fabric, stiffening and wadding (batting) *(see diagrams 1-2)*.
2. Smock the flap *(see diagrams 2-3)*.
3. Make up the bag *(see diagrams 4-5)*.

CUTTING OUT

1. Cut out the fabric *(see diagram 1)*.
2. Cut out vilene (pellon) to size 59 × 10cm (23½ × 4in) *(see diagram 2)*.
3. Cut out wadding (batting) to size 40 × 10cm (15¾ × 4in) *(see diagram 2)*.

SMOCKING

Preparing the dots

1. Take the piece of fabric for smocking 48 × 22cm (19 × 8¾in).
2. The dots are 1cm (⅜in) apart and the same between the rows, but a 1cm (½in) measurement may be used.
3. Make a template *(see page 37)* from the graph paper, using the above measurement. Prick holes with the stiletto or thick needle, and transfer dots by using

powdered chalk or talcum powder, leaving the seam allowance on either side free. If using a smock-gathering machine, leave seam allowance free at the sides. If using smocking dots, leave seam allowance free at the sides.

Gathering the dots

Pick up each dot across the fabric using a contrasting coloured thread.

Pulling up the gathering threads

Pull up the threads to 10cm (4in) and tie off securely.

Transferring the smocking design

1. The design *(see diagram 3)* is transferred to the prepared smocking by the template method *(see page 37)*.
2. Trace the design *(see diagram 3)* on to tracing paper, using a pencil or pen. Take a needle and prick holes along the lines. Some lines will be too close, so choose those which can act as a guide.
3. With the right side facing upwards, pin the prepared piece of smocking to a folded piece of cloth, to act as a padding, or pin into a soft board.
4. Place the design on top of the prepared piece of smocking, right side upwards, and pin in place. Rub chalk or talcum powder through the holes. Lift off the tracing paper and hold the transferred design by using a soft pencil, water-erasable pen or watercolour. Test before using. Leave prepared smocked piece pinned to the cloth. This will help to keep its shape while smocking, which will be on top of the folds only. Alternatively, the design can be transferred by the tissue-paper method *(see page 101)*.

Working the smocking

1. Use three strands of stranded cotton for the lines marked 'black'. Use metallic thread, if available, or use another colour in stranded cotton for the lines marked 'green' *(see diagram 3)*.
2. Work outline stitch across the lines with the thread above the needle.
3. There are three rows of beads. For attaching beads, use a beading needle and sewing thread to match the background fabric, or one strand of stranded cotton to match the fabric. The beads, when added with stem stitch, lie between the folds. To add beads, work one stem stitch, then pick up a bead and slide it down the thread and place in the fold. Work another stem stitch. Repeat along the row. End off securely.
4. When all smocking is finished, remove from padded surface. Remove gathering threads.

Opposite Project 11: Green Bag *(see page 111)* and Project 12: Black Bag *(see page 115)*

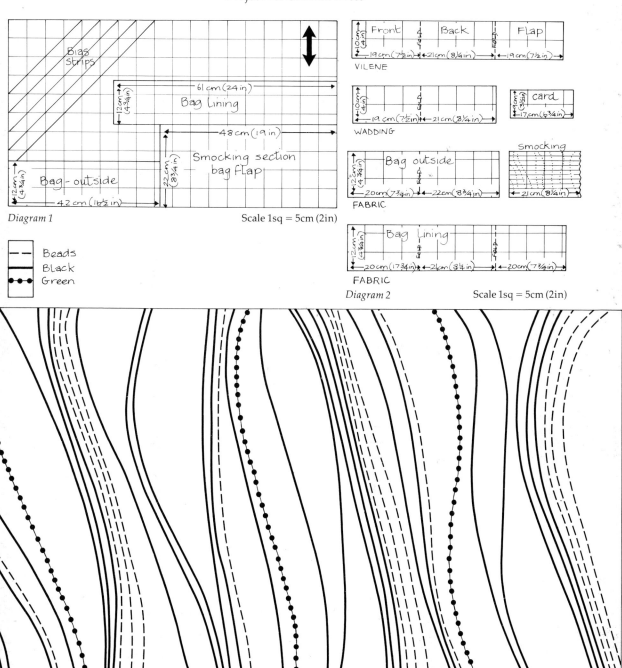

Diagram 1   Scale 1sq = 5cm (2in)

Beads	— — —
Black	———
Green	•-•-•-

Diagram 2   Scale 1sq = 5cm (2in)

Diagram 3   Scale: actual size

MAKING-UP THE BAG

Step 1: Joining the smocked flap to the bag

With right sides together, pin top of smocked flap to the outside piece of the bag. Tack (baste) carefully,

Opposite Project 14: Blue Dress *(see page 127)*

and machine carefully to join. Remove tacking (basting) and trim seam. Steam press to make a flat seam. Take out gathering threads.

Step 2: Preparing the stiffening

Prepare the vilene (pellon) piece by machining along fold lines *(see diagram 2)*.

Step 3: Preparing the outside of the bag

1. Place long outside piece, right side downwards, on to a flat surface. Place wadding (batting) on top of this. Place vilene (pellon) on top of the wadding (batting). Place the card under the vilene (pellon) and under the smocked end as it acts as additional stiffening to the flap (*see diagram 4*).
2. To hold the smocking in place on the flap end, place pins into the side of the card (*see diagram 4*).
3. Turn over seam allowance on to vilene (pellon) and tack (baste) in position (*see diagram 4*). Turn over smocked end of flap and carefully tack (baste) in place.
4. With matching thread, stab stitch through all layers on seam line where the smocking joins the bag back (*see diagram 4*). Work one line of outline stitch across the line, using three strands of black stranded cotton.

Step 4: Lining the bag

Take the lining, turn under the seam allowance and tack (baste) in place on top of the vilene (pellon).

Step 5: Binding the edge

1. Make a test piece of bias for edging the bag before proceeding.
2. Cut a bias strip approximately 4cm (1½in) wide and long enough to go around the four sides of the bag. Press joins flat and trim.

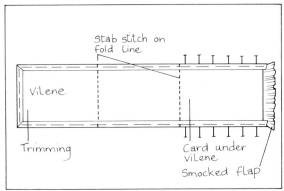

Diagram 4

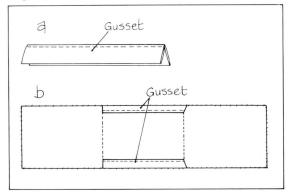

Diagram 5

3. With wrong sides turned to the inside, fold bias lengthwise and press.
4. Pin bias to the outside of the bag, right sides together and raw edges together. Be careful to place the joins of the bias away from the smocked front flap. Tack (baste).

5. Stitch in place. The smocked flap must be very neatly finished with the folds lying evenly. As machine stitching may be awkward, especially around the flap, which has the piece of card inserted, the bias may be attached by hand using tiny back stitches. Trim the turnings and hem bias to the inside, taking care to ensure that the width of the bias binding is kept even.

Step 6: Making the gussets

1. The gussets are made of wide bias strips. Cut two strips, each 5cm (2in) wide and approximately 38cm (15in) long.
2. Take strip, and with right sides together seam down the long side. Turn inside out. Press. Turn each end in 1cm (½in).
3. Double over the strip and stitch on the edge which has already been seamed (*see diagram 5a*). Make another strip in the same way.

Step 7: Attaching the gussets to the bag

With seam edge of the gusset facing inwards, ladder stitch folded edge to stitching line of the binding, starting at the top of the front of the bag, and working around to the top of the back of the bag. This gives a very neat finish. Attach the other gusset in the same way (*see diagram 5b*).

Step 8: Handle

Cut bias strips 2cm (¾in) wide. Join strips to make three lengths, each 72cm (30in). Make narrow rouleaux (bias-strip tubes) 5mm (¼in) by seaming on the wrong side and turning inside out. Plait (braid) rouleaux (bias-strip tubes) and attach to inside back of bag as handles. To neaten, place a small square of fabric over the join and hem in place.

Step 9: Fastening

1. Attach a round black bead to the bag front.
2. Work a buttonhole loop on the edge of the flap.

Step 10: Tassels

Make two simple tassels by wrapping threads around a card; slide off the thread; tie top bunch of threads, winding a thread around the bunch several times. Link these tops together with several threads and finish by wrapping thread around them. Loop this through the buttonhole loop. Cut ends of tassels.

Black Bag

Size: The bag measures approximately 17 × 13.5cm (6½ × 5¼in).

General description: The bag, which is envelope-shaped, is made in two fabrics. Black silk is used for the back and front of the bag, and black/red shot silk taffeta for the flap. The flap is smocked in red and black. The bag is lined in the same black silk and fastens with a snap fastener.

Alternative suggestions: The bag can be made in any colour and in one kind of fabric only, as long as it is firm and will hold the smocking. Silk is preferable, shot silk giving an added depth to the colours. The lining can be in a different colour. As the bag is small, oddments of fabric can be used.

Smocking stitches: Honeycomb stitch and cable stitch, using six strands of stranded cotton, were used.

System for preparing the smocking: A template from graph paper was made. The smocking is unusual in that it forms a semi-circle, the gathering being prepared in an unusual way.

Experience required: Those with experience will be able to follow the making of this bag.

Notes
● It is advisable to try out the whole flap on a spare piece of fabric first to see how the flap is constructed. The smocking does not take long, but the preparation has to be carefully followed and will only work with the given measurements.
● Instead of using a graph, a ruler and soft pencil or water-erasable pen may be used following the diagram carefully.
● A 1cm (½in) seam allowance is included.

MATERIALS

Fabric: 30 × 90cm (⅜ yd × 36in) plain black silk; 30 × 20cm (12 × 8in) silk shot taffeta for flap.

Needles: Crewel embroidery, No. 8, 9 or 10.

Thread for sewing: 1 reel (spool) black mercerised sewing cotton No. 50.

Thread for gathering: 1 reel (spool) mercerised sewing cotton No. 50 in a contrasting colour.

Thread for smocking: 1 skein red stranded cotton; 1 skein black stranded cotton.

Pelmet (drape valence) vilene or heavy vilene (pellon) for stiffening: 1 piece 50 × 20cm (18 × 9in).

Wadding (batting), synthetic, lightweight: 1 piece 50 × 20cm (19 × 9in).

Snap fastener: 1 large snap.

Usual workbox equipment plus graph paper or plain paper; stilleto or thick needle; powdered chalk or talcum powder; soft pencil or water-erasable pen and ruler.

GENERAL INSTRUCTIONS

1. Cut out patterns *(see diagram 1).*
2. Smock the flap *(see diagrams 2-4).*
3. Make up the bag *(see diagrams 5-7).*

CUTTING OUT THE PATTERN

1. Cut out black silk *(see diagram 1).*
2. Cut out vilene (pellon) stiffening. Use pattern for lining *(see diagram 1).* Cut off all seam allowances.
3. Cut out all wadding (batting). Use pattern for lining *(see diagram 1).* Cut off all seam allowances plus an extra fraction.
4. Cut out shot taffeta – 26.5 × 18cm (10½ × 7½in).

SMOCKING

Preparing the dots
1. For smocking the flap, make a template *(see page 37),* and follow diagram 2 very carefully. There are 28 dots across the strip and 11 rows.
2. Using the template, and working on the wrong side, mark the dots carefully with powdered chalk or talcum powder.

As an alternative, a ruler with a soft pencil or water-erasable pen may be used. Mark exactly.

Picking up the dots
Starting on the right with a firm knot, pick up the dots. It is essential to pick the dots up as a running stitch in the exact order as shown. Note that the last dot is on the seamline.

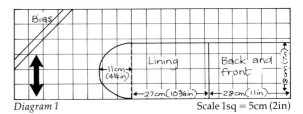

Diagram 1 Scale 1sq = 5cm (2in)

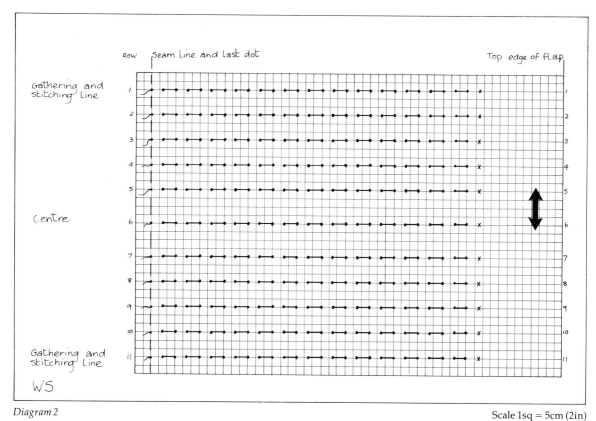

Diagram 2   Scale 1sq = 5cm (2in)

Pulling up the gathering threads

This is an unusual way to pull up the gathers as they are pulled to make a semi-circle.

1. Working on the wrong side, fold the flap in half and seam on seam line and on line of last dots *(see diagram 2)*.

2. Pull up the gathers, pulling row 6, centre, very tightly.

3. Pin flap on to a piece of firm fabric and fan into shape. There will be 14 folds either side of the seam, and the rows will now swing across in the order shown *(see diagram 3)*.

4. Tie off the gathering threads each side of the seam.

5. Work stem stitch on the wrong side along row 6, over the tight bunching in the centre *(see diagram 3)*.

6. The flap is now ready for smocking on the right side.

Working the smocking

1. See diagram 4 to see how the rows are now numbered ready for smocking. Follow the graph for smocking *(see diagram 5)*. Use six strands of stranded cotton. Note the position of the honeycomb rows and where they start to make the folds lie in the direction as shown in illustration facing page 128. Work around each row to the other side of the semi-circle, matching

the ends of the honeycomb rows. Keep flap in position as it is worked.

2. When smocking is finished, remove all gathering threads except the bottom row, rows 11 and 1. These are left in for the stitching line when making-up *(see diagrams 4-8)*.

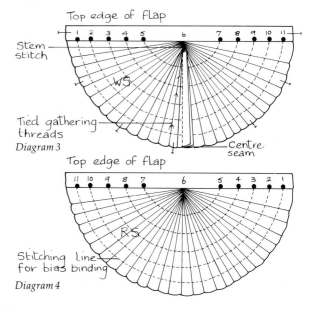

Diagram 3

Diagram 4

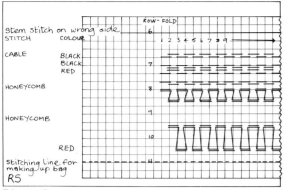

Diagram 5

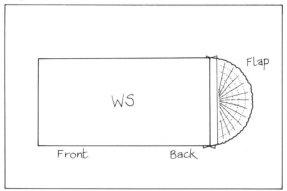

Diagram 6

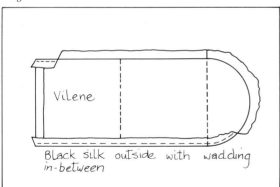

Diagram 7

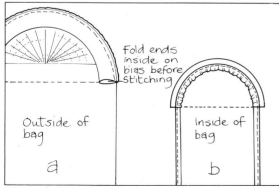

Diagram 8

MAKING-UP THE BAG

Step 1: Joining the flap to the bag back
1. As the flap is cut generously, adjust the top edge only, to the lining pattern.
2. With the right sides together seam flap to the bag back making a flat seam. Press *(see diagram 6).*

Step 2: Preparing the bag
1. Place outside of bag, right side downwards. Place wadding (batting) on top. Place vilene (pellon) on top of wadding (batting).
2. Fold over seam allowances of the outside of the bag, on to the vilene (pellon). Tack (baste) close to the edge, making sure that the folds on the flap form a flat pleat, an inverted pleat, at the honeycomb spots. Trim *(see diagram 7).*

Step 3: Binding the flap
1. Make a test piece of bias binding before proceeding. Cut bias strip to measure approximately 32 × 3.4cm wide (12½ × 1¼in).
2. Fold the strip lengthwise and fold ends of bias inside.
3. Place the bag with the inside facing upwards. Pin the bias to the flap with right sides and raw edges together. Tack (baste) close to the edge *(see diagrams 8a and 8b).*

Step 4: Lining the bag
1. Turn under seam allowances of lining to fit bag. Tack (baste) in place around the bag.
2. Adjust bias to fit flap and stitch the bias in place. Remove tackings (bastings). Hem bias on to underside of flap.
3. Slip stitch lining to the bag.

Step 5: Seaming the bag
Fold to envelope shape and ladder stitch side seams.

Step 6: Fastening the bag
Attach a snap fastener to the underside of the flap and bag front.

Other Forms of Smocking using English Smocking Techniques

Fabrics not requiring smocking dots

Some fabrics are so printed with a regular repetitive pattern that smocking dots are not required *(see Gingham Dress in illustration between pages 88 and 89).* The spot on spot and striped fabrics can also be used as a guide for gathering. Also some printed fabrics can be used in this way. In these printed fabrics gathering can be worked directly on to the fabric as a foundation for the smocking.

By picking up at certain points in the design one pattern will emerge, whereas, if picked up at another point in the design, a different pattern will emerge. Practise on a sample first to see which is preferred.

Any smocking stitch can be used on a fabric which has been gathered up.

Counterchange smocking

This form of smocking is worked directly on to striped, check or spot fabrics and as explained above no dot preparation or gathering is required. One stitch, surface honeycomb stitch, is worked using the pattern of the fabric for guidance *(see right).*

To work counterchange smocking using striped fabric of equal width, approximately 5mm (¼in) wide, work as follows:

1. No preparation is required as the surface honeycomb is worked by eye directly on to the fabric. However, to assist, pencil lines can be lightly marked at rows 2, 5, 8 for guidance *(see diagram 1).*

2. Using two strands of white stranded cotton, start on the righthand side of the dark stripe at position 1 on row 1. Work surface honeycomb stitch, approximately 5mm (¼in) deep, across the row.

3. Work the second row, starting on row 3, also in surface honeycomb stitch and the same depth, across the row.

4. The third row is started on row 4, leaving a space of approximately 1cm (½in).

5. Continue repeating surface honeycomb until the desired pattern is formed.

In this pattern as worked above, the white stripe is predominant in the 1cm (½in) space between the rows, whereas, if the pattern is started on the white stripe, the reverse will be the effect, and the blue stripe will be dominant.

Mock smocking

This form of smocking is worked on gingham of any size. It is simply and quickly worked by picking up corners of squares with honeycomb spots worked from right to left along a row. It is in the form of a back stitch and does not zig-zag as in honeycomb stitch. It

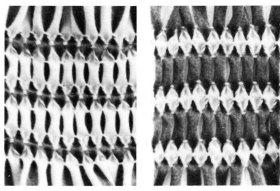

Two examples of counterchange smocking

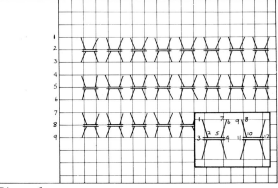

Diagram 1

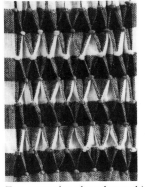

Two examples of mock smocking

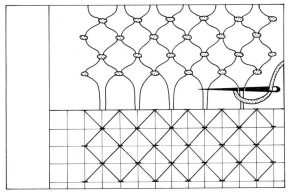

Diagram 2

does not use very much fabric and is slightly elastic. It can also be worked on the diagonal. In the sample *(see photographs above)*, several colours were used for smocking.

Smocked insertions

This is when a piece of smocking is inserted between two edges for decoration only *(see the Blue Dress in illustration facing page 113)*. Any type of smocking can be inserted to decorate a garment, an accessory or an item for the home. Sometimes a lining cut to the same size as the smocking, with the smocking mounted on to it, helps to give a neat finish.

Rich patterns from Central Europe

Smocking has been widely used on folk costume; in Czechoslovakia and Hungary the 'English' type of smocking was richly worked in bands close together to resemble weaving *(see page 30)*. The Black Belt *(see illustration facing page 128)* shows diamond stitch closely worked in rich colours.

PROJECT 13 *(See illustration between pages 88 and 89)*

Gingham Dress

Size: This dress fits a five-year-old child. The measurements are: chest 58cm (23in); finished length from neck edge at shoulder back 63cm (25in); and hem 6cm (2¾in). Instructions are also given for a smaller dress, to fit a three-year-old. The depth of the smocking in the smaller size is not so great. Instructions for the smaller size are given only if there is a variation from the larger size. The measurements for the small size are: chest 56cm (22in) and length 53cm (21in).

General description: This is a very classic style of dress for a growing girl. It is made in cotton gingham in dark blue and white check and is trimmed and smocked in white only. The dress, which opens down the back, has a deep band of smocking 10cm (4in) deep which decorates the top of the skirt front and joins a plain yoke. Self-check bias binding, together with a strip of folded white bias, edge the short puffed sleeves. Collars of double thickness in white are trimmed with self check bias binding. Tie belts, inserted in the side seams, tie at the back.

Alternative suggestions: The dress can be made in gingham of other sizes, but it would be necessary to make a sample first to see the effect. Also, plain fabric can be used, using the same design. Use smocking dot transfers size 9.5 × 9.5mm (⅜ × ⅜in) – Deightons size F. A smock-gathering machine can be used also but it would not be exactly to the given pattern, although near enough. Consider a cream cotton or silk smocked and trimmed in red; the yoke in a plain colour and the rest of the dress in a tiny floral fabric picking up the yoke colour for smocking; the dress in plain fabric with yoke and hems trimmed with stitched-down ribbon, and smocked in colours of the ribbons.

Smocking stitches: Two smocking stitches are used on the dress. Wave is worked forming a trellis pattern, as well as diamond stitch.

System for preparing smocking: As the squares of the check are a guide, the smocking is prepared by picking up dots at regular intervals. No other method of preparation is suitable for gingham.

Experience required: This is a traditional smocked dress for a small girl and can be attempted by anybody with some dressmaking experience. The preparation for the smocking is easy and the smocking itself is simple though very effective.

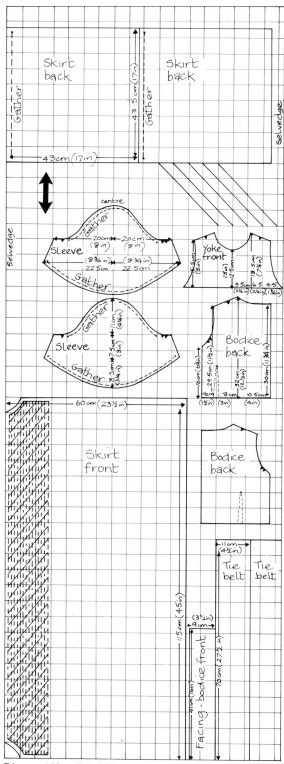

Diagram 1 90cm (36in) fabric Scale 1sq = 5cm (2in)

Pattern and layout for five-year-old child.

Note: For pattern for collar, see diagram 2

Notes

● The size of the gingham square is important. To work this dress exactly, squares 5mm (less than ¼in) are required. Other sizes of squares are also suitable but it would be necessary to work a sample piece first to see the effect of the smocking.

● When preparing for the smocking, use the check squares as a guide. On this dress, the dots are picked up on the white squares on the wrong side, thereby eliminating the white on the right side. Always work a trial piece to see which colour surfaces on the right side to make sure it is the one required.

● Do not use smocking dots or a smock-gathering machine.

● When tacking (basting) and stitching the dress, make sure that the checks meet. Therefore, when cutting out, a little extra can be allowed.

● A French seam may be used. As the sleeve edges have many thicknesses, some machines may have difficulty doing this.

● Check all measurements and adjust before cutting out.

MATERIALS

Dressmaker's Pattern Guide Paper ruled in 1cm (½in) and 5cm (2in) squares or similar. If this is not available use large size plain paper, ruled into the appropriate squares.

Fabric: 2.50 metres × 90cm (2¾ yds × 36in) *(see diagram 1)* or 2 metres × 115cm (2¼ yds × 45in) *(see diagram 2)* wide check cotton gingham (5mm/¼in squares).

● *For the small size:* 2.20 metres × 90cm (2½ yds × 36in) or 1.70 metres × 115cm (2 yds × 45in).

Fabric for collar and bias: 20 × 90cm (¼ yd × 36in) white cotton *(see diagram 3)*.

Needles: Crewel embroidery needles, No. 8, 9 or 10.

Thread for sewing: 1 reel (spool) mercerised sewing thread No. 40.

Thread for gathering: 1 reel (spool) mercerised sewing thread No. 40 in a contrasting colour.

Thread for smocking: 2 skeins white stranded embroidery cotton.

Buttons: 5 small white buttons for fastening.

Usual workbox equipment plus pencil, eraser and ruler.

GENERAL INSTRUCTIONS

1. Draft the pattern. A 2cm (¾in) seam allowance has been included in pattern *(see diagrams 1 or 2, 16 or 18)*.
2. Cut out the dress *(see diagrams 1 or 2, 16 or 18)*.

Note: Diagram 1 is for 90cm (36in) fabric; diagram 2 is for 115cm (45in) fabric. Use same pattern for the white collar and binding *(see diagram 3).*

● For the version for a three-year-old child follow diagrams 16-18 on pages 126-7.

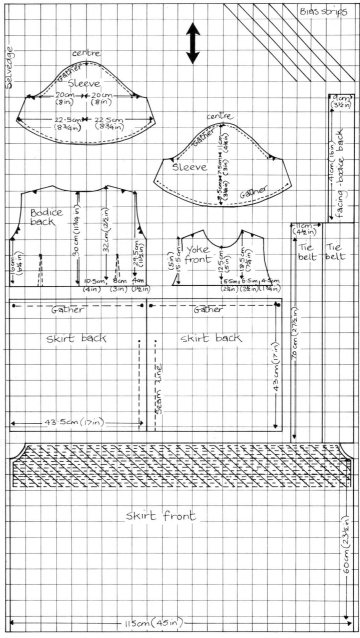

Diagram 2 115cm (45in) fabric Scale 1sq = 5cm (2in)

Pattern and layout for five-year-old child.

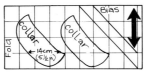

Diagram 3
Scale 1sq = 5cm (2in)

3. Cut out the collar in contrasting colour *(see diagram 3 or 17)*.
4. Smock the skirt *(see diagrams 4-5)*.
5. Make up the dress *(see diagrams 6-15)*.

PREPARATION

Drafting the pattern
1. Draft the following pattern pieces: sleeve; bodice back and yoke. The remainder of the pattern pieces are oblong and can be marked out on the fabric with pins or tailor's chalk *(see diagram 1 or 2, 16 or 18)*.
2. Draft pattern for collar *(see diagram 3 or 17)*.

Cutting out the dress and collar
1. Before cutting out, check measurements and adjust.
2. If the fabric is 90cm (36in) wide follow diagram 1 or 18 for the dress. If the fabric is 115cm (45in) wide follow diagram 2 or 16. Follow diagram 3 or 17 for collar and bias in contrasting colour.
3. As some of the pattern pieces are oblong they may be measured on to the fabric using pins, or marked with tailor's chalk.
4. Mark all seam allowances with tailor's chalk; mark notches; mark centres and darts.

SMOCKING

Preparing for smocking
1. Take skirt front and working on the wrong side on the seam line at top of skirt, pick up a dot in the centre of each white square *(see diagram 4)*.
2. Work fourteen rows of gathering, starting each row with a firm knot and starting on the right, stopping and starting just outside seam allowances at side seams *(see diagram 5)*.

● *For the small size:* Only ten rows of gathering are required. Row 1 will be the seam line and row 10 for gathering only.

Pulling up the gathering threads
Pull up to the width of yoke front less 2.5cm (1in). Tie off securely.

Working the smocking
1. Turn the gathering on to the front side. Having picked up white squares on the wrong side, the right side will show dark blue and pale blue stripes *(see diagram 5)*.
2. Work the smocking in three strands of stranded cotton in white, following the graph *(see diagram 5)*.
3. Starting between rows 2 and 3 work wave stitch up to between rows 1 and 2. Work across the whole front.

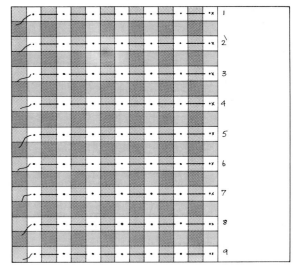

Diagram 4 Scale 1sq = 5cm (2in)

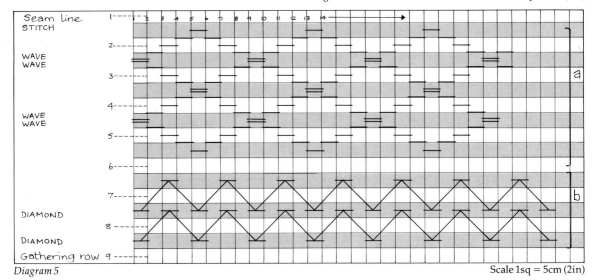

Diagram 5 Scale 1sq = 5cm (2in)

4. Starting between rows 2 and 3 and just below the row just worked, work wave in reverse, down to between rows 3 and 4. Work across the whole front.

5. Repeat these two rows following graph (*see diagram 5*).

6. Starting between rows 7 and 8 work diamond up to between rows 6 and 7.

7. Work another row of diamond starting between rows 8 and 9 and working up to between rows 7 and 8.

8. Repeat section A to complete the design.

9. Remove all gathering threads except the first row which is used for joining.

● *For the small size:* The smocking pattern consists of half A, then B, then half A (*see diagram 5*). Work as follows:

1. Start between rows 2 and 3 and work wave stitch across the whole top.

2. Start immediately below this worked row and work wave in reverse to form diamond shapes.

3. Starting between rows 5 and 6 work diamond stitch up to between rows 4 and 5 and continue across the row.

4. Work another row of diamond stitch starting between rows 6 and 7.

5. Repeat half section A, starting between rows 8 and 9.

MAKING-UP THE DRESS

Step 1: Joining skirt front to yoke

1. Cut across each corner of smocked skirt front, for armholes, approximately 1cm (½in) away from smocking. Do not cut near smocking (*see diagram 6*).

2. With right sides together pin yoke to shirt front, aligning first gathering thread on seam line of yoke. Tack (baste) and stitch carefully. This is an important seam and it must be straight.

3. Trim seam and zig-zag edges together, or whip by hand. Press seam upwards (*see diagram 7*).

Step 2: Joining skirt back to bodice back

1. Working on the wrong side, make small dart at waistline. Pin. Tack (baste) and stitch gradually to a point. Tie off. Press towards centre.

2. Gather skirt back on seam line. Make another gathering line 5mm (¼in) away inside the seam allowance.

3. Pull up to fit bodice back.

4. With right sides together, pin skirt back to bodice back, easing gathers on the skirt. Tack (baste) and stitch. Trim seam. Zig-zag edges or whip by hand. Press seam upwards (*see diagram 8*).

Step 3: Making tie-belts

1. Take tie-belt and with right sides together pin

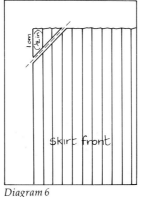

Diagram 6   *Diagram 7*

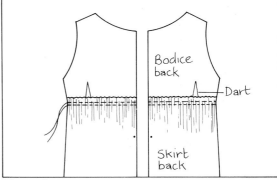

Diagram 8

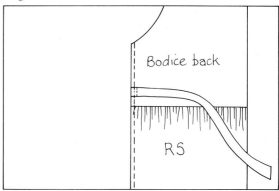

Diagram 9

along the length. Tack (baste). Stitch across end and along length. Trim.

2. Turn inside out. Tack (baste). Press well.

Step 4: Attaching tie-belts

● *Note:* If using French seams, the tie-belts will be attached after Step 10.

1. Working on the right side, place lower edge of tie-belt 2.5cm (1in) above seam line on back (*see diagram 9*).

2. Stitch on seam line. Stitch again.

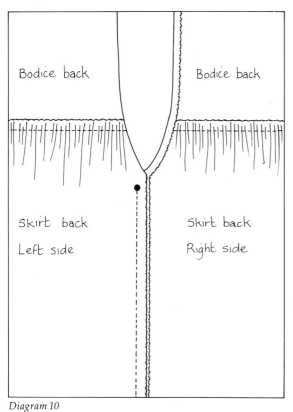

Bodice back   Bodice back

Skirt back   Skirt back
Left side   Right side

Diagram 10

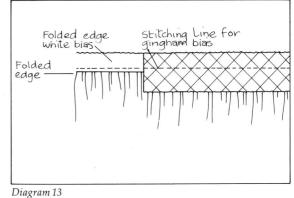

Folded edge
white bias   Stitching Line for
                  gingham bias
Folded
edge

Diagram 13

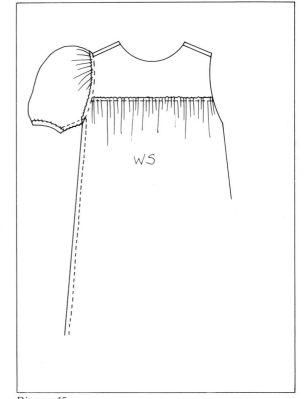

Yoke   Bodice
            back
                    Seam
        Sleeve

Diagram 14

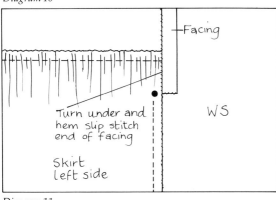

Facing

Turn under and
hem slip stitch
end of facing

Skirt
Left side

WS

Diagram 11

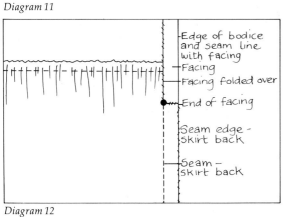

Edge of bodice
and seam line
with facing
Facing
Facing folded over
End of facing
Seam edge —
skirt back
Seam —
skirt back

Diagram 12

WS

Diagram 15

Step 5: Seaming skirt back

1. Allowing seam allowance of 3cm (1¼in), seam below large ● 10cm (4in) below waist seam on skirt backs *(see diagram 10)*.
● *For the small size:* Seam below large ● 9cm (3½in) below waist seam on skirt backs *(see diagram 10)*.
2. Zig-zag or whip by hand the righthand side of seam edging from bodice back neck to hem edge. Zig-zag or whip lefthand seam edge from large ● to hem edge *(see diagram 10)*.

Step 6: Attaching facing to back opening

1. Take bodice back, righthand side and with right sides together pin facing along opening edge, starting at neck edge and ending at large ● on skirt back. Tack (baste) and stitch.
2. Turn under edge of facing and hem on to seam line, on wrong side of bodice back. Slip stitch end of facing at skirt end *(see diagram 11)*.
3. Turn back doubled facing so that bodice opening edge is in line with skirt seam edge *(see diagram 12)*.

Step 7: Joining dress front to dress back

1. With right sides together, pin dress front and dress back at shoulder seam. Tack (baste) and stitch.
2. Trim seam. Press flat. Zig-zag edges or whip by hand. Press again. Alternatively use a French seam.

Step 8: Sleeve and sleeve trimming

1. Cut two bias strips in gingham fabric, each 26.5 × 3cm (10½ × 1¼in) for the sleeve edge.
2. Cut two bias strips in white fabric, each 26.5 × 3cm (10½ × 1¼in) for trimming.
3. Gather sleeve edge on seam line. Make another gathering line 5mm (¼in) away from this line and inside seam allowance. Pull up gathering to 26.5cm (10½in). Tie securely.
● *For the small size:* The bias strips for the sleeve edge and the trimming and the gathering should all measure 25.5cm (10in).
4. Fold over white bias strip lengthways. Press.
5. Place folded edge 2.5mm (⅛in) away from seam line with raw edges together *(see diagram 13)*. Tack (baste) in place.
6. Take gingham bias strip and with right sides together place on top of white bias.
7. Tack (baste) in place, allowing 2.5mm (⅛in) of doubled white bias edging to show when finished *(see cut-away section in diagram 13)*.
8. Trim seam allowance so that when the bias is folded over and hemmed on to the wrong side, the gingham bias will be approximately 5mm (¼in) wide.
9. Care needs to be taken with these trimmings to make sure the folded edge of the white bias is absolutely even.

Step 9: Joining sleeves to dress

1. Gather top edge of sleeve on seam line, from small ● to small ●. Make another gathering line 5mm (¼in) away and within seam allowance.
2. Pull up to fit armhole of dress, matching centre large ● on sleeve with shoulder seam. Match notches. With right sides together, pin, easing gathers. Tack (baste). Stitch on seam line. Stitch again. Trim edges to approximately 5mm (¼in) and zig-zag or whip by hand *(see diagram 14)*. Alternatively, a French seam may be used. Press seam towards sleeve.

Step 10: Joining sides and sleeves of dress

1. With right sides together, pin sides of dress, continuing over sleeve underarm seam *(see diagram 15)*. Tack (baste) and stitch. Trim seam. Press flat. Zig-zag each edge of seam, or whip by hand. The ties will also be stitched in. Alternatively, a French seam may be used, but the ties should be removed and applied by hand after the seaming.
2. Neaten inside of sleeve underarm seam by catching the sides of the seam to the bias.

Step 11: The collar

1. Take two collars and with wrong sides together tack (baste) in place.
2. Cut gingham bias strips 3cm (1¼in) wide.
3. With right sides together pin bias on to collar, raw edges together. Tack (baste) on seam line 1cm (½in) from edge. Stitch, easing the bias. Do not stretch the bias as it will not lie flat.
4. Trim raw edges to 5mm (¼in) and hem bias over on to wrong side on to stitching line. The bias must lie flat.

Step 12: Joining the collars to the dress

1. Overlap backs and mark centre back 1cm (½in) in from edge on left side, and 2cm (¾in) on right side which has folded facing.
2. Trim neck edge by 5mm (¼in).
3. With wrong side of collar to right side of yoke, pin collars around neck edge to centre back where collars must meet without overlapping. Test for size. Adjust neckline seam allowance if necessary. Tack (baste) in place.
4. Using a strip of white bias, pin this on top of the collars at seam line, raw edges together. Tack (Baste) all around neck edge. Stitch. Trim neck edge, snipping carefully so that when the bias is hemmed on to the yoke, it lies flat.
5. Hem bias on to wrong side of yoke and bodice back using tiny stitches. Press flat.

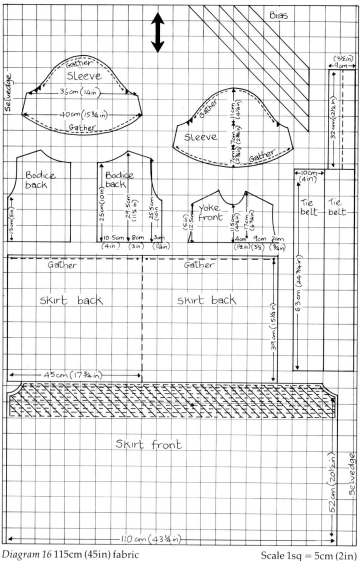

Note: Diagrams 16 and 18 are pattern and layout for the Gingham Dress for a three-year-old child. Diagram 16 is for 115cm (45in) fabric; diagram 18 is for 90cm (36in) fabric. Use the same pattern for the white collar and binding *(diagram 17)*.

Diagram 16 115cm (45in) fabric   Scale 1sq = 5cm (2in)

Pattern and layout for three-year-old child

Diagram 17

Step 13: Finishing the dress

1. Sew four buttons, evenly spaced, on to bodice back above waistline, right side. Sew one button on skirt below waist seam.

2. Working in white cotton, make buttonholes on left side.

3. Adjust hem. Turn under 5mm (¼in) on to wrong side. Stitch 2.5mm (⅛in) away from edge. Slip stitch hem in place, using white cotton and placing stitches in white squares.

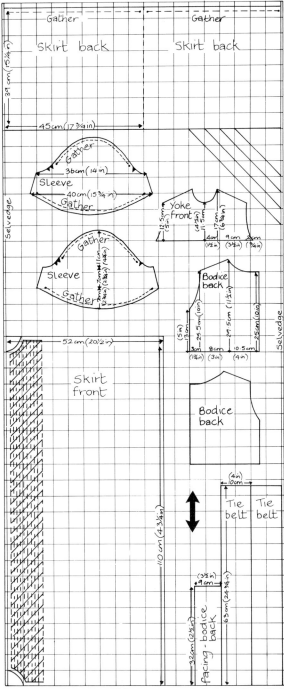

Diagram 18 90cm (36in) fabric   Scale 1sq = 5cm (2in)

Pattern and layout for three-year-old child

Blue Dress

Size: This dress will fit size 87cm (34in) bust.

General description: This very attractive dress, which is made in medium-weight blue cotton, is trimmed with a multi-coloured, narrow-striped fine cotton lawn. The bodice joins the skirt at the waistline and opens down the back with a zip. The four-piece flared skirt is gathered at the waistline. The neckline is finished with a frill and insets of interesting smocking, worked in the five bright colours of the stripe, trim the bodice.

The full sleeves, which are threequarter length, are drawn in with elastic leaving a deep frill (ruffle) which is trimmed with narrow bias binding.

Three rouleau (bias-strip) streamers fall from either side of the waistline where a small rouleau (bias-strip) bow finishes the trimming.

Alternative suggestions: This dress can be made in any fabric but cotton or silk are very suitable. It can be made in any plain colour combination to suit individual requirements, as long as the stripes for the smocking are very narrow.

Consider: a white dress with a narrow stripe in white with another colour; a dress in a plain colour throughout with the smocking insets worked in several colours and using ribbon picking up the same colours for the streamers and the sleeve edge.

Smocking stitches: Two forms of honeycomb stitch are used and these are worked diagonally changing the colours to form an interesting pattern. Stem stitch is also used.

System for preparing smocking: The preparation is simple as the inset is very narrow. Guided by the stripes, the dots are picked up by eye.

Experience required: Those who have experience in smocking will find this quick to work, but special attention is required to follow the sequence of colours in the smocking graph. The dress might appear complicated but is in fact easy to make.

Notes
- Work a small piece following the smocking graph until familiar with the colour sequence.
- The dress is easy to launder, preferably by hand. Press on the wrong side up to the smocking insets, avoiding the smocking.

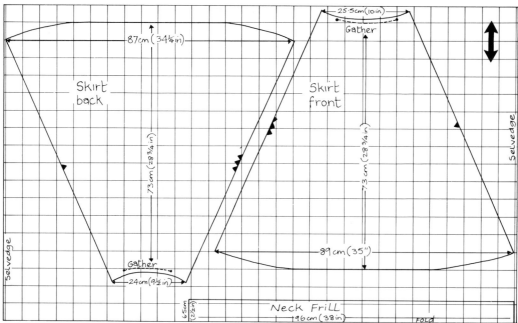

Diagram 1a

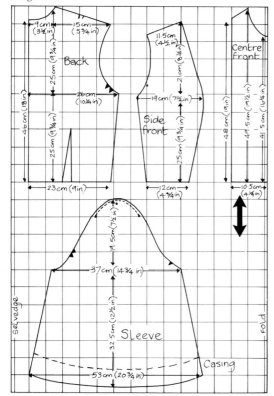

Diagram 1b

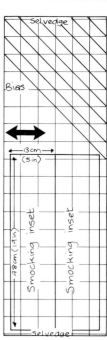

Diagram 2

Opposite Project 15: Black Belt *(see page 132)*; Project 16: Suede Belt *(see page 134)*; and Project 17: Blue Belt *(see page 136)*

MATERIALS

Dressmaker's Pattern Guide Paper ruled in 1cm (½in) and 5cm (2in) squares or similar. If this is not available use large size plain paper, ruled into the appropriate squares.

Fabric for dress: 3 metres × 150cm (3⅜ yds × 60in) wide medium weight cotton in mid-blue.

Fabric for trimming: 30 × 90cm (⅜ yd × 36in) wide fine multi-striped cotton lawn.

Needles: Crewel embroidery needles, No. 8, 9 or 10.

Thread for sewing: 2 reels (spools) mid-blue mercerised sewing thread No. 40.

Thread for smocking: Stranded cotton in blue, red, pink, jade, yellow or to match stripes. Only part of a skein is required.

Elastic: 1 metre (1 yard) 5mm (¼in) wide.

Zip: 54cm (22in) to match fabric.

Usual workbox equipment plus tailor's chalk; soft pencil; bodkin; pencil, eraser and ruler.

GENERAL INSTRUCTIONS

1. Draft pattern for dress. A 2cm (¾in) seam allowance has been included in pattern *(see diagrams 1a and 1b)*.
2. Cut out dress *(see diagrams 1a-1b)*.
3. Cut out striped fabric *(see diagram 2)*.
4. Smock the insets *(see diagrams 3-4)*.
5. Make up the dress *(see diagrams 5-6)*.

PREPARATION

Drafting the pattern
1. Draft the patterns *(see diagrams 1a-1b)*.
2. Make adjustments if necessary.

Cutting out the dress
1. Note the layout for cutting out the pattern pieces for the dress.
2. Place the skirt pieces and neck frill as in layout *(see diagram 1a)*. Note how the fabric is folded double.
3. Place the other pattern pieces as in layout *(see diagram 1b)*.
4. Mark seam allowances, notches, darts and centres. Tack (baste) a line for sleeve casing 6.5cm (2¼in) in from sleeve edge.

Cutting out the striped fabric
1. Cut out two smocking insets, each 13 × 48cm (5 × 19in) *(see diagram 2)*.

Opposite Project 18: Volendam Blouse *(see page 141)*

2. Cut bias strips for trimming the sleeves and for the rouleau streamers 2.5cm (1in) wide from the remainder of the fabric. Keep the longest strips for the streamers.

SMOCKING

Preparing the stripes
1. Note that the stripes lie horizontally across the strip to be smocked and are used as a guide.
2. Only the first row requires to be marked, as the remainder are picked up by eye.
3. Working on the wrong side, mark 10 dots spaced 1cm (½in) apart with a soft pencil. Leave seam allowances by starting 2cm (¾in) down and 2cm (¾in) in from the side *(see diagram 3)*.

Picking up the dots
1. Working on the wrong side and with a firm knot, start on the right and pick up 10 dots across the first row *(see diagram 3)*.
2. Continue picking up dots by eye, each row 1cm (½in) apart, down the strip.

Pulling up the gathering threads
Pull up the gathering threads to approximately 1cm (½in).

Working the smocking
1. Follow diagram 0. Note that apart from stem stitch on the first two rows, two forms of honeycomb are worked. The zig-zag starting on row 3 is worked in ordinary spot honeycomb. The triangular spaces which are created on either side of the zig-zag are filled in with honeycomb stitches worked with the thread showing (not to be confused with surface honeycomb) and not concealed as in spot honeycomb, though working in the same manner.
2. Start by working stem stitch on rows 1 and 2.
3. Starting on row 3 work honeycomb diagonally to row 10. Turn work upside down and work in the other

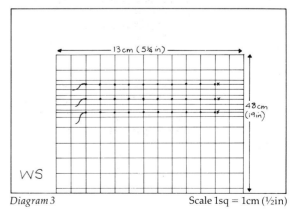

Diagram 3   Scale 1sq = 1cm (½in)

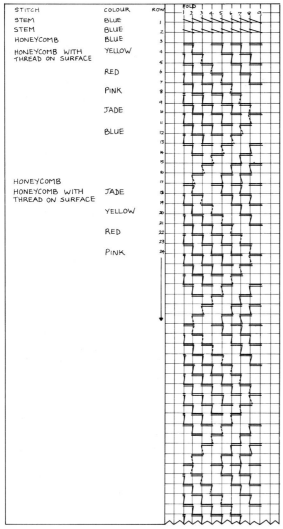

STITCH	COLOUR	ROW
STEM	BLUE	1
STEM	BLUE	2
HONEYCOMB	BLUE	3
HONEYCOMB WITH THREAD ON SURFACE	YELLOW	4
		5
	RED	6
		7
	PINK	8
		9
	JADE	10
		11
	BLUE	12
		13
		14
		15
		16
HONEYCOMB		17
HONEYCOMB WITH THREAD ON SURFACE	JADE	18
		19
	YELLOW	20
		21
	RED	22
		23
	PINK	24

Diagram 4

7. For working the second inset, note that the pattern is reversed by starting the original zig-zag line in the opposite corner and then working the colour triangles from right to left.

8. When both insets are completed, remove the gathering threads.

MAKING-UP THE DRESS

Step 1: Bodice back
Pin, tack (baste) and stitch darts on bodice back. Press darts towards centre.

Step 2: Bodice front
1. Take one smocked inset and with right sides together pin one side of the inset to side front. Pin the other side of the inset to centre front side seam.
2. Repeat for other inset.
3. Tack (baste) both insets in position, making sure that the edge of the smocking is close to the seamline. Stitch. Trim edges. Zig-zag edges (*see diagram 5*).
4. Press seams towards centre of inset, avoiding smocking (*see diagram 5*).

Step 3: Joining bodice back to bodice front
Place bodice front and bodice backs together. Pin at side seams and shoulders. Tack (baste) and stitch. Trim. Zig-zag edges. Press seams flat.

Step 4: Sleeve
1. Gather by hand or by machine, at top of sleeve on seamline and between small ●. Make another gathering line approximately 5mm (¼in) in from this line.
2. Seam sleeves. Trim. Zig-zag edges. Press seam flat.
3. To make casing for elastic, cut bias strip from dress fabric, approximately 55cm (21in) long by 2.5cm (1in) wide.
4. On both long edges of the bias strip turn under 5mm (¼in). Press.
5. Working on the wrong side, pin this strip over tacking (basting) line for casing near edge of sleeve. Turn under ends of bias to abut for an opening. Tack (baste) bias in place. Stitch on both sides of the bias.
6. Measure arm for elastic adding 2.5cm (1in). Using small safety pin thread elastic into casing. Overlap elastic and stitch securely.

Step 5: Binding the sleeve
1. Take bias of striped fabric and with right sides together, pin bias to sleeve edge. Join bias. Tack (baste) bias around sleeve edge. Stitch. Remove tacking (basting) and trim.
2. Turn over on to wrong side and with tiny stitches hem in place. If possible, the finished width of the bias should be approximately 5mm (¼in).

direction to row 17. Turn work and work diagonally to 24. Repeat this zig-zag line down the inset.
4. In the triangular areas created on the left of the inset, work diagonally in the following way, changing colours (*see diagram 4*). Work honeycomb stitch diagonally with the thread showing:
Starting on row 4 work diagonally to row 10.
Starting on row 6 work diagonally to row 11.
Starting on row 8 work diagonally to row 12.
Starting on row 10 work diagonally to row 13.
Starting on row 12 work diagonally to row 14.
5. Now change colour sequence and following diagram 4 repeat to the end of the inset.
6. In the small triangular areas created on the right, work honeycomb in one colour only with the thread showing (*see diagram 4*).

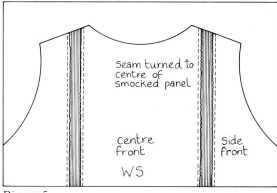

Diagram 5

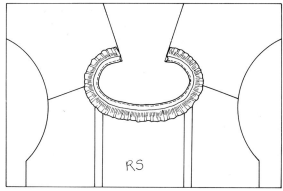

Diagram 6

Step 6: Joining sleeve to bodice

1. With right sides together pin sleeve into armhole of bodice, matching centre of sleeve to shoulder seam of bodice, and underarm seam of sleeve to side seam of the bodice.
2. Pull up gathers of sleeves and adjust. Tack (baste) and stitch. Trim seam to approximately 5mm (¼in). Zig-zag edges together. Press seam towards sleeve.

Step 7: Skirt

1. Gather by hand or machine, on seamline of upper edge of skirt pieces between ●. Gather a second line 5mm (¼in) above seamline.
2. Pin, tack (baste) and stitch centre front seam. Zig-zag edges. Press flat.
3. Pin, tack (baste) and stitch centre back seam from ■ to hem. Trim. Zig-zag edges. Press flat.
4. Pin, tack (baste) and stitch side seams joining front to back. Zig-zag edges. Press flat.

Step 8: Joining skirt to bodice

1. Pin skirt to bodice, matching centre line of bodice to centre seam of skirt and matching side seams of bodice to side seams of skirt.
2. Pull up gathers on skirt to fit bodice. Pin. Tack (baste) and stitch. Trim. Zig-zag edges together.

Step 9: Neck frill

1. With wrong sides together, fold neck frill in half lengthways. Press.
2. Neaten short edges by turning in 5mm (¼in) and slip stitch.
3. Gather by hand or machine along seam line. Make another gathering line approximately 5mm (¼in) away. Pull up to fit neckline.

Step 10: Joining neck frill to bodice

1. Turn under seam allowance on centre of bodice back. Press.
2. With right sides together, pin neck frill to bodice around neckline, easing the gathers to fit. Tack (baste).
3. Cut bias strip 4cm (1½in) wide the length of the neckline plus 2cm (¾in) in blue fabric.
4. Pin this on tacked (basted) seam line, turning over 1cm (½in) at each end. Tack (baste), carefully easing the bias on to the frill. Do not stretch the bias. If it is too tight it will not lie flat. Stitch. Trim *(see diagram 6)*.
5. Trim bias edge. Turn under 5mm (¼in) on to wrong side and stitch bias edge 2.5mm (⅛in) in from edge.
6. Pin and tack (baste) bias flat around the neckline.
7. With matching thread, carefully slip stitch bias in place, making sure that the bias lies flat and that the stitches are hardly noticeable on the right side.

Step 11: Inserting zip

1. Turn under 2cm (¾in) seam allowance on bodice back and skirt back. Press.
2. Pin zip in place. Tack (baste), making sure the turned-in edges meet at the centre of the zip.
3. Stitch 5mm (¼in) each side of centre and across end using a zipper foot or by hand using a back stitch.

Step 12: The hem

1. Try on dress. Adjust length.
2. Turn under 5mm (¼in) on to wrong side. Stitch approximately 2.5mm (⅛in) in from edge. Press.
3. Pin and tack (baste) in position, easing fullness where required. If necessary use gathering stitches to ease fullness. Slip stitch in place. Press well.

Step 13: Making rouleau (bias-strip) streamers

1. Using cut bias strips prepare six streamers in pairs. Each pair should be approximately 44cm (18in), 54cm (22in) and 60cm (24in) long.
2. With right sides together, fold strip lengthways and stitch 5mm (¼in) in from the folded edge to form rouleau (bias strip) 5mm (¼in) wide.
3. Slip stitch both ends of rouleau (bias strip). Press.
4. Attach three streamers, one of each length at waistline.
5. Using rouleau (bias strip) make two small bows and stitch over where the streamers are attached.

Black Belt

Size: To fit waist 64cm (25in). The belt is 6cm (2¼in) wide.

General description: The belt is made of black poplin which is smocked in one long strip with the folds placed vertically. It is stiffened, and edged with a bias binding in the same material. Soft ties fasten the belt. The smocking is worked in scarlet, deep pink, purple, light bright pink and deep orange with added metallic thread.

Alternative suggestions: This most attractive belt can be made in any fine fabric, such as fine lawn or silk and in any colour to suit individual taste.

Work a sampler first to test the balance of the colours chosen. Suggestions for colours on black are: turquoise, blues and greens; white, creams and tan; tones of any one colour; tones of blues and violet with jade on a grey background.

Bronze metallic thread which can be threaded in a needle would look attractive worked on brown or a dark colour.

A narrower belt can be made using either the two top and two bottom lines, or the middle section only. The belt can be made in any length.

Smocking stitches: Diamond stitch, worked very closely, was used throughout. It was worked with six strands of stranded cotton.

System for preparing smocking: A template was made from graph paper and the dots transferred with powdered chalk.

Experience required: This project is suitable for anyone who is familiar with smocking. It is an interesting, though large piece to work.

Notes
● It is advisable to work a sampler first to test for tension and colour.
● A bought transfer can be used, or a smock-gathering machine for preparing the smocking.
● A 1cm (½in) seam allowance is included.
● As the fabric is washable, it is possible to launder the belt. Wash carefully in warm soapy water. Rinse well and dry flat on a towel pulling the belt into shape. Only the ties will need pressing. Steam press the smocked part if required.

MATERIALS

Fabric: 60 × 115cm (¾ yd × 45in) black cotton poplin or polycotton.

Needles: Crewel embroidery No. 8.

Thread for sewing: 1 reel (spool) black mercerised sewing thread No. 50.

Thread for gathering: 1 reel (spool) white mercerised sewing cotton No. 40.

Thread for smocking: 2 skeins each of stranded cotton in the following colours: scarlet, deep pink, purple, light bright pink, deep orange. If available 1 reel (spool) metallic embroidery thread.

Pelmet (drape valence) vilene or heavy vilene (pellon): 70 × 8cm (27 × 3¼in).

Smocking dots: 2 sheets size 8mm × 1cm (⁵⁄₁₆ × ⅜in) – Deighton's size A.

Usual workbox equipment plus graph paper or plain paper; powdered chalk or talcum powder; stilleto or thick needle.

GENERAL INSTRUCTIONS

1. Cut out the belt. A 1cm (½in) seam allowance has been included in pattern *(see diagram 1)*.
2. Smock the belt *(see diagrams 2-3)*.
3. Make up the belt *(see diagram 4)*.

PREPARATION

Cutting out the belt
1. Make a pattern for the tie only. No pattern is required for the rest of the belt as the pieces are straight.
2. Cut out pieces *(see diagram 1)*. The bias strips should not have a join.
3. Mark 1cm (½in) seam allowances on all pieces.

Joining the belt pieces
With right sides together, join the three belt pieces, making one long strip. Trim seams to 5mm (¼in) and press flat. If using a smock-gathering machine, do not join the pieces together yet.

SMOCKING

Preparing the dots
Place strip wrong side upwards. If using the template method, see page 37. Mark seven rows of dots *(see diagram 2 for exact sizing)*. Align the first row of dots on the seamline, and transfer, using powdered chalk or talcum powder. If using smocking-dot transfer, pin one prepared sheet at a time, press and quickly remove. As it is a long stretch across the belt, be careful

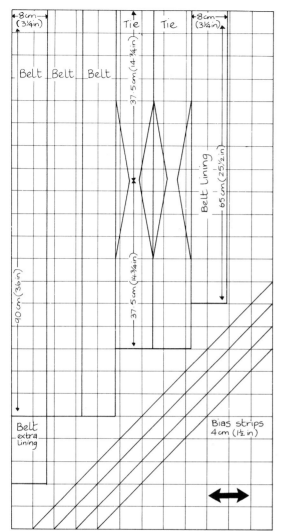

Diagram 1

to match the rows exactly.

If using a smock-gathering machine, do not seam the belt pieces first as they will not go through the machine. Put each piece through the machine and then join as above.

Picking up the dots
Starting on the wrong side, pick up the dots right across the whole length of the belt. Start with a strong knot on the righthand side. Leave the ends free.

Pulling up the gathering threads
Pull up the gathers to approximately 64cm (25in), making sure that a needle can be inserted between the gathers. Tie off very securely.

Working the smocking
1. Work on the right side. Using six strands of stranded cotton in the needle, work diamond stitch right across the belt, using the diagram for colour reference. The rows are worked very closely together (*see diagram 3*).
2. When the smocking has been completed, use metallic thread, if available, to work diamond stitch between rows 1 and 2; rows 3 and 4; rows 7 and 8; and rows 9 and 10.
3. Do not remove gathering threads. The smocked piece is now ready for making-up.

MAKING-UP THE BELT

Step 1: Lining the belt
1. Cut the vilene (pellon) to the size of the smocked piece.
2. Cut the belt lining the same size. This will need joining (*see diagram 1*).

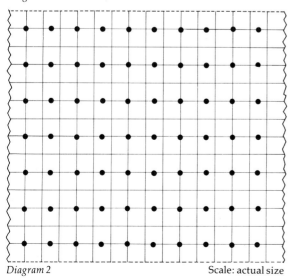

Diagram 2   Scale: actual size

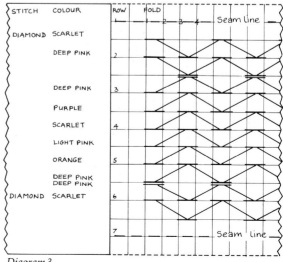

Diagram 3

3. With the wrong side of the belt lining facing the vilene (pellon), tack (baste) both together.

4. Place together belt lining, then vilene (pellon), then smocked piece with the right side uppermost. Pin and tack (baste) all together.

Step 2: Binding the belt

1. Take the bias strip. Double over the strip lengthwise and press.

2. Place doubled bias on first row of gathering threads of smocked piece, right sides together and raw edges together. Pin. Tack (baste), making sure that the line is straight. Machine through all thicknesses carefully *(see diagram 4a)*.

3. Trim all the thicknesses back to 5mm (¼in). Turn folded edge of bias on to the back of the belt and very neatly hem to the stitching line.

4. Repeat 1, 2 and 3 for the bottom edge of the belt.

5. Remove all gathering threads.

Step 3: Preparing the ties

1. Place two ties, right sides together. Pin. Tack (baste). Stitch on seam line, leaving the wide side open. Turn inside out. Press. Make other tie in the same way *(see diagram 4b)*.

2. On the wide end, turn the seam allowance under to the inside and press.

Step 4: Joining the ties to the belt

1. Place smocked belt inside the tie and very neatly hem the tie to the belt *(see diagram 4c)*.

2. Repeat at the other end.

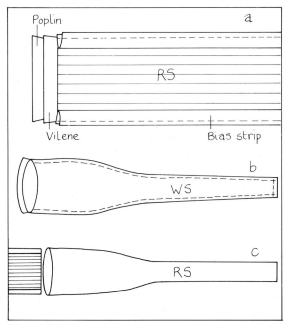

Diagram 4

Suede Belt

Size: To fit waist 66cm (26in). The belt is approximately 9cm (3½in) wide.

General description: This belt is made in soft grey suede, the vertical folds of the smocking leaving a frill at the edge. An adhesive is used to finish the edges. It is simply smocked in three colours. The belt is stiffened and it is fastened with large hooks and eyes.

Alternative suggestions: Though this belt is made in natural suede, synthetic suede can be tried. Make a sample piece before buying the fabric. Other fabrics can be used, but they would need different methods for turnings etc. As the idea is very simple, an experiment can be carried out in a suitable furnishing fabric or fine needlecord.

The length of the belt can easily be extended, allowing approximately 5cm (2in) extra suede for each 2cm (¾in) of extra width.

Smocking stitches: Only one stitch, cable stitch, is used. Black, jade and grey are used for smocking, using six strands of thread.

System for preparing smocking: A template from graph paper was made and the dots transferred by a felt-tipped pen.

Experience required: A knowledge of working on suede or leather is advisable.

Notes
- Care is necessary when selecting a skin to see that it is of an even texture and thickness, as thin areas pull together more closely and will give an uneven appearance.
- Various tests should be carried out before cutting out the belt, which will have joins. Test machining seams to see if the suede will sew, if not the seams can be stitched by hand, using an ordinary sewing needle.
- Test the adhesive to see that it is suitable. It should be a clear adhesive.
- Test marking the dots with a felt pen or ball point pen.
- Plain paper can be used instead of graph paper. The dots can be marked using a ruler and a felt-tipped pen or a ball point pen.
- Work a trial piece of smocking using an ordinary sewing needle. Do not use a leather needle as it will tear a fine suede skin.

- To stop the suede slipping whilst sewing, Sellotape (adhesive tape) can be temporarily used on the wrong side of the suede.
- A 1cm (½in) seam allowance is included.
- This suede belt is not suitable for laundering or dry cleaning. If there are marks, try lightly rubbing with very fine sandpaper.

MATERIALS

Skin: A piece of suede approximately 64 × 44cm (25 × 17in) to make a strip 168 × 11cm (66 × 4¼in).

Needles: Crewel embroidery, No. 8.

Thread for sewing: 1 reel (spool) mercerised sewing thread No. 50 to match skin.

Thread for gathering: 1 reel (spool) mercerised sewing thread No. 50 in a contrasting colour.

Thread for smocking: 1 skein each of grey, black and jade in stranded cotton.

Petersham ribbon or stiffening (crisp ribbon with a pronounced weft rib, resembling heavy gros grain ribbon): 70 × 4.5cm (27 × 1¾in).

Clear adhesive: Copydex or any adhesive which is suitable for suede and dries clear.

Hooks and eyes: 2 large hooks and eyes for fastening.

Usual workbox equipment plus graph paper or plain paper; stilleto or thick needle; felt-tipped pen or ball point pen; ruler; Sellotape (adhesive tape) and newspaper for pattern.

GENERAL INSTRUCTIONS

1. Make the pattern.
2. Cut out the belt from the skin.
3. Prepare the edges of the belt.
4. Smock the belt *(see diagram 1)*.
5. Finish the belt *(see diagram 3)*.

PREPARATION

Making the pattern
From newspaper, cut out a pattern 168 × 11cm (66 × 4¼in). This includes a 1cm (½in) seam allowance.

Cutting out the belt
1. Using the pattern above as a guide, cut out the skin, allowing extra for joining.
2. Working on the wrong side and using matching colour, seam the strips together starting on the fold line on the top edge, and stopping at the fold line of the bottom edge *(see diagram 1)*. Tie seams off securely. Trim seams back to 5mm (¼in).

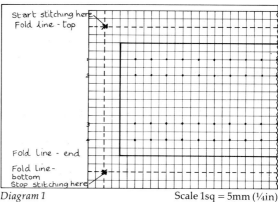

Diagram 1   Scale 1sq = 5mm (¼in)

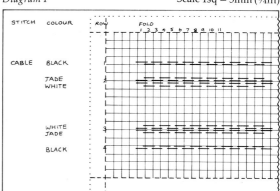

Diagram 2

Preparing the edges of the belt
1. Turn edges on to wrong side at fold line top, and fold line bottom. Glue these in place.

Preparing the dots
1. The dots are 1cm (½in) apart and the same between rows 1 and 2, and rows 3 and 4.
2. Either make a template from graph paper or plain paper *(see page 37)* or use a ruler and felt-tipped pen or ball point pen. Mark dots according to diagram *(see diagram 1)*.

Picking up the dots
Working on the wrong side, and using a contrasting coloured thread, pick up each dot across each row, starting on the right with a firm knot.

Pulling up the gathering threads
1. Pull up the threads so that the whole belt measures approximately 66cm (26in).
2. Tie off securely.

Working the smocking
1. Only one stitch, cable stitch, is used. The belt is simply worked *(see diagram 2)*. Make sure that the cables worked on rows 2 and 3 form straight folds.
2. Remove gathering threads.

MAKING-UP THE BELT

1. Turn face down and place petersham (stiffening) centrally. Hem top and bottom edges to wrong side of belt *(see diagram 3a)*.
2. Fold ends back and glue *(see diagram 3b)*.
3. Bring ends edge to edge *(see diagram 3c)*. Sew two hooks and eyes to the petersham (stiffening).

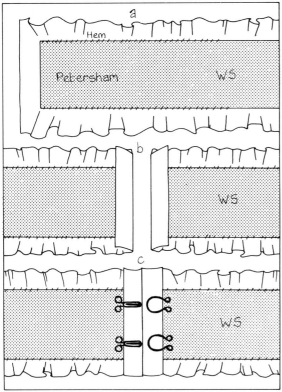

Diagram 3

Blue Belt

Size: To fit waist 66cm (26in). The belt is approximately 4cm (1½in) wide. The ties are 22cm (8½in) long.

General description: The belt is made from striped cotton jersey fabric which is cut on the bias. The folds forming the smocking run horizontally and are lightly smocked at intervals. The belt is stiffened and lined. It is fastened with two ties.

Alternative suggestions: A similar belt can be made from dressweight cotton or silk which is soft and drapes well.

It can be made in any colour to match an outfit. Suggestions might be: making a belt in the same fabric as the dress and smocking it in a contrasting colour; using a black evening fabric with a lurex stripe.

A wider belt could be made in a multi-coloured stripe, or it could be made longer.

Smocking stitches: Working vertically, one stitch, stem stitch, is used throughout. The smocking, at intervals on the front of the belt, is simply worked in stem stitch. To hold the folds in position, the belt is smocked on the reverse side, also in stem stitch.

System for preparing smocking: A template was made from graph paper and the dots transferred on to the fabric with powdered chalk.

Experience required: For anyone accustomed to working with bias strips, this is a very simple belt to make.

Notes
• The belt can be made in any length and the ties can be longer.
• The belt was made in lightweight cotton jersey. Heavier jersey might present problems when making-up. A sampler should be made to try out the suitability of the fabric and threads. When using striped fabric on the bias, be very careful when joining, to match the stripes accurately.
• Dots may be marked on the wrong side of the fabric using a ruler and a soft pencil or water-erasable pen.
• Note that when preparing and working the smocking the belt is worked vertically.
• A 1.5cm (¾in) seam allowance is included.
• The belt can be laundered by hand. Dry flat on a towel and pat into position while damp.

MATERIALS

Fabric: 50 × 115cm (½ yd × 45in) wide lightweight cotton jersey.

Needles: Crewel embroidery, No. 8, 9 or 10.

Thread for sewing: 1 reel (spool) mercerised sewing thread No. 50 in matching colour.

Thread for gathering: 1 reel (spool) mercerised sewing thread No. 50 in a contrasting colour.

Thread for smocking: 1 skein stranded cotton in matching colour to fabric.

Petersham (stiffening): 70 × 4cm (27 × 1½in) in suitable colour.

Usual workbox equipment plus graph or plain paper; powdered chalk or talcum powder; stiletto or thick needle; soft pencil or water-erasable pen and ruler.

GENERAL INSTRUCTIONS

1. Cut out the belt. A 1.5cm (¾in) seam allowance has been included in pattern *(see diagram 1)*.
2. Smock the belt *(see diagrams 2-4)*.
3. Make up the belt *(see diagram 5)*.

PREPARATION

Cutting out the belt
Cut out the belt *(see diagram 1)*.

Seaming the bias strips
1. Seam the strips of bias, carefully matching stripes *(see page 49)*. Trim seams. Press flat.
2. Cut this strip to measure approximately 74cm (29in) long by 17cm (6¾in) wide.

SMOCKING

Preparing the dots
1. Make a template from graph paper or plain paper, marking the dots 1.3cm (½in) apart, and the rows 1.3cm (½in) apart *(see diagram 3)*. Pierce the dots with a stiletto or thick needle.
2. Working on the wrong side, mark centre of belt *(see diagram 3)*. Place graph on to the belt so that the vertical single line of dots is positioned over the single vertical line as in diagram 2 matching A's, B's etc.
3. Mark the dots by rubbing chalk or talcum powder through the holes.
4. If using a ruler with a soft pencil or water-erasable pen, follow diagrams 2 and 3.

Picking up the dots
1. Place the belt in a vertical position.

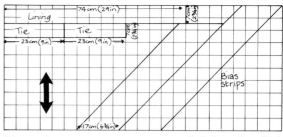

Diagram 1 Scale 1sq = 5cm (2in)

Note: As the belt is worked in a vertical position, diagrams 2-4 are shown vertically.

Diagram 2

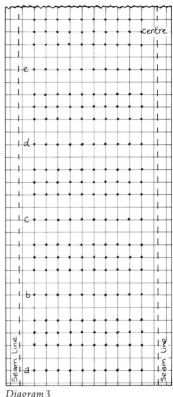

Diagram 3

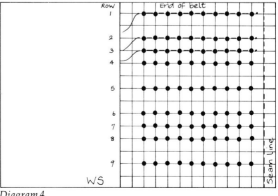

Diagram 4

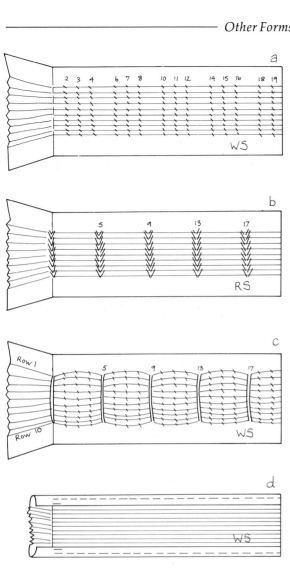

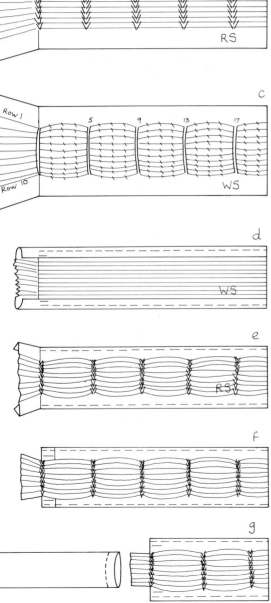

Diagram 5

2. Working on the wrong side, pick up each dot across each row. There are only 10 dots to each row. It may help to pick up rows 1 and 5 etc. in a different colour, as these rows are for the smocking on the right side (*see diagram 4*).

Pulling up the gathering threads
Pull up all the threads and tie off securely. Note that this will make 10 folds on the wrong side and 9 folds on the right side.

Working the smocking
1. Working on the wrong side with a matching thread, either sewing thread or one strand of stranded cotton, work stem stitch across each fold on rows 2, 3, 4; 6, 7, 8; etc. along the entire length of the belt (*see diagram 5a*).
2. Working on the right side, smock the front of the belt, using three strands of stranded cotton, on rows 1, 5, 9 etc. with two rows of stem stitch (*see diagram 5b*). Work stem stitch by working the first row with the thread under the needle, and the second row close to it, with the thread above the needle. This gives a 'mock chain' stitch.
3. Working on the wrong side, pull folds 1 and 10 together to give a slight scallop to the effect on the front (*see diagram 5c*).
4. Take out gathering threads.

MAKING-UP THE BELT

Step 1: Adding the stiffening
1. Place belt, wrong side upwards. Place petersham (stiffening) centrally on top. Turn over seam allowance on top and bottom edges and tack (baste) in place. The petersham (stiffening) should end on the last smocking line (*see diagrams 5d and 5e*).
2. Turn under seam allowance on ends and tack (baste) in place, leaving central bunch of gathers free (*see diagram 5f*).

Step 2: Lining the belt
Turn under seam allowance on lining. With the belt wrong side upwards, place lining on top. Trim corners to neaten. Pin. Tack (baste). Slip stitch in place all around the belt. Take out tackings (bastings).

Step 3: Adding the ties
1. On the wrong side, fold the tie lengthwise and pin and tack (baste) in position. Stitch across the end and down the side. Remove tacking (basting). Turn inside out and press. Make second tie.
2. Attach ties to each end of the belt by turning under the seam allowance and slip stitching on to the bunch of folds (*see diagram 5g*).

6

Other Types of Decorative Smocking

On a Tightly-gathered Foundation

SMOCKED PATTERN DARNING

In this technique, which is seen in Europe and in Mexico, but not in Britain, this form of smocking is worked on a tightly-gathered foundation in which the gathering threads are left in. A pattern is then darned with running stitches of varying lengths, according to the pattern, across the tightly-gathered folds. The pattern can be worked in one colour or several colours depending upon the design. This form of smocking is not elastic.

The following samples (*see photographs page 140 and diagrams 1-3*) were worked on a white self-stripe cotton fabric, each stripe 2.5mm (⅛in) apart, using black Perle No. 5 for the darning. (Mediumweight cotton fabrics are suitable for this work.)

To do smocked pattern darning, work as follows:
1. Cut fabric for a sample, approximately 23cm (9in) square, and whip or turn under edges.
2. On the wrong side, mark lines 1cm (½in) apart, using a ruler and soft pencil. The patterns are not deep, so several different designs can be worked on the same sample.

Gathering the fabric

Work on the wrong side with strong thread which matches the background fabric. Start with a firm knot or two small stitches at the top of a fold, and go under 2.5mm (⅛in) and over 7.5mm (⅜in) across the sample, leaving a border approximately 2.5cm (1in) either side of the sample. Leave thread hanging at the end of each row (*see right*). Always allow an extra row either side of a pattern as this helps to keep the pattern even. Although these samples were gathered every 1cm (½in), traditionally they are gathered every 2.5mm (⅛in) or less.

Right Preparing fabric for smocked pattern darning

Pulling up the gathering threads

Working on the wrong side of the fabric, pull up the gathering threads as tightly as possible to form the folds. Pull on the ends of the threads in order to straighten the folds.

Straightening the folds

It is important to make sure that the folds are straight. To do this, pin a side edge of the fabric to the side of a piece of graph paper or a sheet of paper with a straight edge. Release threads slightly, approximately every 5mm (¼in). Pin other edge of fabric to paper, making sure the sides are parallel.

Fastening off the gathering threads

1. Still working on the wrong side, fasten each row by working tiny stitches on the top of the nearest fold.

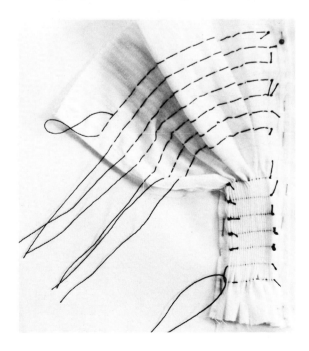

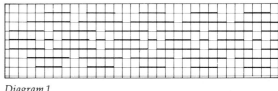

Diagram 1

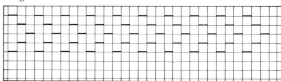

Diagram 2

Left Two examples of smocked pattern darning *(see diagrams 1 and 2 above)*

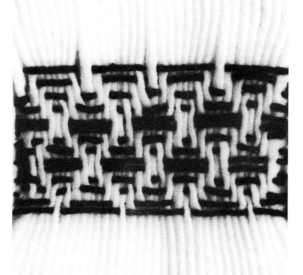

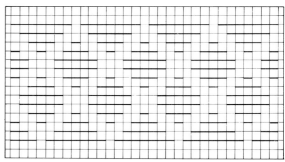

Diagram 3

Left Another example of smocked pattern darning *(see diagram 3 above)*

2. Stroke folds in place with a blunt needle, so that they are evenly placed across the fabric.
3. Remove fabric from paper. Turn sample on to right side and it is now ready for darning.

Working smocked pattern darning
1. Work a darning stitch, following the graph pattern, by stitching through some folds, and going over others. When stitching through a fold, pick up only a few threads down from the top of each fold.
2. Start each row at the same side. Work, fasten off and cut thread before starting next row. An alternative way is to work one row, then fasten thread at end, but do not cut it off; turn work upside down and continue working until the thread finishes at the nearest end. Do not join in the middle of the pattern. The distance

between each row of darning varies according to the pattern, but usually the rows are very close together.

3. It is easier to complete one stitch at a time, rather than take up two or more stitches on the needle, as is usually done in ordinary darning.

It is interesting to note that in Mexico, the fabric was prepared by working a gathering thread at the top of the work and another at the bottom of the work *(see page 32).* The fabric was then dampened and the gathering threads pulled up tightly and pulled into shape while drying. This helped to set the gathers for the remaining gathering rows which were worked less than 2.5mm (⅛in) apart.

Smocked pattern darning with beads

Mexican examples show exotic use of smocked pattern darning incorporating beads. In these pieces the beads, which lie between the folds, form the colourful pattern *(see page 32).*

SATIN STITCH ON FOLDS

This is worked in various countries in Europe and was used on the Volendam Blouse *(see illustration facing page 129).* Instructions for working this type of smocking are given with the project.

From the Balearic Isles there is an apron in The Embroiderers' Guild Collection *(see page 28)* which shows an interesting use of satin stitch. The apron is made of ribbed fabric rather like a coarse needlecord. On the top part of the apron satin stitch is worked down the vertical stripes in alternating colours of pink and gold. The apron is then further decorated with superimposed motifs of needleweaving.

OTHER DECORATIONS ON TIGHT GATHERS

An Italian shirt of the seventeenth century (in the Victoria and Albert Museum, London) *(see page 27)* shows an interesting use of satin stitch over a tightly-gathered foundation. The foundation is worked with gathering threads approximately 2.5mm (⅛in) apart, and over this flowers are worked in satin stitch which goes through to the wrong side.

Another example of stitchery on a tightly-gathered foundation is to be seen on aprons from the Biano do Castelo area of Portugal where chain-stitch embroidery decorates the tight gathers.

PROJECT 18 *(See illustration facing page 129)*

Volendam Blouse

Size: To fit bust size 90cm (36in); length from shoulder back neck seam to bottom edge: 66cm (26in); finished smocked wrist measurement 19.5cm (7¾in).

General description: This blouse has been inspired by the traditional 'Bontje' or apron worn on weekdays in Volendam in Holland. There is another form of dress for Sundays.

This traditional apron is made from multi-coloured striped cotton fabric which is sold especially for the purpose in Volendam. The apron is worn long, about 1 metre (1 yard) in length; the width of the fabric, which is 1.20 metres (47in), being smocked at the waist in a form of smocking traditionally worked in this town. The apron is tied around the waist and finishes in the front with a bow of white ribbon. On larger women, the bow is tied at the back.

The blouse has been made in traditional fabric bought in Volendam, and smocked in the traditional way by Joppa Valk of Amsterdam. It is plain at the front and at the back with vertical stripes. The sleeves, also with vertical stripes, are long and full and are set into a square armhole. The neck finishes with a high-standing collar. The sleeves are decorated at the wrists with rich smocking worked in traditional colours of red, yellow, green, white and black.

The blouse opens down the front with a concealed opening fastened with four removable tabs which are also decorated in this type of smocking from Volendam. It can be worn loose over a skirt or trousers. It can also be worn with a belt picking up one of the colours or tucked into a skirt.

Alternative suggestions: This blouse can be made in any plain-coloured fabric as well as certain striped fabrics. The smocking is very rich, and therefore the stripes should not be too striking otherwise they will detract from the smocking. Consider: any plain-coloured fabric smocked in tones of one colour and with the darkest colour outlining the diamond. Work the remaining tones towards the centre. For evening wear, consider adding a bead in the centre of the design and edging the cuff with the same beads.

Many exciting patterns can be worked following the design theme in this piece of smocking. Use graph paper to plan your design for a geometrical effect, or work freely for an exciting creative effect.

Smocking stitches: This is an unusual way to smock which is explained in the text.

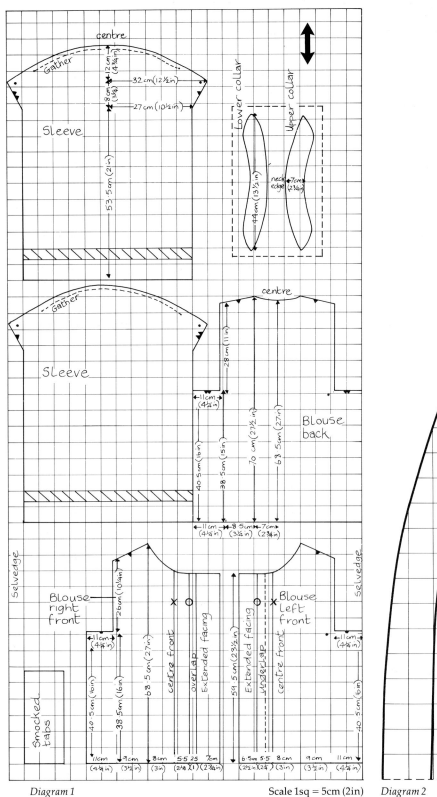

Diagram 1

Scale 1sq = 5cm (2in)

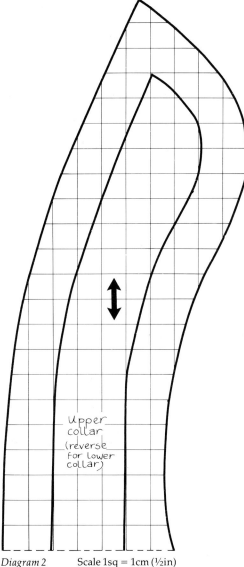

Diagram 2

Scale 1sq = 1cm (½in)

System for preparing smocking: A foundation of gathering threads is worked. These threads are left in. As this is an unusual way to prepare smocking, see the text for detailed explanation.

Experience required: Those familiar with embroidery would enjoy working this unusual form of smocking. For constructing the blouse, dressmaking experience is necessary.

Notes

● The gathering must be worked as specified. If using striped fabric, a sample must be worked to see the effect. The smocking is very dense and covers the area completely; it is not elastic, therefore a sample is required to estimate the wrist measurement.
● If coton à broder thread is not available, stranded embroidery cotton using three threads can be used. Adjust the number of strands to the effect required. The stitches must lie evenly and must not be too thick.
● Pattern pieces for the bodice fronts are named as worn on the person. For following directions for concealed closing of bodice front, practise on the paper pattern or fold a small piece of paper to help as a guide.
● The collar must fit well. It is advisable to make a sample collar before cutting out the fabric, or leave the cutting out of the collar until this stage is reached.

MATERIALS

Dressmaker's Pattern Guide Paper ruled in 1cm (½in) and 5cm (2in) squares or similar. If this is not available use large size plain paper, ruled into the appropriate squares.

Fabric: Traditional Volendam width: 2.25 metres × 120cm (2½ yds × 47in); or 3.20 metres × 90cm (3½ yds × 36in) or 2.40 metres × 115cm (2¾ yds × 45in) striped cotton.

Interfacing: 45 × 10cm (18 × 4in).

Needles: Crewel embroidery needles, No. 8, 9 or 10.

Thread for sewing: 2 reels (spools) white or to match mercerised sewing thread.

Thread for gathering: 1 reel (spool) white or to match mercerised sewing thread.

Thread for smocking: Coton à broder No. 16, one skein each in black, white, red, yellow, green or alternatives. If not available, stranded embroidery cotton can be used.

Snap fasteners: 7 small snaps.

Buttons: 10 small shirt-type buttons.

Usual workbox equipment plus soft pencil, eraser and ruler.

GENERAL INSTRUCTIONS

1. Draft pattern. A 2cm (¾in) seam allowance has been included in pattern (*see diagram 1*).
2. Cut out blouse (*see diagram 1*).
3. Smock sleeves and tabs (*see diagrams 3-5*).
4. Make up the blouse (*see diagrams 6-10*).

PREPARATION

Drafting the pattern

Draft the following pattern pieces: blouse right front; blouse left front (these are not the same size); blouse back; sleeve; and collar.

Cutting out the blouse

1. Before cutting out check your measurements against pattern pieces and adjust if necessary.
2. Cut out pattern pieces (*see diagram 1*). Use diagram 2 as a template for the collar pieces, reversing for the other half of the collar.
3. Mark all seams, notches, and gathering lines. Tack (baste) all details on both bodice fronts. It is important to mark them accurately.

SMOCKING

THE SLEEVE

Preparing the sleeve

Zig-zag around all edges of the sleeve.

Gathering the sleeve

1. Prepare gathering by using same sewing thread as for making-up the garment. The thread must match the fabric. Work on the right side as follows:
2. Measure 10cm (4in) up from wrist edge and lightly mark a line with a soft pencil from seam edge to seam edge. The remainder of the rows can be judged by eye with just an occasional mark.
3. Start on the righthand side with a firm knot, just inside seam allowance, and work over 3mm (⅛in) and under 4mm (¼in) to the end of the row. Leave end of thread. Work a total of seven rows, 5mm (¼in) apart. Do not pull up (*see diagram 3*).

Hemming the wrist edge

Turn under 3.5cm (1½in) on to wrong side and blind stitch to wrong side just below gathering line. Press.

Pulling up the gathering threads

1. Pull up threads and check the number of folds on the right side. There should be 73 for the pattern. Adjust at this stage. The gathers should pull up to approximately 18cm (7in).

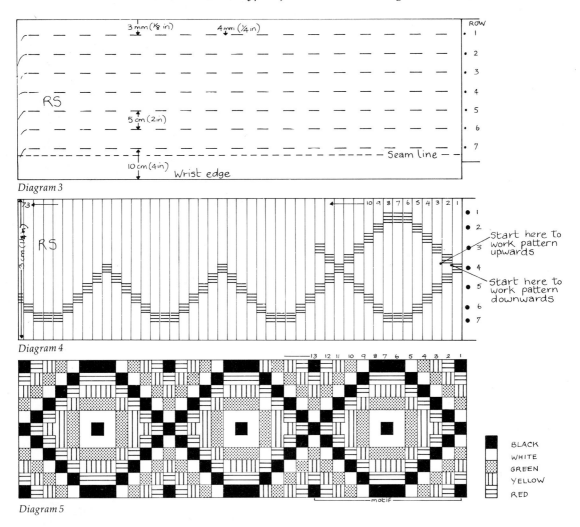

Diagram 3

Diagram 4

Diagram 5

BLACK
WHITE
GREEN
YELLOW
RED

2. Tie gathering threads in pairs. Tie securely as they are left in permanently. The work is now ready for smocking.

Working the smocking
This is an unusual form of smocking. The stitch is worked like a satin stitch in blocks of 4 stitches on each fold, and is worked right through the fabric. It does not decorate just the top of the fold. The stitches have to be worked evenly and without showing the background fabric. This form of smocking is not elastic.

The smocking is worked from right to left. Do not turn the work. The motif, which measures 3cm (1¼in) across when finished, is repeated six times for the wrist which will stretch slightly to approximately 19.5cm (8¾in).

In this pattern work the black diamond pattern first by working the bottom 'wave' first. Then come back

and work the top 'wave'. This must be accurately worked otherwise the pattern will not fit.

Working the pattern
1. Start to work the bottom 'wave' of the pattern, in black, in a single thread of coton à broder, by commencing on the right side of the pattern *(see diagram 4)*.
2. Bring the needle out just above row 4, which is the middle, on the left side of fold 1 *(see diagram 4)*.
3. Pull thread through, leaving 7cm (3in) on the wrong side. Later this is threaded for finishing off.
4. Take needle across fold 1, and going through to the back, come out at left of fold 1 just below the first stitch. Make a total of three stitches in this way, working the stitches close together. The fourth stitch is worked across the fold and taken through to the

Opposite Project 19: Mexican Blouse *(see page 149)*

back, then emerging at the lefthand side of fold 2. Continue working the pattern in blocks, working one colour at a time *(see diagrams 4 and 5)*.

5. Finish each starting thread, which has been left at the back, before starting a new thread.

6. Remember to leave gathering threads in. They should be covered by the smocking.

THE TABS

Preparing the smocking for the tabs
1. The tabs are worked, one under the other, on a strip of fabric.
2. Cut a strip 12cm (4¾in) wide and 28cm (11in) deep *(see diagram 1)*.

Gathering the tabs
1. Working on the right side of the fabric, start 2cm (¾in) down from top edge and 2cm (¾in) in from right edge. Work seven rows of gathering, each row 5mm (¼in) apart. Gather over 3mm (⅛in) and under 4mm (¼in). Note that this is not the same spacing as on the sleeve.
2. Check on the right side that there are thirteen folds for each tab.
3. The second tab starts 4cm (1½in) under the first tab. Gather tabs 3 and 4 in the same way.
4. Pull up all tabs.

Pulling up the gathering threads
Pull up the gathering threads to 3cm (1¼in) in width.

Working the smocking
The smocking is worked in exactly the same way as for sleeve except that only one motif per tab is required *(see diagram 5)*. Work all four tabs.

MAKING-UP THE BLOUSE

Step 1: Joining the shoulders
With right sides together, pin bodice front right and bodice front left to bodice back at shoulders. Tack (baste) and stitch. Press flat. Trim. Zig-zag edges.

Step 2: Joining sleeve to bodice
1. Stitch gathering line on seam line at top of sleeve. Stitch another line 5mm (¼in) away and within seam allowance.
2. Join the top of the sleeve to the bodice armhole by placing right sides together. Match shoulder seam on bodice to centre of sleeve. Match large ● on bodice with large ● on sleeve. Note that these large ●s are at the corner of the seam allowances for both edges. Ease

Opposite Project 20: Ribbon Waistcoat *(see page 155)*

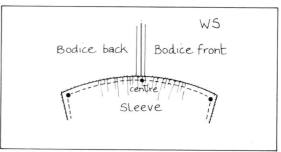

Diagram 6

gathers around sleeve. Pin. Tack (baste). Stitch together from large ● and around sleeve top to large ● on other side of sleeve *(see diagram 6)*.
3. On bodice front and bodice back, carefully snip seam allowance to near large ● at corner. These are important corners and care must be taken.
4. Continue armhole seam from large ● to edge *(see diagram 6)*.
5. Trim. Zig-zag edges together. Press flat towards bodice.
6. Turn blouse on to right side and top stitch approximately 2.5mm (⅛in) away from seam line. Make sure the corner is neat and well defined *(see diagram 7a)*.
7. With right sides together, pin sleeve together, starting 2cm (¾in) above smocking and continue down sides of bodice. Tack (baste) and stitch. Trim. Zig-zag edges. Press flat.

Step 3: Hemming edge of blouse
Turn under 2.5cm (1in) at the bottom edge of the blouse. Zig-zag edges. Blind stitch in place. Press.

Step 4: Bodice – left front
1. Fold the extended facing on tacked (basted) line to the right side of fabric.
2. At neck edge, stitch on seam line from centre of underlap, the dotted line on pattern layout *(see diagram 1)* to folded edge *(see diagram 7b)*. Tie thread ends securely.

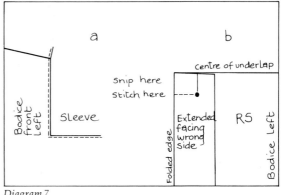

Diagram 7

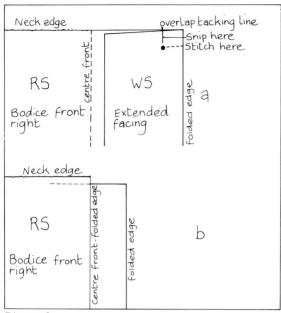

Diagram 8

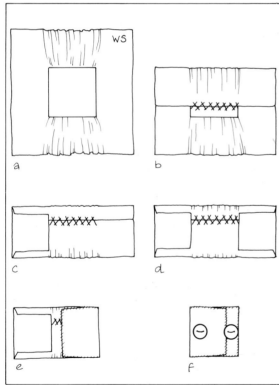

Diagram 9

3. Carefully snip seam allowance at underlap centre and turn extended facing to the wrong side *(see diagram 7b)*. This forms the concealed closing.

4. Working on the right side of the blouse (outside), fold at centre front tacking (basting) line (**x**) and fold over to underlap tacking (basting) line (**o**). Tack (baste) in place.

5. Zig-zag edges of facing. Press.

Step 5: Bodice – right front

1. Fold extended facing, tacked (basted) line, to the right side of the fabric.

2. At neck edge, stitch on seam line from folded edge of extended facing to overlap tacking (basting) line (**o**) *(see diagram 8a)*. Tie threads securely.

3. Carefully snip on seam allowance at overlap tacking (basting) line *(see diagram 8a)*, and turn extended facing to the wrong side. This forms the concealed closing *(see diagram 8b)*.

4. Fold on centre front tacking (basting) line (**x**) and bring across to overlap tacking (basting) line (**o**). Tack (baste) in place.

5. On the inside place raw edge of the facing to pleat edge and zig-zag all edges together. To do this, trim back the seam so that the overlap is flat. Press.

Step 6: The collar

1. Cut out interfacing, using the collar pattern without seam allowance.

2. Place interfacing to wrong side of upper collar. Tack (baste) together.

3. Pin upper collar to under collar, right sides together. Tack (baste). Stitch on outside edge of collar from the interfacing side. Trim.

4. Turn collar inside out. Tack (baste) outside edges.

5. With right sides together, pin upper collar to neck edge, from centre front to centre front. Tack (baste) on seam line. Stitch, being careful not to stitch the underlap on bodice left front. Trim. Press seam towards collar.

6. Turn under seam allowance and hem to stitching line.

7. With upper collar facing upwards top stitch approximately 2.5mm (⅛in) away from the edge of the collar.

Step 7: Finishing the tabs

1. Cut each tab from the strip.

2. Press around edges of smocking. Do not press smocking *(see diagram 9a)*.

3. Working on the wrong side, fold over top edge and stitch with small herringbone stitches *(see diagram 9b)*.

4. Fold over bottom edge and stitch with small herringbone stitches *(see diagram 9c)*.

5. Cut away surplus fabric *(see diagram 9d)*.

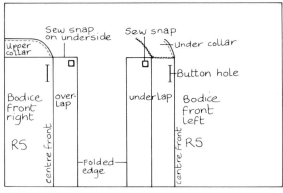

Diagram 10

6. Fold righthand side of fabric over and hem in place.
7. Fold lefthand side of fabric over and hem *(see diagram 9e)*.
8. Attach small flat shirt buttons to the back *(see diagram 9f)*.

Step 8: Finishing the blouse opening
1. Place the overlap over the underlap so that the centre fronts meet.
2. Sew snap fasteners to folded edge of bodice front right, on the inside, and to bodice front left, on the outside *(see diagram 10)*.
3. Work four pairs of buttonholes, one on each side of the bodice, to fit buttons on tabs, spacing them approximately 13cm (5in) apart.
4. Close blouse and fasten with snap fasteners; place tabs in position, and button them through the button-holes.

Step 9: Finishing the sleeve opening
1. Turn back seam allowance on to wrong side at opening of sleeve so that it edges the smocking.
2. Stitch a small hem by hand.
3. Sew a button on to the wrong side of the smocking, midway.
4. Work a buttonhole loop on the edge so that the sleeve fastens to show the smocking in a continuous pattern.

On Pleated Fabric

Instead of gathering a fabric to control the fullness, pleating is another technique to use. As pleating gives a flat surface, it lends itself to further forms of decoration.

In Britain a form of pleating called 'laid pleat work' was worked on children's clothes. In this form of decoration, the pleats which were approximately 5mm (¼in) wide, were individually tacked (basted) in place. A foundation was then made with running stitches, using a thread to match the background, and working under and over the pleats. These were worked in rows approximately 5mm (¼in) apart and were worked in a basket pattern by starting one row with the thread over the first pleat, and the next row under the first pleat, and working with the pleats, not against the pleats. After this preparation, a coloured thread was used to whip in and out of the foundation stitches to form a pattern.

Pleating is decorated in another way in Mexico. The Mexican Blouse *(see illustration facing page 144)* was inspired by blouses from that country. In this garment, chain, satin and herringbone stitches are used to decorate a trailing design which holds the pleats in place.

Children's dresses in The Embroiderers' Guild Collection, which were worked in Europe, show interesting embroidered decorative pleats. The dresses are cut in one piece from shoulder to hem and where the pleating covers the yoke, this part is decorated with attractive embroidery.

On folk costume in Europe, where the fullness of the garment is pleated, mainly on skirts and blouses, pleating is decorated in a similar way.

The skirt of the folk costume in certain parts of Czechoslovakia is pleated around the waist. Over this pleating, down to about the hips, a rich pattern of flowers, leaves and scrolls is embroidered. The skirt is usually dark blue and the embroidery is worked in very bright colours, using chain, buttonhole and satin stitches. In other parts of Czechoslovakia, as well as other forms of decoration, the pleated part of the skirt is plainly finished by simply holding the pleats in place by hemming, and the rich embroidered decoration is then placed at the hem.

In the Far East, costume for the peasants, as well as for the rich, uses pleats to control fullness.

A skirt from the Shuan Miao tribe of North Yunan in China, collected in 1949, and a skirt of 1966 from the Blue Meo Hill tribe, Thailand, have the same form of decoration on pleats *(see photograph on page 148)*. To work this unusual decorative detail for holding pleats in place, work as follows *(see diagrams 1 and 2, page 148)*.

Detail of a skirt of 1966 from the Blue Meo Hill tribe, Thailand

1. Use plain cotton fabric for a sample approximately 15cm (6in) deep and any length. Using a pencil or water-erasable pen, mark dots every 5mm (¼in) across the fabric. Fold over to make pleats 5mm (¼in) wide. Tack (baste) in place at top and bottom of pleats. Press.

2. Mark a line across the pleats as a guide for working.

3. Turn pleats so that they face the worker, and work so that the stitches are worked away from the worker, instead of forwards.

4. Come up at position 1 *(see diagram 1)*, which is slightly to the left of the line and take needle forward across the first pleat and under the second pleat, emerging at position 2 on the line.

5. Take the needle across to position 3 which is slightly to the right of the line, and under to position 4, going through the thickness of the pleat and pulling tightly. Repeat across the sampler.

6. Check that the stitch is correct, by turning on to the wrong side to see that the last stitch is through the pleat, and is parallel to the pleats.

In Chinese costume the silk skirts of ladies' costume are richly pleated using a form of tacking (basting) stitch which is worked on the wrong side to hold the pleats in place. With movement the pleats part and show a honeycombing effect, which varies according to the way the stitches were placed. Usually the stitches are closer together at the top of the skirt. Other forms of pleating are used, and as the silk is very fine, exquisite effects are obtained by holding very narrow pleats down with running stitches, making a wavy pattern across the pleats. Others show pleats edged with fine bias and then held in place with bullion knots (bouillion stitches). In other examples many colours are joined together before pleating and tacking (basting).

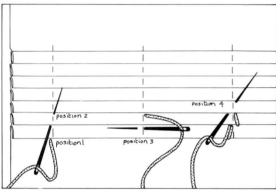

position 4

position 2

position 1   *position 3*

Diagram 1

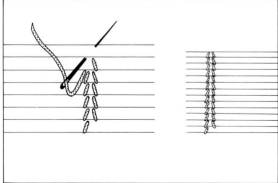

Diagram 2

PROJECT 19 (*See illustration facing page 144*)

Mexican Blouse

Size: To fit bust sizes 83-90cm (32-36in). As the blouse is very full, it will fit several sizes.

General description: This attractive sleeveless blouse is made in white cotton fabric and is simply cut with a full bodice which draws into the waistline with a threaded ribbon. There is a short back opening at the neck. The feature of the garment is the pleated frill at the neckline which is decorated with embroidery to hold the pleats in place. The colours of the embroidery are orange, red, cerise pink, dark maroon and intense blue, colours which are reminiscent of Mexico from where the inspiration for the blouse came.

Alternative suggestions: This form of decoration can be very exciting used on any plain-coloured fabric and worked in colours to suit individual taste. A fabric which presses into pleats must be used and therefore natural fibres, such as cotton, silk or fine linen are suitable. Synthetics are not recommended.

Any design which has a trailing effect is suitable. The design must be continuous as the embroidery holds the pleats in position. Consider using stitch combinations on a machine, or working free machine embroidery. Very narrow ribbons combined with machine or hand stitchery can be most effective. For evening, beads can be incorporated.

System for preparing smocked pleats: This is a form of decoration on pleats, the foundation for which has to be pleated by hand and tacked in place before decorating with embroidery.

Embroidery stitches: Chain, satin, herringbone stitches as well as French knots are used.

Experience required: The preparation of the pleated foundation takes time, though no more than ordinary gathering, and has to be carefully done before working the embroidery. Little dressmaking experience is required as it is a very simple pattern.

Notes
● Work a sample piece of the pleating before attempting the pleated frill. Also work a sample of the embroidery design before starting the blouse.
● The blouse washes perfectly in warm soapy water and with rinsing in plenty of water. Press while damp, placing the embroidered sections face down on to a towel and pressing on the wrong side.

MATERIALS

Dressmaker's Pattern Guide Paper ruled in 1cm (½in) and 5cm (2in) squares or similar. If this is not available use large size plain paper, ruled into the appropriate squares.

Fabric: 2 metres × 90cm (2¼ yds × 36in) wide white cotton lawn.

Needles: Crewel embroidery needles, No. 8, 9 or 10.

Thread for sewing: 1 reel (spool) white mercerised cotton thread No. 50.

Thread for tacking: 1 reel (spool) mercerised cotton thread in a contrasting colour.

Thread for embroidery: Coats stranded cotton, 2 skeins each of following colours: Orange (0925); Red (0335); Cerise Pink (089); Maroon Red (072); Blue (0410).

Ribbon for waist: 2 metres × 2cm (¾in) wide white.

Button: 1 shirt-type button.

Usual workbox equipment plus soft pencil or water-erasable pen; eraser and ruler.

GENERAL INSTRUCTIONS

1. Draft the pattern. A 2cm (¾in) seam allowance has been included in pattern (*see diagram 1*).
2. Cut out the blouse (*see diagram 1*).
3. Pleat frill (*see diagram 2*).
4. Embroider frill (*see diagrams 3-4*).
5. Make up the blouse.

PREPARATION

Drafting the pattern
Both bodice front and bodice back are the same size, so draft only one pattern.

Cutting out the blouse
Cut out following diagram 1. Note that the fabric is folded over on one side to cut the bodice front and back. The pleated frill is cut in one long strip the length of the fabric.

SMOCKING

Preparing the frill
1. Cut off selvedge from edge.
2. Turn under and make a small hem 5mm (¼in) wide along one long edge and at both ends. Hem by hand.

Pleating the frill
1. To make the pleats lie flat around the neckline, they are pleated so that they are closer together at the neckline.

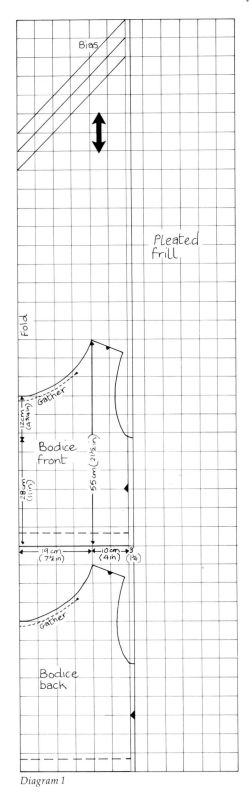

Diagram 1

2. This project was pleated by 'eye' with pleats approximately 1cm (½in) apart. For accuracy, use a soft pencil to mark dots at 1cm (½in) intervals around the neck edge of the frill.

3. Pin pleats, sloping gently at the neck edge, and tack (baste) using small tacking (basting) stitches about 1cm (½in) away from neck edge to hold pleats in place. Make another tacking (basting) line approximately 8cm (3in) away. Care is needed to make the pleats slope gradually inwards and at the same time to swing around the neckline, and lie flat. The finished length of the frill, when pleated, is 78cm (30¾in) approximately *(see diagram 2)*. Press pleats in place.

Working the embroidery at neck edge of frill

1. Mark a line with tacking (basting), or with a soft pencil, 5cm (2in) from neck edge.

2. Work herringbone stitch *(see diagram 4a)* just above this line, all around the frill.

3. Work another line of herringbone stitch at neck edge just below top tacking (basting) line which is 1cm (½in) down from neck edge.

4. Work row of chain stitch *(see diagram 4b)* 3cm (1¼in) below neck edge. The stitches must go right through the pleats. This forms the foundation for the design *(see diagrams 2 and 3)*.

5. Work the remainder of the design except the French knots following diagram 3.

6. The design can be copied by marking dots with a soft pencil where the design crosses the straight chain stitch line. Then by 'eye' pencil in the trailing design. Alternatively, the design can be embroidered directly on to the pleats.

Working the embroidery at edge of frill

1. Work herringbone stitch starting 2.5mm (⅛in) up from hem edge.

2. Work another line of herringbone stitch 4cm (1½in) from hem edge, leaving a space of 3cm (1¼in) in between.

3. Mark a line in the centre from which to work triangles in satin stitch *(see diagram 4c)*.

4. Work the rest of the embroidery *(see diagram 3)*. The trailing line can be lightly pencilled in as a guide.

MAKING-UP THE BLOUSE

Step 1: Finishing the pleated frill
Stitch 5mm (¼in) in from neck edge.

Step 2: Joining bodice front to bodice back
Join with a French seam. With wrong sides together, pin bodice front to bodice back, at shoulder seam and side seam. Tack (baste) and stitch. Trim seam to 5mm (¼in). Turn on to wrong side and stitch again.

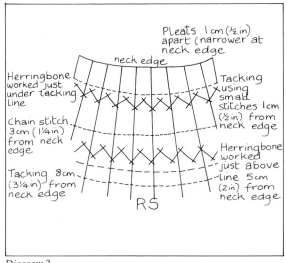

Diagram 2

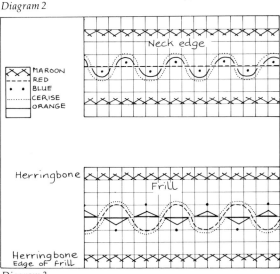

Diagram 3

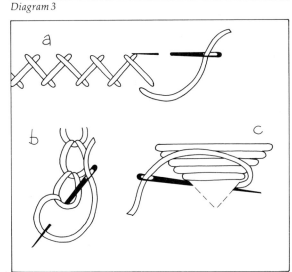

Diagram 4

Step 3: Making buttonhole for ribbon
1. At bottom edge of front, mark centre.
2. Mark 3cm (1¼in) up from edge.
3. Mark buttonhole, 2cm (¾in) long, up from this mark again.
4. Work buttonhole, which is vertically placed.

Step 4: Hemming the blouse
1. Turn up approximately 3cm (1¼in) on to the wrong side to make a hem at the bottom edge. Check that the edge of the buttonhole is not turned over on to the wrong side, as it must lie flat on the front of the blouse, but near the hem edge.
2. Pin hem. Tack (baste) and stitch.

Step 5: Neck opening
1. On bodice back, at centre of neck edge, make opening 8cm (3in) long.
2. Bind opening with bias strip by placing right sides together. Trim to make a narrow binding. Turn over and hem to stitching line.

Step 6: Attaching pleated frill to bodice
1. Gather bodice front and bodice back *(see diagram 1)*, using a gathering stitch on the seam line. Stitch another line 5mm (¼in) away and within seamline. Pull up to fit pleated frill.
2. Tack (baste) pleated frill, right side upwards, on to bodice right side, with stitched line of frill on top of seam line of blouse and 5mm (¼in) in from neck edge.
3. Pin bias strip approximately 2.5cm (1in) wide along neck edge, right sides together, turning up ends of bias at opening edge. Tack (baste) all thicknesses together, matching seam lines. Stitch. Trim edges back to 5mm (¼in) away from seamline. Trim bias and turn over on to stitching line and hem in place making a narrow binding. This is an important finish and must be neatly done. The bias must be the same width all around the neckline.

Step 7: Binding armholes
With right sides together pin bias to armhole seam line. Tack (baste) and stitch. Trim seam allowance back to 5mm (¼in). Turn bias over on to wrong side and hem to stitching line making a narrow binding.

Step 8: Finishing the blouse
1. Pin pleated frill to bodice around neck edge. Tack (baste) in place on lower line of herringbone stitching. Work French knots, *(see diagram 29, page 47)* through all the thicknesses, stretching from one French knot to the next. This helps to keep the frill in place.
2. Sew button to blouse at opening back.
3. Make buttonhole loop to fit button.
4. Thread ribbon through buttonhole.

On Shirred and Gathered Fabrics

Shirring is another technique for controlling fullness, and there are several ways to work it decoratively. Shirring is usually worked with small running stitches across a given area, so that when the stitches are pulled up, the area is gathered up without a pattern.

However, in certain countries in Europe, an advanced form of shirring, with running stitches making a pattern, has evolved; it has been worked on folk costume in Latvia in the USSR, parts of Hungary which are now in Romania, Portugal and Spain as well as in Italy.

ITALIAN SHIRRING

This form of shirring from Italy is sometimes referred to as 'Italian shirring' or 'Italian smocking' and is seen on men's shirts from as far back as the seventeenth century. However, before World War I, it was known to have been worked by peasants for decoration at the neck and sleeves of their cotton blouses. One area where this is known to have been worked was in the foothill towns and villages near Naples.

Working Italian shirring

There are two ways to work this particular type of shirring. One way is the Italian way which was traditionally worked in Italy and is worked with the fabric drawn up as the work progresses. The other way is to work the pattern flat, as for ordinary shirring by hand, and draw up the threads after this preliminary preparation. The results are the same, the only difference being that with the Italian method, less thread is used.

Suitable fabrics are those which are fine, such as fine cotton lawn and silks, or mediumweight cottons. The threads for gathering should be strong and suitable for the fabric. Coton à broder or Perle No. 5 are suitable for mediumweight cottons. For the sample in the photograph above (which was made in fine cotton lawn), one strand of stranded cotton was used. For the sample in the photograph right (which was made in a fine striped cotton), sewing thread was used. These threads are suitable for small areas when using fine fabrics, but for stronger fabrics and larger areas, a stronger thread should be used.

If making a sample, choose a cotton fabric with small equal stripes and work as follows:

1. Mark a straight line by either gently creasing, or marking lightly with a pencil and ruler on the right side of the fabric.

2. Work on the right side and start with a knot. Starting on row 1 at the righthand side, bring needle up

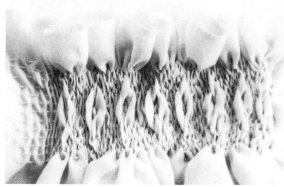
Italian shirring in fine cotton lawn

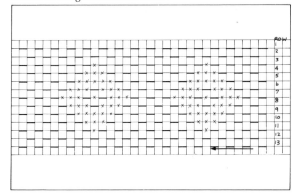
Diagram 1

Italian shirring in fine striped cotton

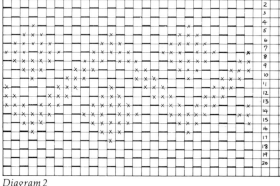
Diagram 2

and run in and out of the stripes across the row. End by taking needle through to the back and leave the thread hanging *(see diagrams 1 or 2 and photographs opposite).*

3. Pull up this first gathering row and using a needle stroke the folds into place.

4. Start row 2 approximately 2mm (1/16in) below row 1 and where a gather is formed, take the needle over and work across the row. Work one stitch at a time, pulling tightly, until the end of the row is reached. As the end stitches must all be in line, work half a stitch to finish. Tighten work, and again, using a needle, stroke the folds into position. A basket weave pattern will emerge and this will form the background to the pattern.

5. Continue to work pattern with each row 2mm (1/16in) apart *(see diagrams 1 or 2).*

6. When completed, adjust gathers and then twist all the end threads into a cord which will be a secure way to end the work. Alternatively, each thread may be stitched separately on the back.

Instead of starting each row with a knot as in Italian work, a piece of thread twice the length required for each row may be used by turning the same thread at the righthand side, thus obviating untidy startings.

If working the shirring flat, it can also be started in the Italian way, depending upon the size of the work. When drawn up, it is finished in the same way as for the Italian type of shirring.

SHIRRING ON PATTERNED FABRICS

Interesting decorative effects can be obtained by using stripes. By working several rows of running stitches in one way, and then by reversing the colour of the stripe which is picked up, interesting patterns can be made. *(see photograph below).* This form of shirring called *Vlagrimpelen* is used on the jacket worn by women in Volendam, Holland, where a patterned cotton fabric in black, brown and cream is traditionally used for the purpose.

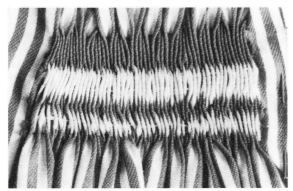

Shirring on stripes

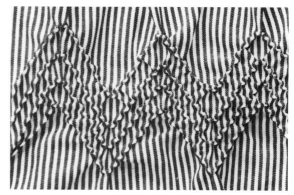

Zig-zag shirring on stripes

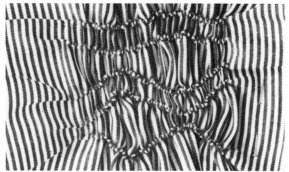

Wavy line shirring on stripes

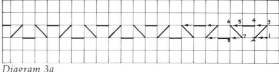

Diagram 3a

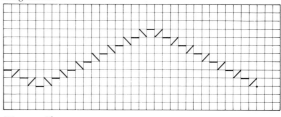

Diagram 3b

To obtain a zig-zag effect with shirring, running stitches can be worked *(see diagram 3a and photograph top).* In this case stripes were used as a guide.

In the sample with wavy lines *(see photograph above)* this effect was obtained by working the lines *(see diagram 3b)* which is shown in a straight line. To obtain a wavy effect curve the lines gently.

A more sophisticated effect can be obtained by gathering stripes to a pattern *(see photograph page 154).* In this sample, the fabric used is a very fine cotton lawn in very narrow black and white stripes, and the gathering is worked in red cotton Perle No. 5 in rows 2.5mm (1/8in) apart. The red of this gathering

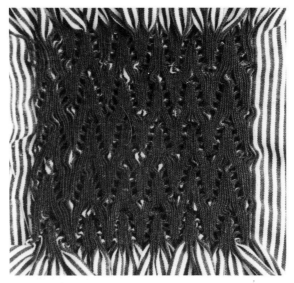

Patterned shirring on stripes

thread shows slightly through the background of the pattern to give an interesting effect against the predominance of the black.

To work the pattern *(see diagram 4)*:

1. Working on the right side of the fabric, and starting with a firm knot, come up to begin row 1 at the right-hand side.

2. Pick up the black stripes by working in and out of the centre of the white stripes. Follow diagram 4, noting where it is stepped at rows 11-12 and rows 13-14. Work across this row. Leave thread hanging.

3. Work 2nd, 3rd and 4th row. These four rows so worked form the pattern *(see diagram 4)*.

4. Repeat the pattern the required number of times. It was repeated five times for the sample.

5. When all the pattern has been worked pull up the gathering threads tightly until the pattern emerges. In this sample, as the fabric was very fine and the stripes were very narrow, less than 2mm (1/16in) in width, the pattern pulled up to one seventh of the original

worked area. Tie off the threads on the wrong side by taking two threads together to tie off securely with the next two threads.

LATTICE SMOCKING

This form of decorative gathering is worked by picking up certain points on the wrong side of the fabric, which produce a lattice effect on the right side.

Fabrics for this type of smocking should be firm, such as mediumweight woollen, velvet and stiff satin. The sample *(see photograph opposite)* was worked on fine leather. Use strong thread, depending upon the fabric.

If worked on a small scale, it can be used in various ways on clothing, depending upon the fabric. If worked on leather it can be used as an inset for a bag or belt. Interesting effects on fabric can be obtained by decorating further by spray dyeing with fabric dye.

A template is required to mark dots on to the wrong side of the fabric. To make a template, mark out on graph paper *(see diagram 5)* and then paste this on to a thin piece of card. Then, taking a thick needle or a stiletto, pierce the dots. The template can be made to any spacings between the dots and worked to any depth or width.

To work lattice smocking

1. Using the template, mark dots on to the wrong side of the fabric. The pattern is then commenced and is worked downwards, working row 1 first and finishing at the bottom, then working row 2.

2. Pick up dot 1, as for picking up dots for smocking, and work small stitch over it. Pick up dot 2, return to dot 1 and pick it up again. Pull 1 and 2 tightly together.

3. Pick up dot 3. With thread above the needle, slip the needle under the thread between dots 1/2 and 3 and pull tightly to make a knot, keeping the fabric flat between dots 1/2 and 3.

4. Pick up dot 4. Then pick up dot 3 and pull tightly together and make a knot.

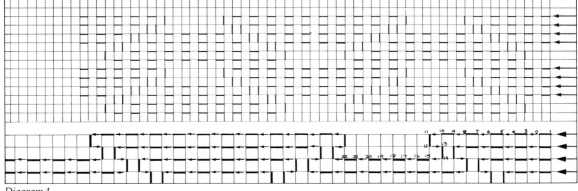

Diagram 4

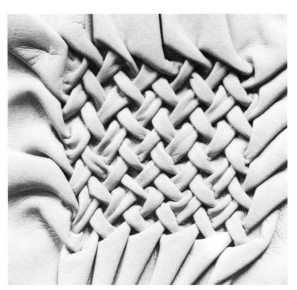

Lattice smocking

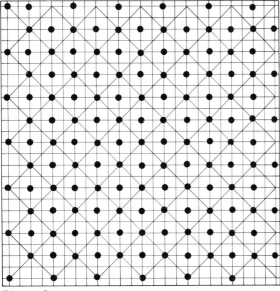

Diagram 5

5. Pick up dot 5 and with thread above the needle, slip needle under the thread between 4 and 3 and make a knot. Repeat down the sample and finish row 1 and then start row 2.

CONTEMPORARY SHIRRING

Interesting effects can be obtained by shirring on a machine and then using this foundation to elaborate further by using threads or fine ribbons. A strong thread suitable for the fabric must be used for the shirring. For decorating with ribbon, see Ribbon Waistcoat *(see illustration facing page 145).*

PROJECT 20 *(See illustration facing page 145)*

Ribbon Waistcoat

Size: To fit 87-90cm (34-36in) bust. This is a loose fit. The finished back length from shoulder neck edge is 55.5cm (21¾in).

General description: This loose-fitting waistcoat which is suitable for evening wear, is made in cream dull polyester satin. The front is most unusually gathered and smocked in a very narrow teal-coloured polyester ribbon. The back is plain. The waistcoat is lined in the same fabric and is finished with a self bias binding around the armholes and the edging.

Alternative suggestions: Fabrics such as silk, taffeta and crêpe de Chine can make very rich garments. As the ribbon, which must be very narrow, is smocked across in rows, it forms stripes and interesting patterns which can be used to advantage. A contrasting colour can be used as a lining. Consider: a plain-coloured waistcoat smocked with double-faced ribbon which has one colour on one side and another colour on the second side; a shot silk or a shot taffeta waistcoat picking up one of the colours for the ribbon smocking; a plain-coloured waistcoat smocked in ribbon in tones of one colour with the lightest colour at the top and the darkest colour at the bottom; a waistcoat in any plain colour smocked in several bright-coloured ribbons; a black waistcoat smocked in black ribbon which is interwoven with a metallic thread; a plain-coloured waistcoat smocked in a contrasting colour and using the contrasting colour for the lining.

Smocking stitches: This is a very unusual way of decorating gathers using ribbon instead of thread.

System for preparing smocking: This is not ordinary smocking. The preparation is worked on a sewing machine, stitching lines at regular intervals across the waistcoat fronts. These are then gathered up to fit the size of the waistcoat fronts in readiness for trimming with the ribbon.

Experience required: Those with experience in dressmaking and using a sewing machine and who wish to make an unusual garment would enjoy this creative use of smocking.

Notes
● The gathering takes time and must be done carefully. Therefore it is essential to have a sewing

machine with a quilting foot to do the gathering, as gathering by hand is not suitable.

• A sampler must be made to test: the suitability of the fabric; the thread for gathering which must be strong; and the size of needle. Make sure that the needle will take the width of ribbon for threading, also that it has a blunt end and that the ribbon will lace freely through the gathering threads.

• Be careful at all planning stages to see that the right front and the left front match.

• Dry cleaning is recommended for this garment.

MATERIALS

Dressmaker's Pattern Guide Paper ruled in 1cm (½in) and 5cm (2in) squares or similar. If this is not available use large size plain paper, ruled into the appropriate squares.

Fabric: 2.30 metres × 115cm (2½ yds × 45in) wide dull polyester satin in cream.

Ribbon: 45 metres (47 yds) × 2mm (¹⁄₁₆in) wide teal colour polyester double-face satin.

Needles: Tapestry needle, No. 20, 22 or 24.

Thread for sewing: 3 reels (spools) each 100 metres (100 yds) synthetic or mercerised sewing thread No. 60 or 50 depending upon testing.

Usual workbox equipment plus pencil, eraser and ruler.

GENERAL INSTRUCTIONS

1. Draft pattern *(see diagram 1)*.
2. Cut out waistcoat *(see diagrams 1 and 3)*.
3. Prepare gathering on machine *(see diagram 2)*.
4. Ribbon smock the gathering *(see diagram 4)*.
5. Make up the waistcoat *(see diagram 5)*.

PREPARATION

Drafting the pattern
This is a simple pattern to draft as only two pieces are required *(see diagram 1)*.

Cutting out the waistcoat
1. Note the pieces for smocking the waistcoat fronts. They are cut to size 82.5 × 65cm (32½ × 25½in) and are not shaped until *after* the smocking is finished.
2. Note that seam allowances are 2cm (¾in) on shoulder and side seam, and 1cm (½in) around armholes and edging.
3. Cut out the back lining and back plus two pieces of front lining and two smocking pieces, each 82.5 × 65cm (32½ × 25½in). Leave areas for cutting bias strips when required.

SMOCKING

Gathering by machine
1. Before machining gathering lines on front pieces of waistcoat it is essential to work samples first.
2. Working on the right side of the fabric, test for correct tension and stitch length using the smallest stitch which will gather well; practise machining in parallel lines 5mm (¼in) and 2cm (¾in) apart *(see diagram 2)*. Use a quilting attachment on the machine; pull up threads to test strength of thread; thread a piece of ribbon into a tapestry needle to test that the ribbon will thread easily into the gathering. Make sure that the gathering thread is strong enough.
3. When experiments are satisfactorily carried out proceed to machine the entire front piece starting and stopping 5mm (¼in) in from each edge.
4. Work the second front, making sure that the rows will match the first piece.

Pulling up the gathering threads
1. Working on the right side, pull up the top thread, the one which lies on the surface.
2. Pull up the entire piece to the width of the widest part of the waistcoat front pattern.

Cutting out gathered waistcoat front
1. Place gathered waistcoat front, face upwards, and then place waistcoat front pattern on top. Pin in place.
2. Mark with pins around the entire edge of the pattern. Remove pattern.
3. Pull threads through and tie off at the edge of the pattern. The threads must be tied very securely as this is the foundation for the lacing of the ribbon. For extra security the threads may be stitched.
4. Replace pattern to check *(see diagram 3)*. Tack (baste) around the pattern edge. Remove pattern.
5. Cut out waistcoat, being extra careful to avoid gathering threads as on no account must these be cut.
6. Be most careful when cutting out the second waistcoat front to make sure that the pattern is reversed.

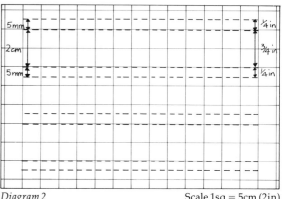

Diagram 2 Scale 1sq = 5cm (2in)

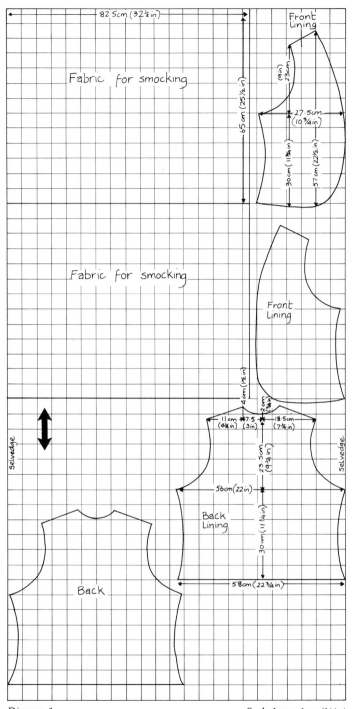

Fabric for smocking

Fabric for smocking

Front Lining

Front Lining

Back Lining

Back

82.5cm (32½in)

65cm (25½in)

23cm (9in)

27.5cm (10¾in)

30cm (11¾in)

57cm (22½in)

4cm (1½in)

2cm (¾in)

11cm (4¼in)

7.5 (3in)

18.5cm (7¼in)

23.5cm (9¼in)

56cm (22in)

30cm (11¾in)

58cm (22¾in)

Selvedge

Selvedge

Diagram 1

Scale 1sq = 1cm (½in)

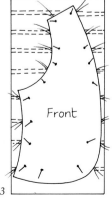

Front

Diagram 3

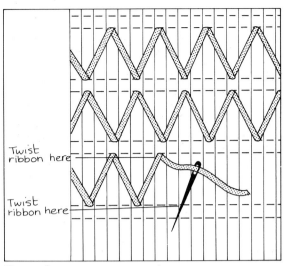

Twist
ribbon here

Twist
ribbon here

Diagram 4

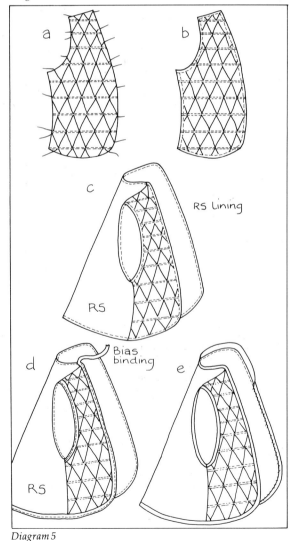

a

b

c

RS Lining

RS

d

Bias
binding

e

RS

Diagram 5

Smocking with ribbon

1. Allow approximately three times the width of the row for the length of ribbon. Cut one row at a time.

2. Thread ribbon into tapestry needle and leaving a short end, start to lace the ribbon from top row to bottom row, picking up a gathering stitch at regular intervals. The ribbon is turned at an angle on the top row, as well as on the bottom row *(see diagram 4)*.

3. When working the second waistcoat front, be careful to see that the two fronts, when placed edge to edge, match.

4. When the ribbon smocking is entirely finished machine stitch approximately 5mm (¼in) in from edges to secure cut ends of ribbon. Trim excess ribbon *(see diagrams 5a and 5b)*.

MAKING-UP THE WAISTCOAT

Step 1: Joining the waistcoat

1. With right sides together, pin and tack (baste) fronts to back along shoulders and side seams. Stitch.

2. Press seams flat, being careful not to press the smocking.

Step 2: Joining the lining

Join as for waistcoat. Press seams flat.

Step 3: Attaching lining to waistcoat

1. With wrong sides together, pin lining to waistcoat.

2. Tack (baste) together. Stitch around armholes and all around edge of waistcoat in readiness for binding. Stitching approximately 5mm (¼in) in from edges *(see diagram 5c)*.

Step 4: Binding the waistcoat

1. Cut bias binding strips 4cm (1½in) wide and join *(see diagram 5d)*.

2. With right sides together, pin bias all around the waistcoat edges and armholes. Tack (baste) carefully in place. Stitch 1cm (½in) from edges *(see diagram 5d)*.

3. Turn under edge of binding and hem neatly to the inside, making sure that the binding is even *(see diagram 5e)*.

SELECT BIBLIOGRAPHY

Historical

Adburgham, Alison. *Liberty's – A Biography of a Shop*. Allen & Unwin, London, 1975.

Birbari, Elizabeth. *Dress in Italian Painting 1460-1500*. John Murray Ltd, London 1975; Allanheld & Schram, Montclair, New Jersey, USA, 1976.

Cunnington, Phyllis and Buck, Anne. *Children's Costume in England 1300-1900*. A & C Black Ltd, London, 1965; Humanities Press Inc, Atlantic Highlands, New Jersey, USA, 1972.

Hall, Maggie. *Smocks*. Shire Publications Ltd, Princes Risborough, Buckinghamshire, 1979.

Jekyll, Gertrude. *Old West Surrey*. Longmans Green, London, 1904. Reprinted S. R. Publishers Ltd (A & C Black), London, 1971.

By a Lady. *The Workwoman's Guide*. Simpkin Marshall 1838 London. 2nd ed. 1840. Reprinted Owston Ferry, Bloomfield Books, Sudbury, Suffolk, 1975.

Liberty's 1875-1975 – An Exhibition to mark the firm's centenary. Victoria and Albert Museum, London, 1975.

Newton, Stella Mary. *Health, Art and Reason: Dress Reformers of the 19th. Century*. John Murray Ltd, London, 1974; Allanheld & Schram, Montclair, New Jersey, USA, 1976.

Oakes, Alma and Hamilton Hill, Margot. *Rural Costume – Its Origin and Development in Western Europe and the British Isles*. B. T. Batsford Ltd, London, 1970; Van Nostrand Reinhold, New York, 1970.

Ribaric/Szenczi. *Yugoslavian/Croatian Folk Embroidery*. Van Nostrand Reinhold, New York, 1975.

Wingfield Digby, George. *Elizabethan Embroidery*. Faber & Faber Ltd, London 1963.

Useful museum leaflets and booklets: 'Smocks in the Buckinghamshire County Museum'; 'Smocks in Hereford and Worcester County Museum'; 'Smocks in Luton Museum'; 'Warwickshire Museum Costume Collection'.

Technique

Armes, Alice. *English Smocks with directions for making them*. The Reeves Dryad Press, Leicester, 1980. Now distributed by B. T. Batsford, London.

Cave, Aenone. *English Folk Embroidery*. Mills and Boon, London, 1965.

Durand, Dianne. *Complete Book of Smocking: Techniques and Projects*. Van Nostrand Reinhold, New York, 1982.

Frew, Hannah. *Three-Dimensional Embroidery*. Van Nostrand Reinhold, New York, 1975.

Howard, Constance. *The Constance Howard Book of Stitches*. B. T. Batsford Ltd, London, 1979; Charles T. Brandford Co, Newton Center, Massachusetts, USA, 1980.

Marshall, Beverley. *Smocks and Smocking*. Alphabooks, Sherborne, Dorset, 1980; Van Nostrand Reinhold, New York, 1981.

Maile, Anne. *Tie and Dye as a Present-day Craft*. Mills and Boon, London, 1971.

Nichols, Marion. *Encyclopedia of Embroidery Stitches including Crewel*. Dover Publications Inc, New York, 1974.

Thom, Margaret. *Smocking in Embroidery*. B. T. Batsford Ltd, London, 1972.

Articles

Bishop, Elizabeth. 'A Family Heirloom' in *Embroidery*, Summer 1972.

Clive Couture Collection 1971 in *Embroidery*, Summer 1971.

Evans, Alice B. 'Smocking Part I and Part II – A Revival of an Old English Handicraft' in *Embroidery*, 1909.

Farwell, Ann. 'A Gathering of Smocks' in *The Countryman*, Spring 1968.

Keay, Diana. 'New Ideas for Smocking'. An Embroiderers' Guild leaflet.

Littlejohn, Jean. 'Free Smocking' in *Embroidery*, Autumn 1980.

'Military Skirt', ref. Metropolitan Museum Bulletin, 1922, vol. 17.

Rolleston, E. 'Smocks Past and Present' in *Embroidress*, 1924.

'An Unusual Smock' in *Embroidery*, Summer 1974.

ADDRESSES OF SUPPLIERS

For British readers

The Campden Needlecraft Centre, High Street, Chipping Campden, Gloucestershire.

de Denne, 159-61 Kenton Road, Kenton, Harrow, Middlesex.

Deighton Brothers Ltd, Riverside Road, Barnstaple, Devon. (For smocking dot transfers.)

The Handworkers' Market, The Shire Hall, Shirehall Plain, Holt, Norfolk.

The Ladies Work Society Ltd, Delabere House Embroideries, Moreton-in-Marsh, Gloucestershire.

John Lewis, Oxford Street, London.

Liberty and Co. Ltd., Regent Street, London.

Mace & Nairn, 89 Crane Street, Salisbury, Wiltshire.

Needle and Thread, 80 High Street, Horsell, Woking, Surrey.

Christine Riley, 53 Barclay Street, Stonehaven, Kincardineshire, Scotland.

The Royal School of Needlework, 25 Princes Gate, London SW7. (A shop as well as classes.)

Spinning Jenny, Bradley, Keighley, West Yorkshire and also Market Place, Marsham, Ripon, North Yorkshire.

Templetons Mill Shop, Mill Street, Ayr, Ayrshire, Scotland.

Unicorn Fabrics, Woodstock, Oxfordshire.

For classes and courses: The Smocking Group of The Embroiderers' Guild, The Embroiderers' Guild, Apartment 41a, Hampton Court Palace, East Molesey, Surrey.

Magazine: Embroidery is published quarterly by The Embroiderers' Guild.

For North American readers

Beverly Andrews Designs, 111 Bonita Drive, Birmingham, AL 35209.

Briar Patch Designs, Inc., Becky Summers, 2753 Acton Road, Birmingham, AL 35243.

The Cotton Patch, 1025 Brown Avenue, Lafayette, CA 94549.

Charles Craft, Inc., P.O. Box 1049, Laurinburg, NC 28352. (Guildford gingham.)

The Gathering Place, 1046 Lancaster Avenue, Bryn Mawr, PA 19010.

Heirloom Designs by Judith Wood, P.O. Box 804, Redmond, Washington 98052.

Allyne Holland, 1907 Adelphi Road, Richmond, VA 23229.

Sandy Hunter, Inc., P.O. Box 706, Flat Rock, NC 28731.

Little Elegance, P.O. Box 14567, Richmond, VA 23220.

Little Miss Muffet, P.O. Box 10912, Knoxville, TN 37939.

Little Stitches, P.O. Box 76769, Atlanta, GA 30328.

McCarn Enterprises, Inc., Ellen McCarn, P.O. Box 75047, Birmingham, AL 35253.

A. T. Newell Co., 415 South 64th Place, Birmingham, AL 35212.

Peggy Penton Smocking, 830 Prospect Avenue, Van Wert, OH 45891.

Margaret Pierce, 1816 Pembroke Road, Greensboro, NC 27407.

Martha Pullen Co., 805 Madison Street, Huntsville, AL 35801.

The Smoc Box, P.O. Box 10562, Knoxville, TN 37939.

Smocking Unlimited, 1238 Devonshire Road, Windsor, Ontario N8Y 2M7, Canada.

The Smock Shop, 1615 E. Fourth Street, Charlotte, NC 28204.

The Smocking Basket, Inc., P.O. Box 2365, Gaithersburg, MD 20879.

Thai Silks, 252 (H) State, Los Altos, CA 94022. (China silks, crêpe de chines, raw silk noils, silk dupionni, etc.)

Utex Trading, 710 9th Street, Suite 5, Niagra Falls, NY 14301. (China silks, crêpe de chines, raw silk noils, silk dupionni, etc.)

Utex Trading, 111 Peter Street, Suite 212, Toronto, Ontario M5V 2H1, Canada.

Resources: Smocking Arts Guild of America, P.O. Box 75, Knoxville, TN 37901. (Publishes *The Smocking Arts*, SAGA newsletter.)

Embroiderer's Guild of America, 6 East 45th Street, New York, NY 10017.

National Standards Council of American Embroiderers Correspondence School, Carnegie Office Park, 600 Bell Avenue, Carnegie, PA 15106. (Offers a correspondence course in smocking.)

Other Publications of Interest: Handmade, Lark Communications, 50 College Street, Asheville, NC 28801. (Smocking is featured in the April '84 issue.)

INDEX